CYBORGS AND B

This book is for Dan

CYBORGS AND BARBIE DOLLS

FEMINISM, POPULAR CULTURE AND THE POSTHUMAN BODY

KIM TOFFOLETTI

I.B. TAURIS
LONDON · NEW YORK

Published in 2007 by I.B.Tauris & Co Ltd
6 Salem Road, London W2 4BU
175 Fifth Avenue, New York NY 10010
www.ibtauris.com

In the United States of America and Canada distributed by Palgrave Macmillan
a division of St. Martin's Press, 175 Fifth Avenue, New York NY 10010

ISBN: 978 1 84511 467 1

A full CIP record for this book is available from the British Library
A full CIP record is available from the Library of Congress

Library of Congress Catalog Card Number: available

Printed and bound in Great Britain by TJ International Ltd, Padstow, Cornwall
From camera-ready copy edited and supplied by the editor

Contents

List of Illustrations

Acknowledgements

Many people have contributed to this book, whether by way of reading and providing comments and suggestions, or other forms of assistance and support. I am indebted to Anne Marsh, JaneMaree Maher, Rachael Fensham, Maryanne Dever, Angela Ndalianis, Susan Broadhurst, and the Departments of Women's Studies and Visual Culture at Monash University, where this book first took shape as part of my doctoral research.

I am grateful to Deakin University who, by way of funding and teaching relief, enabled me to complete this book. My colleagues have been a great emotional and intellectual resource, especially Estelle Barrett, Grazyna Zajdow, Peter Mewett, Marilyn Poole and Mel Irenyi, all who have put up with me while writing. The advice of Sarah Paddle and the magical signature of David Lowe helped ensure this project made it to book form.

I also wish to acknowledge the staff at I.B.Tauris, particularly Susan Lawson, for guiding me through the world of book publishing. Her helpful and positive correspondence has been much appreciated. Sincere thanks to Patricia Piccinini for allowing me to reproduce her wonderful artwork, and to Mark Rashleigh and Carolyn Leslie for their contributions.

My gratitude goes out to the family and friends who have provided endless encouragement, nurturing and optimism. Thank you to the Toffoletti and Silkstone clans for their unwavering support and faith in what I do. Thanks also to Jo, Greta, Liz, Katie, Tom, Sarina and Miranda for last minute proofreading. The Westside crew have provided welcome and necessary distractions. Despite living in different states most of the time, Bec has always been there. As always, much love and affection to Dan for keeping the home fires burning, putting things in perspective, reading everything and keeping me sane.

Chapters four, five and six have been expanded, revised and updated from previously published works. Chapter four appeared in an earlier incarnation in 2003 as 'Catastrophic Subjects: Feminism, The Posthuman and Difference' in *Thirdspace: A Journal of Feminist Theory and Culture* 3(2). Sections of chapter five were adapted from 'Media Implosion: Posthuman Bodies at the Interface', published in *Hecate* 29(1) in 2003. An abridged version of chapter six was published as 'Imagining the Posthuman: Patricia Piccinini and the Art of Simulation' in *Outskirts: Feminisms Along the Edge* 11 (2003).

Introduction

This book is about the posthuman. More specifically, it is about how the posthuman is represented in popular culture, and how useful these images might be for thinking about the subject in an age of biotechnologies, information networks and digital worlds. If you find yourself reading this, chances are that you are probably interested in popular culture and use technologies in your day-to-day activities. Without reducing readers to a stereotype, I'd imagine that readers of books like this one have the privilege of education and/or economics, and often along with those privileges comes the opportunity to inhabit high-tech worlds, whether that be in the form of medical advances, media communications or digital devices. This isn't to say that those without social or economic capital are outside of the circuits of technology. From CCTV cameras on the street to the offshore call centres servicing the West's communication needs, there are very few spaces on the globe where the effects and consequences of technology are not felt.

Myself? I'm not an outrageously high-tech girl. Wouldn't recognise a chat room if I stumbled into one. Although I can admit to owning an iPod, I have limited knowledge of how to file share. Virtual worlds leave me cold and mobile phones are trouble. My first and only experience of mowing a lawn was a success. That's dealing with technology, isn't it? I'm sensing that by this stage any credibility I might have had as an 'expert' on our hyper–nano–digi–techno–cyber–micro–bioengineered–society has been undermined by my professed lack of technological savvy. Before writing me off, let me just say five simple words: *The Six Million Dollar Man.* As a child of the seventies, this television series provided one of my earliest memories of the techno–human encounter. Although the actual feats of the title character, Steve Austin (played by Lee Majors), are vague in my mind, I clearly remember the opening sequence of each series and those immortal lines:

Narrator: *Steve Austin: astronaut. A man barely alive.*

Oscar Goldman: *Gentlemen, we can rebuild him. We have the technology. We have the capability to make the world's first bionic man. Steve Austin will be that man. Better than he was before. Better…stronger…faster.*

This is just one of many examples across art, advertising, film and television where human beings have been portrayed as a fusion of technological and natural components, a mixture of species and in some cases, of indeterminate gender. Tellingly, the character of Steven Austin first appeared in the 1972 Martin Caidin novel *Cyborg*, which is a now-commonplace term to describe the (con)fusion between the human and the machine. The story of how I came to undertake this research, then, stems from an ongoing fascination with how the relationship between humans and technology has been represented.

So this book is also about representation. As I will go on to discuss, various writers have offered different meanings and interpretations of the posthuman as it has been imagined in culture. Their goal has been to consider what the image can tell us about ourselves. Underpinning this kind of approach to representation is an assumption that images are in some way connected to reality. I question this assumption by arguing that the function of representation is not just to reference reality. Rather, its changing status prompts us to reflect on how we understand reality in a posthuman age. While the role of image culture in subject formation is predominantly understood as the site where meaning and identity are secured, the possibilities for disabling identity at the level of the image remain largely unexplored in studies of the posthuman. This has led me to consider the impact of the visual on theorising the relationship between the self and the world.

Simulated Realities

In this climate of biotechnologies, virtual worlds and digital manipulation, a relationship between the organism and the machine emerges that contests organic bodily boundaries, the locus of identity and the status of the human. Clear distinctions between what is real and what is virtual, where the body ends and technology begins, what is nature and what is machine, fracture and implode. Given this context, how can one understand what the self is, what a human is, what a man or a woman is? How are we to make sense of media images in a posthuman, post-gender world?

I believe that as dialectical modes of thought are destabilised, we can begin to rethink the human condition. Through questioning an oppositional style of thinking, the potential emerges for alternative embodiments, new formulations of the subject and fresh means of experiencing our surrounds through posthuman figurations. These entities are neither real nor imaginary, but products of a simulation order where dichotomies of value implode as the sign/origin relationship collapses. It is at this point of implosion that the transformative potential of the posthuman resides, and also where I situate my analysis.

At the heart of this argument is a theory of simulation. Jean Baudrillard's writings on our visual world enable new articulations of the subject at the advent of the twenty-first century, where digital, biological and information technologies invite a reconsideration of what it means to be human. In *Cyborgs and Barbie Dolls*, simulation is used to establish a theory of the posthuman at the collapse of the relation between representation and reality. This strategy questions a structural approach to representational practice that upholds a system of meaning reliant on an origin or referent. By dissolving the relationship between the sign and reality, Baudrillard's theory of simulation encourages us to engage with representation and subjectivity in a way that is beyond signification. A theory of images and signs is vital to this book because it helps us to understand how posthuman images may create new articulations of the subject that exceed dialectical thought, and the impact of such images on notions of identity, the body and selfhood.

Part of the process of conceptualising the world as simulation requires that we take on board an alternative logic outside of the categories of traditional Western thought. This is Baudrillard's challenge to us—to think about images, reality and the self in quite new ways. This is not to say that Baudrillard's ideas are beyond reproach (as a survey of critiques of Baudrillard in chapter two indicates), but that they offer another framework through which to conceive of the relationship between reality and images. Baudrillard's 'strategy of "radical thought" could appear trivialising, insincere, pointless, irresponsible, or just plain absurd, even mad' to some, as Victoria Grace has pointed out (Grace 2005: 1). Yet it is in the undoing of an assumed and coherent sense of reality that Baudrillard's 'fatal theory' may prove tactically useful for feminist interrogations of how posthuman images operate.

Posthuman Subjects

The necessity to imagine alternative modalities for the subject is what feminist theorist Rosi Braidotti promotes when she writes:

> What counts as human in this posthuman world? How do we rethink the unity of the human subject, without reference to humanistic beliefs, without dualistic oppositions, linking instead body and mind in a

> new flux of self? What is the view of the self that is operational in the world of the "informatics of domination"? (Braidotti 1994b: 179).

Braidotti's questions recognise the difficulties of talking about the self as a coherent entity in an increasingly technologised world. The tension between the subject and technology that is present in her statement is typical of the kinds of anxieties and possibilities that have circulated around this relationship. What follows will explore the various ways that the techno–human relationship has been characterised, using feminist, philosophical, media studies and posthuman perspectives.

While asking us to engage in a way of thinking 'without reference to humanistic beliefs', Braidotti's interrogation elicits a cascade of inquiries with respect to theory, methodology and ontology (Braidotti 1994b: 179). Indeed, for the purposes of this book, Braidotti's questions motivate my analysis of how the posthuman affords new possibilities for rethinking the subject. In order to contextualise my argument, I look to feminist debates about the relationship between women and technology. This is because a study of the posthuman is in many ways an extension of the question of *man's* relationship to technology, and accordingly, the status of the human. Throughout this book, the idea of the human (as it has been understood in Western philosophical thought) is questioned. For these purposes, it is useful to explore feminist approaches to technology as a way of understanding the posthuman. I survey the shifts in feminist conceptualisations of technology to chart how the human/technology interaction has been interpreted by feminism. A reading of the posthuman is developed that brings together feminist studies of technology and a theory of simulation.

By examining the changes in contemporary social operations and our engagements with representational practice, I want to provide a way of thinking about the subject that is not founded on ideas like the 'real me', a 'true identity' or an 'authentic self'. The posthuman figurations discussed in this book do this by circulating as sites of contest, challenging an established set of values based in dialectical thought. A tension between the human and technological is indicative of the posthuman. And it is this tension that disrupts traditional understandings of selfhood, identity, the body and reality. It is for this reason that posthuman images can be appealing. It is because they are contradictory and unstable, not because they transcend the body or offer a better version of human existence.

Underpinning this reformulation of the subject is a shift in social relations that sees narratives of time, space and history as radically altered by engagements with technology. When the limits of the body and identity are called into question by an acceleration of information and media, where does the human reside? It becomes apparent that origins have no place in an order of simulation where history is replayed in the endless propagation and proliferation of signs. Indeed, it has been said that history disappears when the original and the real no longer exist as coherent categories (Baudrillard 1986). What will become clear in the course of reading this book is that the posthuman inhabits a space beyond the real where time and history defy linear progression. The images of the posthuman explored here will be shown to disrupt origin stories, contest understandings of being, and create the potential to configure the subject outside of temporal narratives of evolution and progress.

How to Read this Book

Cyborgs and Barbie Dolls is organised so that it can be read cover to cover, or the chapters may be read separately and in no particular order. Although each chapter stands alone, the first two chapters build the theoretical background informing much of the discussion that follows. These introductory chapters provide a comprehensive overview of how the posthuman has been understood in critical theory, feminist thinking about technology and the posthuman, as well as a study of the visual climate in which we consume images and how this impacts on our engagements with images of the posthuman.

From chapter three onwards, the book is devoted to analysing particular examples of the posthuman body in popular culture. Each of these chapters demonstrates various tropes by which the posthuman challenges signification. Plasticity frames an exploration of Barbie in chapter three. Studies of Marilyn Manson in chapter four and TDK advertising in chapter five configure the posthuman in terms of catastrophe and the interface respectively. Chapter six looks at the work of Australian artist Patricia Piccinini using the ideas of the code and the clone. It is in these pages that I showcase my argument for understanding posthuman figurations as transformative possibilities that reside beyond signification. Given this structure, it is possible to read these as stand-alone chapters.

At the outset of each chapter, I have tried to provide the reader with a sense of how I came to each image, and what it was about these particular images that prompted me to explore them further. The main reason they were chosen was because of their ambivalence. On seeing each of these images, I felt that there was something about them that didn't make immediate sense. For me, what these images share is an uncertainty that makes it difficult to define what is being represented in definitive terms of man or woman, real or illusion, self or Other, human or non-human. In this respect, they operate as contested sites; spaces of ongoing boundary play where meaning is up for grabs. In this act of destabilising meaning and problematising origins, these images open up possibilities for new articulations of posthuman experience. So even though the contradictions of technology as simultaneously a 'threat and promise' has been recognised within feminist studies of technoscience, the productive possibilities of such ambiguities for subject formation have remained considerably under-theorised.

One of the most obvious questions to ask about the posthuman is: 'What is it?' What characteristics does it embody and what attributes typify something as posthuman? How is it different to other techno–human or hybrid bodies in culture? This book begins with a broad survey of the key writers and thinkers on posthuman studies as a way of responding to such questions and introducing the reader to the field. What emerges from this analysis of the posthuman literature is a need to think about what constitutes reality in our discussions of posthuman existence.

Cyborgs and Barbie Dolls moves us beyond current literature on the posthuman by exploring the role of representation in understanding the posthuman at the point where the material and the virtual collapse. This study speaks to feminist scholarship on the posthuman by taking into account the economy of the visual where images of the posthuman circulate, and the ensuing shift in feminist conceptualisations of the operations of representation on subject formation.

This review forms the basis of chapter one, which proposes that alternative models of the woman/technology relationship are needed to account for the ambiguity and contradictory nature of posthuman representations. The tendency of feminist analysis of the relationship between women and technology has been to interpret technology as largely beneficial or detrimental to women. I position myself within this debate as neither affirming nor critiquing technology itself. Instead, the feminist dialogue informing this relationship is reoriented to facilitate another understanding of how figurations of the posthuman operate in popular culture. I argue that these images belie easy distinctions of good or bad, circulating rather as ambivalent and contested sites that act to create confusion, and accordingly, incite a challenge to our perception of reality.

Given that the ideas of French thinker Jean Baudrillard are central to my approach, I take some time to provide a general overview of his key ideas in chapter two and tease out their applicability to posthuman images. His studies of simulation and hyperreality provide a context in which to analyse the circulation of the posthuman across contemporary cultural sites. This chapter establishes Baudrillard's theory of image culture as tactically useful to a feminist analysis of representations of the posthuman. In making this argument, I trace the shift in visual technologies from the Renaissance to our current digital age to show how the relationship between reality and its representation has altered over time. Accordingly, I suggest that new visual technologies offer new ways of interpreting the posthuman and understanding the gendered self.

In chapter three I turn my attention to Barbie—the first of four representations of the posthuman in this study—to apply my thinking about images as transformational to feminist debates on women, technology and the body. I situate Barbie as a posthuman precursor; a type of plastic transformer who embodies the potential for identity to be mutable and unfixed. In this regard, Barbie acts as a 'bridging' figure between debates surrounding gender and representation and posthuman, post-gender figurations. Starting with a photograph of Barbie dolls taken at a local flea market, I re-read Barbie as something other than that which has been put forward in the stereotypical feminist interpretation, which argues that she is a bad role model for girls. To pursue another approach to Barbie, I draw on the history and theory of plastics, feminist studies of consumerism and cosmetic surgery, and Jean Baudrillard's concept of the 'trans' state of being. In linking these diverse discourses, I trace a vision of Barbie as a 'posthuman prototype'; an icon for a new femininity brought about by the implosion of the categories of woman, consumerism, technology and the body.

Chapter four examines the idea that posthuman forms erase social and biological differences, and considers the implications of this for understanding gender difference. The idea of catastrophe, as it is understood by Baudrillard, is used here to explore the question of difference in a world of simulation where the distinction between things is eroding. Through images of the goth rock star Marilyn Manson from his 1998 album *Mechanical Animals,* I demonstrate how digital images of the posthuman promote a model of difference that is exponential rather than oppositional. In recognising that the posthuman acts as an unstable form, we can highlight the similarities between the posthuman and other liminal figures like the monster and cyborg, as well as explaining how the posthuman is different to these other non-human entities. What is shown is how the emergence of the posthuman within the context of digital media creates new ways of thinking about gender identity and its representation.

New digital forms of communication also alter how we interact with others and understand ourselves in the media landscape. In chapter five I discuss the effects of being immersed in communication and what this means for women's place in a new media society. My case study here is one of the images from the TDK advertising campaign 'Evolve to TDK', depicting a baby with square eyes and oversized ears. Questioning accounts that position the subject as either an active participant or passive receiver of information in communication networks, I argue for a new understanding of the relationship between women and communication technologies. In contrast to analyses that see the body and the media as distinct, a model of the body as an interface system is proposed that takes pleasure from diverse communication forms.

Having looked at how posthuman representations transform our perceptions of the self by extending beyond the limits of the body, chapter six examines the inverse: What happens when the boundaries between the body and technology collapse inward? It is this 'miniaturisation of the body', to paraphrase Baudrillard, which forms the focus of the final chapter. Feminism has often been critical of biotechnologies such as cloning and genetic engineering. Here I examine these debates to pose another way of approaching posthuman representations of the biotechnological future, drawing on the works of the Australian visual artist Patricia Piccinini to develop my argument.

In concluding this chapter and this book, I return to the question of technology and representation to highlight the parallels and differences between the approaches of feminist thinker Donna Haraway and Jean Baudrillard. Through this book, I hope to open up further dialogue between feminist thought and the writings of Baudrillard to better understand the role played by posthuman representations in our perceptions of technology, selfhood and the real. What ensues is a theory of the posthuman that is an amalgam of feminist theory and postmodern image culture.

In claiming that posthuman forms like Marilyn Manson and Barbie enable new formulations of the subject, I don't mean to offer a better or truer account of what these images say. Rather, this book aims to reflect on how posthuman representations occupy the status of simulacrum, how this displaces the notion of an original, and the implications of this for theories of identity. Manson, the TDK baby, Barbie and Piccinini's mutant organisms do not mask or reflect reality; they become our reality.

Neither is it my purpose to advocate a utopian or futuristic ideal of the subject. Or to imply that posthuman figurations transcend the materiality of the body or corporeal experience. I resist such readings, preferring to call into question our understandings of the real, representation, the body and identity. The potential for posthuman figurations to offer new imaginings and subjectivities does not necessitate the repudiation of corporeality. But neither can these concepts be understood in the same way any more. As it has been throughout the history of visual technologies, simulation demands new articulations of the self more suited to a postmodern, posthuman experience of technology and the visual.

1

Feminism, Technology and the Posthuman

Not long ago while I was at the pub, a friend who I hadn't seen for a while handed me a video tape. Although I knew I would be meeting up with her, I wasn't expecting to receive anything, and given the context, it came as a bit of a surprise. Especially when the handover was accompanied with an enthusiastic and unnervingly loud 'You MUST watch this. It's about women who get implants in their spinal cords so they can have orgasms'. Righto. I'll admit that I was intrigued by the content, but slightly troubled that it was being directed at me. In a pub. Surrounded by drunk people. Without warning. She followed it up with 'I immediately thought of you when it came on the telly so I taped it'. I'm not showing any signs of being outright offended at this stage, choosing instead to act politely confused. Given I was writing this book at the time, I'll give her the benefit of the doubt and presume that when she thought of me, it was my fascination with posthuman bodies and not a hint that my sex life could be better.

The contents of the tape proved fascinating. It was a documentary about the development of a device called the Orgasmatron. Not to be confused with the album of the same name by heavy metal outfit Motörhead, or that funny bag-thing in the Woody Allen movie from the 1970s which people climbed into in order to reach their sexual peak. And we are definitely not talking about the overpriced 1990s fad that passed off a few bits of wire as a head-massaging gadget. The Orgasmatron in question involves the insertion of a remote controlled device into a woman's spinal column which, when activated, electronically stimulates the body's nervous system, specifically those neural pathways leading to coital nirvana. As described by Grace Dent in *The Guardian* newspaper:

> "When we turned on the power, she let out a moan and began hyperventilating," claims Dr Stuart Meloy, unveiling his revolutionary new Orgasmatron, a machine that he claims has a 91% chance of

> making women reach orgasm. Just plug yourself into the mains, flip the switch and enjoy as your toes curl, your pupils dilate and your neighbours wrinkle their noses and turn up the TV volume in dismay (Dent 2005).

Given the prevalence of these kinds of enhancements of the body in contemporary culture, it's likely that for many readers, medical developments such as the Orgasmatron are hardly novel or surprising anymore. The pages that follow offer more examples of these kinds of techno–human fusions and explore how the self has been imagined through representations of the techno–human encounter, and how this has informed our engagements with such images. Technologies like the Orgasmatron lead us to consider what the implications are of these kinds of posthuman realities for women. And prompt us to ask how empowering or enabling they may be.

I'm certainly not the first to wonder about such things. In their edited collection, *Mapping the Subject: Geographies of Cultural Transformation*, Steve Pile and Nigel Thrift reflect on the products of popular culture to ask: 'What novel kinds of discursive images of the self and experience, what different kinds of identity, what fresh image–concepts, what new maps of subjectivity, which new figurations are available?' (Pile and Thrift 1995: 17). As a counter to images of the technologically enhanced woman in culture, such as the above-mentioned Orgasmatron, feminism has given us a range of evocative and powerful figurations to imagine new ways of being a subject in the world. Alongside her own model of the nomadic subject, Rosi Braidotti cites both Luce Irigaray's 'two lips' and Donna Haraway's cyborg as two well-known feminist figurations (Braidotti 1994a: 3).[1] They operate as 'performative images that can be inhabited' (Haraway 1997: 11), and offer conditions of possibility or ways of thinking that look beyond the phallocentric, or male-centred, subject of humanism. As we'll see throughout this book, the posthuman can also be a useful model for understanding women's existence in an age of biotechnological manipulation, digital networks and genetic alterations. In order to see how it might do this, it is first necessary to consider the cultural significance of the posthuman and survey how it has been interpreted and understood.

What is the Posthuman?

As early as 1977, Ihab Hassan reflected on posthumanism in the following way:

> We need to first understand that the human form—including human desire and all its external representations—may be changing radically,

> and thus must be re-visioned. We need to understand that five hundred years of humanism may be coming to an end, as humanism transforms itself into something that we must helplessly call posthumanism (Hassan 1977: 212).

Since then, many writers have articulated visions of a posthuman future that interrogate the status of the body and the self in a technological age (Badmington 2000, Foster 2005, Fukuyama 2002, Graham 2002, Halberstam and Livingstone 1995, Hayles 1999, Terranova 1996). While most have explored the possibilities afforded by a posthuman existence, albeit with a critical eye, some have appeared understandably anxious about a shift toward a posthuman way of being. As recently as 2002, Francis Fukuyama reiterated the long-held anxiety that comes with the reformulation of the body in an age of biotechnological manipulation. Human nature, he argues, will be profoundly altered by these technologies and as a consequence we risk social and political instability across all levels of society (Fukuyama 2002: 7). This interpretation is troubling for a number of reasons. First, it assumes that 'human nature' is an inherent and universal quality at the core of all individuals, regardless of the social and cultural factors that might influence the range and limits of existence at any given moment in history. Second, it takes the view that once humans begin down the path away from a 'natural' state of being then humanity is over, despite the fact that 'nature' as a category has always been contested by everyday human interactions with technologies ranging from the primitive hand axe to the most recent computer games (McKenzie 2002).

Implicit in Fukuyama's treatise on the posthuman future is a fear that technology will take us over. This is not a new concern, but a question that philosophers such as Martin Heidegger have sought to explain. In his 1955 essay on the 'Question Concerning Technology', Heidegger observes that forces external to the self, such as technology, increasingly compromise the free will of the modern subject. What Heidegger calls technology's *Gestell*, or enframing, is the process whereby technology, rather than the individual, comes to define the purpose of, and motivations for, human existence. Following this line of thinking, machines can no longer be conceptualised as neutral tools that are appropriated by human beings to control and master their environment. Rather, *Gestell* shatters any sense that humans are distinct from their surroundings. While technology may enframe objects by bringing them into being for human resource, people too, can be enframed by technology as objects to be used and manipulated.

Heidegger's argument taps into the fear that humans will become powerless because they are no longer able to fully control either technology or nature.

Not only are human beings disempowered, they risk becoming another resource in the service of technology, or what Heidegger calls 'standing reserve' (Heidegger 1977: 298). A point of crisis ensues for the subject as humans increasingly rely on technology to control the unpredictable forces of nature, yet concurrently, the 'other-than-human' machine poses a threat to our very existence. From this tension emerges a new understanding of the subject; 'a decentred form of explanation' (Rothfield 1990: 124) that acknowledges the subject's engagements with its surroundings help to shape its sense of self. As Hubert Dreyfus' interpretation of Heidegger suggests, the agency that humans can assert is not one of mastery and domination over nature and technology, but the possibility of rethinking traditional values in order to transform our perception of reality and understanding of being (Dreyfus 1993: 307).

Heidegger's substantive approach to technology is in some ways akin to a poststructural project to destabilise the centrality of the subject in explanations of human identity and existence.[2] While for Heidegger, the techno–human interaction decentres the subject, it does not necessarily signal the end of the human, as Fukuyama fears it might. And despite the productive changes technology can bring to our thinking about the self and the world, social anxieties about technology still have considerable cultural purchase, as Fukuyama's vision of the posthuman future suggests.

One response to this kind of concern is to read the 'post' prefix in the term 'posthuman' as signalling something that comes after the human, but remains in a continuum of human existence and change. In this interpretation, the posthuman becomes part of the process of being human, which involves shaping and being shaped by our environments. As Katherine Hayles suggests, the posthuman doesn't have to mean the end of the human or the rise of the antihuman, it can signal a shared partnership between human and non-human forms that in the process of this engagement challenges the boundaries between the two (Hayles 1999: 286–91).

This vision is very different to the popular image of the posthuman found in cyberpunk literature, where the posthuman comes to embody a state of transcendence of the 'real world' through virtual technologies. Writing on the representation of the body in the science fiction novel *Neuromancer*, Scott Bukatman observes that 'the body is paradoxically extended by its own disappearance—the subject's control is increased by its implosion within the cyberspaces of electronic technology' (Bukatman 1993: 315). The male protagonist of the novel is empowered by entering cyberspace and leaving behind all the perceived inadequacies associated with the human corpus, including death, for a state of virtual immortality. Here, information technology acts as a tool to move beyond the limitations of bodily existence.

What needs to be stressed at this point is that the posthuman condition cannot simply be explained by the transcendence, extension or penetration of the human body via technologies. Rather, it is the bodily transformations and augmentations that come about through our engagements with technology that complicate the idea of a 'human essence'. The posthuman emerges by interrogating what it means to be human in a digital age. If the human mind can be downloaded into a machine, as imagined by Hans Moravec in his controversial book *Mind Children* (1988), then does bodily experience count for nothing? Indeed, is it the mind or the body that makes us human? When our corporeal experiences and our interactions with others are changed by technology, do we stop being human?

These questions attack the very foundation of humanist thinking, which tells us that the modern subject is an autonomous agent whose sense of being remains constant, regardless of the factors that impact on the experience of day-to-day living. In a human-centred universe, external factors count for very little when seeking to understand the 'essence' of being human. For the Enlightenment subject, understanding the fundamental characteristics of humanity demands a transcendence of historical and social contexts in favour of an interpretation of the self as self-mastering and universal. In Enlightenment thinking, the human subject is the primary locus of existence (Kohanski 1977). It follows, then, that an individual's 'true self' is immutable, unchanging and unaffected by the specificities of location, history, culture and the body. The modern self is understood as 'one that contains the ground of intentional consciousness as an inherent property, it is a self that is "self constituting" in being itself "the source and agent of all meaning"' (Marshall cited in Prado 1995: 54).

As a way of getting around this human-centric way of thinking, I take a view of the posthuman in genealogical terms, which rejects a singular or universal interpretation of human existence. A genealogical approach, as outlined by Michel Foucault, disrupts a linear account of history and subject constitution (Foucault 1984a: 77). Unlike a search for origins, which is oriented in a sequential way, genealogy looks for shared sensibilities and affiliations that can be made across time and place. Genealogy allows me to look for connections, relations and resonances across historical moments, rather than taking a unified, linear account of the emergence of the posthuman.

It offers a way of moving beyond an interpretation of the posthuman in 'evolutionary' terms, whether technological or biological (Stelarc 1998). I'm not interested in finding the origins of posthuman existence or charting humankind's progress from 'human' to 'posthuman'. The posthuman doesn't supersede the human subject or offer a 'better' or more advanced model of the human. It doesn't necessarily want to leave the body behind.

Instead, interpreting the posthuman as a process of reformulating established categories of being creates the possibility of transforming identity politics based on dialectical relations.

Feminist Approaches to the Posthuman

Amidst the fears and possibilities evoked by theories of the posthuman, two important feminist texts have emerged that contest the correlation between posthumanism and disembodiment found in much cyberpunk literature. Judith Halberstam and Ira Livingstone's collection of essays from 1995, *Posthuman Bodies,* and Katherine Hayles' *How We Became Posthuman: Virtual Bodies in Cybernetics, Literature and Informatics* (1999), interpret the body as a site where what it means to be human in a contemporary age is fundamentally contested. They do this by focusing on the idea of embodied difference, which has been a central question for feminism, particularly in studies of women's relationships to technology. In taking some time to explore the arguments presented by these books, we can further consider how women might approach posthuman representation.

For the editors of *Posthuman Bodies,* it is neither possible nor useful to offer an all-encompassing definition of the posthuman. Instead of determining the posthuman in terms of what it is or isn't, Halberstam and Livingstone imagine the posthuman in terms of the processes though which it emerges. They rely on concepts put forward by the thinker Gilles Deleuze like multiplicities, becomings and assemblages to explain the fragmentation of established narratives structuring notions of bodies, identity and humanness. The posthuman body is thus located at the interstices of 'postmodern relations of power and pleasure, virtuality and reality, sex and its consequences' (Halberstam and Livingstone 1995: 3). Their posthuman bodies are the queer body, the technobody and the contaminated body; bodies that rupture a coherent narrative of the human subject in favour of the body in crisis (Halberstam and Livingstone 1995: 3–4).

A number of the essays in this collection see mutants, aliens, monsters and cyborgs as forms of posthuman existence. Such hybrid forms are no longer futuristic ideals, utopian myths or nightmarish fantasies. Instead, these new imaginings of the human circulate as possibilities, potentialities and processes that shatter the conventional divide between reality and fantasy or fact and fiction. The posthuman is a point at which we never arrive (Pepperell 2005). In this sense, the posthuman operates as a site of ambiguity, as a transitional space where old ways of thinking about the self and the Other, the body and technology, reality and illusion, can't be sustained. From this perspective, it is difficult for women to identify definitively with the kinds of posthuman bodies they see represented in popular culture, or indeed to outright reject them. Throughout *Posthuman Bodies*, the idea that individual identity can be secured through social categories, such as gender, sexuality and ethnicity, is called into question.

While *Posthuman Bodies* is oriented toward discursive strategies through which the body may be productively re-imagined, Hayles' response to the posthuman is very much directed toward interrogating the associations between posthumanism and disembodied forms of existence. She aims to re-embody the virtual spaces and digital technologies that have often ignored or denied women's bodies and their lived experiences of the world. According to Hayles, the posthuman is best understood as a historically and culturally situated construction, emerging from the interplay between popular discursive formations and narratives within cybernetics and literature. *How We Became Posthuman* examines the question of posthuman existence in contemporary society by addressing three key areas—the dislocation of information from the body, the creation of the cyborg as a technological artefact and cultural icon, and how a historically specific construction called 'the human' is giving way to a different construction called 'the posthuman' (Hayles 1999: 2). To this end, she provides a historical assessment of cybernetics, interspersed with literary critique, to investigate how scientific discourses and popular literary texts work in tandem to reshape notions of the human. This approach to posthuman identity charts the trajectories of cybernetic discourse and literary articulations of posthuman existence to expose the narratives of anxiety that prevail at the collapse of bodily boundaries.

This differs considerably from the approach taken by Halberstam and Livingstone, who think that 'history is inefficient as a method of processing meaning; it cannot keep up' (Halberstam and Livingstone 1995: 3). Like them, I consider the posthuman from the position of a 'past and future lived as present crisis' (Halberstam and Livingstone 1995: 4). The body and identity are not only radically transformed by everyday interactions with technology, but are projected into futures without histories. I'll return to this idea in the next chapter, where I talk about the disappearance of history, as it is understood by Jean Baudrillard.

Both Hayles' *How We Became Posthuman* and Halberstam and Livingstone's *Posthuman Bodies* expose how a posthuman existence can be advantageous for women. This is because the posthuman contests old categories of identity formation that function to essentialise and exclude women and replaces them with a more complex range of subject positions.

But Hayles is also aware of some of the difficulties of embracing the posthuman as an empowering figuration for women. If, as she argues, the posthuman derives from the specific moment where information is separated from a material substrate, then what happens when the material world and all the elements associated with it, including the body, are left behind?[3] As a product of modernist thinking about intelligence and being, cybernetics constructs the human as a set of information processes, privileging mind over body and erasing the embodied experience of the corporeal subject. As a result, 'this separation allows the construction of a hierarchy in which information is given the dominant position and materiality runs a distant second' (Hayles 1999: 12). The discourse of cybernetics can thus be interpreted as being at odds with a feminist politic that seeks to redress the negation of female subjectivity, embodiment and experience. It is the cybernetic myth of disembodiment that is based on the construction of 'information and materiality as distinct entities' (Hayles 1999: 12) that Hayles wants to overcome by repositioning the posthuman as an embodied mode of being.

Hayles is critical of a cybernetic version of the human that puts the mind and its informational patterns, rather than embodied experience, at the core of being human. Her project, then, is to contest the divide between information and materiality to challenge the construction of the cybernetic subject as disembodied. Although the (con)fusion between the corporeal and the cybernetic does not necessitate an absolute obliteration of bodily materiality,[4] Hayles' project is to reinstate and revalue the body in a humanist narrative that traditionally separates man from woman, mind from matter and technology from the body (Hayles 1999: 5). The way that she challenges the material–informational divide is by highlighting the interplay of discursive formulations of embodied subjecthood and the cybernetic desire for disembodiment. For Hayles, it is this parallel tension between abstraction and embodiment that produces the posthuman subject. By building and expanding on feminist studies of technology, cyberspace and embodiment, Hayles puts the body back into information, revaluing the posthuman as an embodied mode of being.

As it is necessary to critically intervene in the discourses arising from computer technology to prevent posthuman subjects being rewritten from a disembodied position, how might we do this without simply returning to an unproblematised notion of material reality, as I think Hayles does, to redress the cybernetic myth of bodiless information? She advocates for an embodied virtuality that perceives human life as 'embedded in a material world of great complexity' (Hayles 1999: 5), and cautions us about 'the fragility of a material world that cannot be replaced' (Hayles 1999: 49). And while I agree that subjects—posthuman or otherwise—are forged by symbolic practices of signification as well as everyday interactions with technologies in society (Hayles 1999: 29), I'm not convinced that we can speak unproblematically about material existence, especially in a context where the distinctions between real and virtual worlds are no longer clear.

While both *Posthuman Bodies* and *How We Became Posthuman* address the posthuman as an embodied state, little has emerged in the literature on the posthuman to suggest how such figurations might operate in a culture of simulation to radically contest notions of reality, being and identity. It is at the site of the collapse between reality and fiction, referent and image, that I locate the posthuman as a figuration that reformulates identity as a process of transformation.

My proposition that a transformation in signification allows feminism to refigure notions of identity, representation and reality does share similarities with the argument Hayles puts forth in chapter two of her text. In 'Virtual Bodies and Flickering Signifiers', Hayles forges valuable insights toward refiguring the signifier/signified relationship by way of a shift from the presence/absence dialectic to one of pattern/randomness. In a world where the emerging cultural aesthetic of the digital is transforming our very mode of signification, Hayles contends that discursive formations that rely on a presence/absence dialectic are no longer effective in making meaning in a virtual world. Theories of the subject discussed in these terms make little sense in a digital domain characterised by simulation and virtuality because signifides and signifiers have no direct relationship and meaning is no longer grounded by a fixed origin.

Drawing on the typewriter as an example, Hayles explains how mechanical technologies of inscription maintain a proportionate relationship between signifier and signified. That is, the physical act of striking a key produces a directly corresponding letter. This relationship is quite different to the domain of digital technology, where the signified and signifier no longer correspond in a one-to-one relationship. In a virtual environment, 'text-as-flickering-image' may be manipulated entirely by a single keystroke, thus fundamentally altering the signifier/signified relationship based on a one-to-one association (Hayles 1999: 26). The computer is an exemplar of a new model of signification based on randomness.

She proposes a new theory of signification based on pattern and randomness to replace Cartesian dualisms of presence/absence (Hayles 1999: 28). Extending on the Lacanian idea of the floating signifier, Hayles suggests that 'information technologies create what I will call *flickering signifiers*, characterized by their tendency toward unexpected metamorphoses, attenuations, and dispersions' (Hayles 1999: 30). While this concept offers an effective tool to consider how technologies of textual production affect signification, it cannot be sustained at the point where the circulation of signs has no relation to the material world. By replacing presence and absence with pattern and randomness, and establishing a divide between the material (presence/absence) and the virtual (pattern/randomness), Hayles maintains an approach to signification based in a dialectical logic. These kinds of concerns form the focus of the next chapter, where I engage with the ideas of Jean Baudrillard to explain how the order of simulation collapses a mode of sign exchange against a 'real', thus confusing the very categories of virtuality and reality.

Feminist Critiques of the Subject

Amidst the debates about the posthuman, it is important to recognise that the idea of the hu*man* has been fraught for feminists and other marginalised groups prior to the advent of technologies that blur the boundaries of the human. Neil Badmington neatly summarises this point when he remarks that 'the crisis in humanism is happening *everywhere*...the reign of Man is simultaneously being called into question by literature, politics, cinema, anthropology, feminism and technology. These attacks are connected, part of the circuit of posthumanism' (Badmington 2000: 9). For some time now, the notion of the subject in crisis has been the central concern of many poststructural thinkers. As traditional formulations of the human are called into question by the poststructural and postmodern dissolution of absolute systems of value, so, too, are entrenched notions of the body and identity scrutinised.

Michel Foucault reminds us that 'the extent to which a type of philosophical interrogation—one that simultaneously problematizes man's relation to the present, man's historical mode of being, and the constitution of the self as an autonomous subject—is rooted in the Enlightenment' (Foucault 1984b: 42). And much of the destabilisation of the human subject, whether it is through feminist, postmodern or technology studies, centres on an interrogation of the modern Western subject that was forged during the Enlightenment period.

Feminism has been critical of an Enlightenment mode of thinking that understands being human as intimately associated with the qualities of reason, rationality and maleness. Throughout her keynote text, *The Man of Reason: 'Male' and 'Female' in Western Philosophy* (1984), feminist philosopher Genevieve Lloyd confronts and unpacks the gendered assumptions linking Enlightenment values of reason to the construction of the human as an implicitly male subject. According to Lloyd, the universality of reason, while challenged by relativism, is the defining feature of contemporary philosophical interrogations of the self. She notes that:

> Reason has figured in western culture not only in the assessment of beliefs, but also in the assessment of character. It is incorporated not just into our criteria of truth, but also into our understanding of what it is to be a person at all, of the requirements that must be met to be a good person, and of the proper relations between our status as knowers and the rest of our lives (Lloyd 1984: ix).

As well as identifying reason as the pre-eminent characteristic of the Enlightenment model of being, Lloyd explains how reason operates within a hierarchical logic of binary difference. She argues that rational knowledge, constructed as the transcendence, antithesis and domination of natural forces according to dialectical thinking, subsequently determines the status of the gendered subject (Lloyd 1984: 2). As woman is aligned with nature, irrationality and the body, in direct opposition to culture, reason and the mind, she cannot occupy the position of the human subject. Woman is never 'fully' human.

In writing about the relationship between the mind and the body, Elizabeth Grosz shares Lloyd's criticism of the dualistic modes of thought that structure traditional notions of subjectivity. For Grosz, the dichotomisation of masculine and feminine subject positions is implicitly tied to a mind/body relation prevalent throughout the history of philosophy. Grosz describes this relationship as mutually exclusive, whereby the mind is a conceptual entity, positively associated with reason, culture, public, self, subjectivity and masculinity. Incompatible with the mind is its non-conceptual binary opposite: the body. As the negation of the mind, the body, along with its correlates of passion, nature, private, Other and femininity, is relegated to the status of 'object' (Grosz 1987: 4). Grosz emphasises the connection between women and the body when she writes: 'Thus excluded from notions of subjectivity, personhood or identity, the body becomes an "objective", observable entity, a "thing"' (Grosz 1987: 5). By extension, woman comes to define all that is not human, fixed to a corporeal, natural and essential state.

Both of these writers draw on a French feminist philosophical tradition to interrogate the exclusion of woman from full subjecthood. One of the key proponents of this movement, Hélène Cixous, attributes the non-existence of woman to the dual and hierarchical nature of oppositional thinking that sustains phallogocentrism, or the privileging of the phallic signifier in language and culture (Cixous 1980: 91). In exposing the constructed nature of gendered oppositions, feminist critiques of dualistic thought serve as political gestures to displace phallogocentrism as the foundation of humanist subjectivity and reclaim the status of the female subject. This crisis of the modern subject informs not only feminist endeavours to assert female subjectivity, but throws into question the very origins of selfhood on which human existence is grounded.

These kinds of feminist revisions of the subject have been influential to analyses of the relationship between women and technology. As critical accounts of techno–human interactions are largely constructed in accordance with the dialectical principles that govern Western thought, feminist analyses of the gendered nature of technology have provided a much needed critical intervention in a male-dominated debate where the machine is equated with the feminine while remaining the exclusive domain of the masculine (Jardine and Feher 1987: 156). Feminist critiques of technology are therefore part of feminism's ongoing attempt to refigure the human by challenging the dualisms of philosophical thought through which identity has been constructed. We find that the ambiguity arising from technologies that collapse the distinctions between nature and artifice, mind and body, organism and machine, offers the potential for new forms of subjectivity beyond oppositional frameworks.

Feminism and Technology: Past and Present Issues

Along with feminist writings about the posthuman, the history of women's relationship to technology—its artefacts, imagery, design and use—can give us a clue as to how women have been situated relative to technology up to this point. In critical debates about technology, feminist theory has explored the benefits and limitations of technology for configurations of the subject, particularly the female subject. It has done this by, amongst other things, questioning established categories such as organic and artificial, nature and machine, man and woman, mind and body. Although this strategy has been valuable for exposing the gendered assumptions that underpin techno–human interactions, it tends to position women as either victims of technology or liberated by it. The rest of this chapter investigates how technology has been interpreted by feminism as broadly 'utopian' or 'dystopian'. As many of the debates about the posthuman are informed by technofeminist thinking, an overview of its central tenets can provide a useful background for developing a more complex picture of identity, sexuality and subjectivity in contemporary posthuman culture.

Perhaps the most ubiquitous example of women's relationships with technologies is embodied in the cyborg figure. Back in 1985, Donna Haraway published the germinal article 'A Manifesto for Cyborgs: Science, Technology, and Socialist Feminism in the 1980s' where she instigated a whole new way of thinking about not only women's relationship to technology, but the conventional model of the subject based on origins, essences and organic existence. As 'a cybernetic organism, a hybrid of machine and organism, a creature of social reality as well as a creature of fiction' (Haraway 1985: 65), the cyborg is a feminist boundary rider that contests the dualisms of nature/artifice, organism/technology and self/Other. By confusing the categories of nature, culture, organism and machine, Haraway challenges the myth of original unity and its intimate associations with the natural. The cyborg figuration thus serves as a subversive and empowering strategy with which to reconsider women's relationships to each other, technology and notions of the human subject. Most importantly, the cyborg provides new modes of conceiving both social and bodily realities and the universal notion of women's shared experience.

The cyborg operates as a positive indicator of what might emerge from the alliance between feminism and technology and, in my mind, still remains influential in these debates despite over 20 years having passed since its creation. The posthuman, like the cyborg, exhibits a confusion of fact and fiction, science and technology, the virtual and the actual. But while the cyborg operates as a figure through which women may better understand the self in the context of changing technologies, I want to mobilise the posthuman as a figure that disavows identity. Although, as I will go on to discuss, many feminist writers construct the relationship between women and technology as a productive and subversive alliance, the posthuman makes no such assumptions. In a posthuman landscape, technology is neither friend nor foe, but emerges as a possibility or potentiality to refigure bodies and identities outside of self/Other relations.

This is not to take away from the significance of the cyborg in feminist thinking about technology. In Haraway's pursuit of a techno-inspired feminist politics, her cyborg functions as a circuit breaker to strategically disrupt an established line of thinking that locates women as irrevocably estranged from technology. The idea that women and technology don't mix is typified by the writing of feminist scholars such as Judy Wajcman. In her landmark study *Feminism Confronts Technology* (1991) Wajcman identifies the link between masculinity and technology, suggesting this association perpetuates unequal power relations between the genders. In her words:

> ...the traditional conception of technology is heavily weighted against women. We tend to think about technology in terms of industrial machinery and cars, for example, ignoring other technologies that affect most aspects of everyday life. The very definition of technology, in other words, has a male bias. This emphasis on technologies dominated by men conspires in turn to diminish the significance of women's technologies, such as horticulture, cooking and childcare, and so

> reproduces the stereotype of women as technologically ignorant and incapable. The enduring force of this identification between technology and manliness, therefore, is not inherent in biological sex difference. It is rather the result of the historical and cultural construction of gender (Wajcman 1991: 137).

By documenting the historical, social and cultural alignment of men with technology, she exposes how male values and agendas have shaped the way technology has been produced and used.

Coming from a socialist feminist background, Cynthia Cockburn also argues that technological tools are used by men to maintain power over women (Cockburn 1991). Referring to the sexual division of labour in the workforce, she notes that 'the technical competence that men as a sex possess and women as a sex lack is an extension of the physical domination of women by men' (Cockburn 1985: 7). For Cockburn, women's lack of technical competence operates as a structural barrier to exclude women from technology, hence restricting their access to the benefits technology may bring.

The argument that technology is gendered extends to digital technologies. Although many Western women use computers in their everyday lives, feminists have suggested that women's marginalisation from the technosphere persists. Given that the majority of the world's poor are women, economics are a very real limitation to purchasing computer equipment and getting online. Women's low literacy and educational levels pose another barrier to inhabiting cyberspace (Kramer and Kramarae 2000: 206–7). Even for those women who do have access to the Internet, factors such as the language, content and structure of the Net (Spender 1995), the metaphors surrounding computer use (Braidotti 1996, Sofia 1992), the design of hardware and programs (Cooper and Weaver 2003), and gender patterns of socialisation (Turkle 1988), make cyberspace a hostile and unappealing place at times.

In earlier radical feminist debates surrounding reproductive technologies, it was not so much women's exclusion from the design and use of technologies that posed a problem inasmuch as technology itself was considered to be inherently patriarchal and hence incompatible with women. Here the relationship between women and technology is considered to be an exploitative and unequal one that situates women at the receiving end of technology's domination over nature and the body (Arditti, Klein and Minden 1984, Corea 1985, Spallone and Steinberg 1987). By advancing a theory that science and technology are inherently patriarchal, then technology can only be detrimental to women whose ultimate status is to be passive victims under patriarchal control. From this perspective, even if women choose to access and use technology it nonetheless remains the epitome of patriarchal values of domination, force and exploitation. The solution of radical feminism is to resist technology and revalue the organic body as the site of female power; a strategy that has been criticised for essentialising women as it positions them as inherently closer to nature and the body.

In some ways, feminist criticism of the gendering of technology is more complex than simply arguing that women are seen as incompatible with technology. While in many instances women have been structurally excluded from accessing technology (in schools and the workforce, for example), they are often symbolically aligned with technology. One of the early cultural sites where the notion of technology as feminised is enacted and represented is the 1927 Fritz Lang film, *Metropolis*. In his analysis of this film, Andreas Huyssen exposes how the female protagonist's body is constructed as a technological artefact and a potentially destructive force, hence an object to be manipulated and controlled. In this film, the social anxiety towards technology as a threat to human existence, as discussed previously in the chapter, is displaced onto the feminine. When the main character (Maria) is made into a robot, she is denied an autonomous identity because hu*man*s exert power over her machinic body (Huyssen 1986: 75). It is through the gendered assumptions inherent in a definition of humanity and subjectivity that woman is Othered, paradoxically as both nature and technology, thus exploitable and subject to masculine mastery. Accordingly, the masculinist projection of women vis-à-vis technology and nature establishes the woman–machine as a double threat to rational patriarchal order (Huyssen 1986: 71). Like Sigmund Freud's 'dark continent', the feminised 'black box' of technology occupies the status of uncontrollable and unknown territory, replaying the male castration anxiety and thus legitimating the mastery and domination of the nature/technology/woman triad by male reason.

More recently, film critics such as Mary Ann Doane and Barbara Creed have analysed the representation of women in science fiction films. What they observe is that the image of the dangerous woman–machine gives way to a more nuanced inscription of the feminine threat, which often takes the form of monstrous and unnatural reproductive technologies (Creed 1993, Doane 1990). For instance, Creed observes that in David Cronenberg's 1979 film *The Brood*, the female protagonist Nola is threatening because of her reproductive power. Nola gives birth to deformed creatures, which are conceived in the absence of a father. Pre-empting the fears of cloning technologies, what makes woman monstrous in this film is not only her ability to reproduce but her ability to do so without man. Ultimately, Nola's offspring are doomed to failure as they are the product of abnormal reproductive process (Creed 1993: 44–5). Even though feminist film analysis suggests that there has been a shift in how women are depicted relative to technology in film, there still remains an 'insistent history of representations of technology that work to fortify—sometimes desperately—conventional understandings of the feminine' (Doane 1990: 163).

Despite the entrenched associations between masculinity and technology, a number of feminists have sought to endorse a productive and positive relationship between women and machines. Popularly known as cyberfeminism, this strand of feminist politics emerged in the nineties, and has been fundamental to contesting the ideological associations between masculinity and technology. It does this in part through a revaluation of the feminine and the body in a technological landscape that has been conventionally hostile to women. A cyberfeminist sensibility, as seen in the digital artwork of VNS Matrix and in online publications such as *geekgirl* (www.geekgirl.com.au), is optimistic about the kinds of interactions women may forge with technology.

Characterised by a rejection of the traditional coupling of technology and masculinity, cyberfeminism is fundamentally concerned with claiming cyberspace for women. As active agents in cyberspace, women can shake off the tag of 'technology's victims' and inhabit technocultural spaces for their own pleasure (Albury 2003, Creed 2003), and for purposes such as political organising, networking and acts of resistance (Kramer and Kramarae 2000, Wakeford 1997, Wong 2003). By endorsing cyberspace as female space, cyberfeminism strives to challenge and change the male-defined technological landscape.

One of the best-known advocates of cyberfeminism, Sadie Plant, argues for a radical break with deep-seated gendered perceptions of technology. She claims that women are in fact more suited to the new economy of the digital (Plant 1996). Rather than suggesting that women's difference positions them outside of technology, she contests the negative associations between women and technology *from the site of difference.* For Plant, '(c)yberspace is the matrix not as absence, void, the whole of the womb, but perhaps even the place of woman's affirmation' (Plant 1995: 60).[5] In reclaiming a space for women to occupy the masculine domain of technology, Plant suggests that woman, like the computer and cybernetic system, is a simulation mechanism, performing and imitating the self in a political gesture that usurps the categorical construction of woman as nature (Plant 1995: 58–9). Woman and cyberspace share an 'outlaw' status. Both are illusory and artificial. In Plant's worldview, women's difference in cyberspace is not a hindrance, but something that can undermine the very notion of male power from within. As Plant aptly puts it, '(l)ike woman, software systems are used as man's tools, his media and his weapons; all are developed in the interests of man, but all are poised to betray him' (Plant 1995: 58).

While Plant bridges the division between women and cyberspace by re-inserting the feminine into the equation, not all feminists are convinced of the potential of technology to empower women (Klein 1996, Squires 2000, Wajcman 2004). And one of the central concerns arising from a feminist reclamation of cyberspace is the disappearance of the material body in the virtual landscape. As noted earlier, the project of reasserting embodied experience in accounts of subject formation and technology, particularly in cyberspace, has been prevalent in feminist challenges to phallogocentric liberal–humanist theories of the subject. When you consider the gendered values inscribed in technology and nature, as Zoe Sofia does, there is good reason to be anxious. Technology occupies a revered status in phallocentric culture, with cybertechnologies enabling the utopian fantasy to transcend corporeal embodiment. Concurrently, cyberspaces are coded as womb-like and feminine, just waiting to be penetrated and mastered (Sofia 1992: 16). The desire to transcend bodily confines via technology is in keeping with the masculinist fantasy to escape the limitations of a corporeality coded 'feminine'. This utopian, technological rhetoric envisions the human merging *with* the machine. Rather than technology acting as a threat to humanity, it assists man in his endeavours to transcend bodily limitations and reach a pure state of selfhood. Evidently, this desire is grounded in a fear of the feminine and its associations with the body and abjection that threaten the primacy of rational humanism. By becoming like the machine, man may control and contain the body, and accordingly, nature and the feminine.

How, then, might women redress the privileging of the mind, the machine and the masculine over matter, materiality and the feminine? In a similar vein to Hayles' notion of the embodied posthuman mentioned earlier, Anne Balsamo suggests that we need to return to a materialist foundation to understand the subject's engagements with technology. She claims that 'the material body remains a constant factor of the postmodern, post-human condition. It has certain undeniable material qualities that are, in turn, culturally determined and discursively managed; qualities that are tied to its physiology and to the cultural contexts within which it makes sense, such as its gender and race identities' (Balsamo 1995: 220). Similarly, Susan Hawthorne responds to cyberfeminist celebrations of the techno–human by asking us to recognise the importance of the 'real world' over virtual enactments. She is sceptical of a virtual, decontextualised cyberspace that poses a threat to the reality of women's lived existence (Hawthorne 1999). Not only does Hawthorne assume that women maintain a privileged relation to the real over the virtual, she upholds an unproblematic notion of the real and what counts as a 'real' body (Hawthorne 1999: 217).

I suggest that a feminism that celebrates the coupling of women and technology, and one that opposes it, both serve as political gestures to revalorise the feminine, yet risk replaying the binary dualisms that associate women with nature and the body. Surveying the various debates regarding women's relationships to technologies uncovers a profound gap between the proponents of technology as beneficial, and those who deem it detrimental for women. This feminist dialogue follows a broader trend of theorising the relationship between technology and society in black and white terms whereby technology is viewed as either beneficial or detrimental to humanity. For example, scholars such as Theodore Rozak (1970) and Arthur and Marilouise Kroker (1996) adopt a dystopic approach to techno–human relations, signalling the dangers of technology to our sense of self, being and existence. Others, such as Howard Rheingold (1991) and Bill Gates (1995) espouse an uncritical and utopian rhetoric of technology as potentially beneficial to all humanity, thus failing to assess who new technologies may serve and to what ends (Jones 1995).

In the project of revaluing technology and the feminine, an affirmation of the woman–technology relationship employs a deterministic 'pro-technology' approach that aligns technology with women's values and interests. This suggests that technology exists as a neutral tool outside of practices of signification in which a traditional 'masculine' set of values may simply be substituted for 'feminine' values, paying little attention to the historical, social and cultural specificities through which gender shapes technology and technology shapes gender. Thinking instead about techno–human relations as a dynamic process highlights that technology is only ever a social artefact, and in doing so, contests technologically determinist approaches that interpret technology's progress as inevitable and unstoppable.

Neither can the posthuman be located in a narrative of technology as either beneficial or detrimental to a theory of female subject constitution. Instead, I think that the posthuman can offer feminism a different way of thinking about the subject–technology relationship, and in turn, a politics of identity. When read in the context of a transformation in signifying practices, posthuman figurations can work against a feminist valuation of technology in dichotomous terms of good or bad. The posthuman is a figuration that exceeds signification; in Baudrillard's terms it 'disappears' in the process of transforming into something else beyond the effects of technology as affirmative or negative for women.

Sherry Turkle: The Machine and the Self

Poststructural formations of the subject encourage a consideration of the socio-cultural forces that inform the relations between gender and technology. One such proponent of this approach is Sherry Turkle, who circumvents the debates that position technology as a neutral tool to be appropriated productively by women, or used against them. Instead, Turkle's feminist scholarship seeks to explain how computer culture poses alternative means of thinking about subjectivity and the self.

In the landmark text *The Second Self: Computers and the Human Spirit* (1984), Turkle documents the responses of children, adolescents and adults interacting with new digital communications. This ethnographic study highlights how humans perceive themselves in the wake of new digital technologies and raises fundamental philosophical questions about identity in the digital age. For Turkle, the advent of computer culture incites a radical rethinking of who we are and the nature of being human. Central to her analysis is the issue of how individuals forge a sense of self in relation to an emerging computer culture. As she explains:

> Technology catalyzes changes not only in what we do but in how we think. It changes peoples' awareness of themselves, of one another, of their relationship with the world. The new machine that stands behind the flashing digital signal, unlike the clock, the telescope, or the train, is a machine that "thinks". It challenges our notions not only of time and distance, but of mind (Turkle 1984: 13).

By exploring the diversity of relationships individuals may occupy to the computer, Turkle's research assesses the impact of these relations on understandings of the self. From her perspective, the issue is not whether technology is good or bad for people and society, but how it serves as a means by which the self may be articulated. For Turkle, 'the machine can act as a projection of part of the self, a mirror of the mind' (Turkle 1984: 15), or as she goes on to state, 'computers enter into the development of personality, of identity, and even of sexuality' (Turkle 1984: 15). She isn't suggesting here that the computer is a passive screen or neutral entity onto which the self is projected. Rather, it is how the individual perceives themselves and their relationship to the world that is radically altered through the virtual medium.

Turkle's studies of computer–human relations have made an important contribution to thinking toward a posthuman mode of being. An alternative means of theorising identity is posed by the author—one that recognises the context, location and embodied experiences, which impact on the formation of the subject. Just as Turkle advocates a subject that is neither unified nor fixed, but constantly formulated and reconstructed through her/his diverse relationships with computer culture, to be posthuman is to construct a notion of self within a culture of simulation, virtuality and the digital. It is a new mode of existence by which the subject comes into being, as distinctions collapse between nature and artifice, self and computer, virtual and real, animate and inanimate.

The confusion around where the human ends and the non-human begins raises the pivotal question in an analysis of posthuman existence: 'what is most essential about being human?' (Turkle 1984: 24). By examining people of varying age groups and their relationship to computer culture, Turkle uncovers a blurring of the boundaries between the categories of the human and the machine. The computer is an 'evocative object', that 'seems to stand betwixt and between the world of alive and not alive' (Turkle 1984: 106). A simple example of this is the analogies that people make between themselves and machines, as shown by Turkle in the case of a boy called George. She documents how George uses the computer metaphor of debugging to explain how he intends to deal with his feelings of depression. From George's point of view, his mind could be equated with a computer, which once 'debugged' would be fixed (Turkle 1984: 161–2). By drawing parallels between computer and human elements, the distinction between organism and machine is confused, and the very nature of self is questioned.

Although the computer–human interaction has opened up new ways to think about the self, there is still a pervasive tendency to secure human identity as something that can be differentiated from a machine. The characteristics that are commonly defined as essential to being human, such as emotion and intuition, are the qualities computers as supposedly unable to emulate. For Turkle, 'human' comes to define all that the computer is not (Turkle 1997: 177). Like Jacques Lacan's theory of the subject, where identity is forged through the process of differentiation from the m/other, the computer serves as an Other from which the human is defined.

So what we see in Turkle's version of the development of the self is a simultaneous affiliation to, and disassociation from computers. Even though she shows that technology impacts on how the self is perceived and experienced, the boundaries between self and Other remain distinct, rather than collapsing. For Turkle, computer technology affords a means to reflect upon real life, rather than problematise the very status of the real. This proves problematic to a rethinking of the status of the human subject as a posthuman entity, in that the self remains a separate entity from the machine.

For example, in critically surveying the construction of the self within a culture of simulation, namely the virtual environments of Multi User Domains (MUDS), MUD Object Oriented (MOOs) and virtual chat rooms, Turkle suggests the life enacted within the virtual realm often infiltrates the real life of participants. Such experiences have emerged within what Turkle perceives as a broader cultural trend. It is the context of 'eroding boundaries between the real and virtual, the animate and inanimate, the unitary and multiple self, which is occurring both in advanced scientific fields of research and in the patterns of everyday life' that enables a new cultural aesthetic and philosophy of existence (Turkle 1997: 10).

MUDs offer an interactive space where multiple users from vastly different locations and contexts may simultaneously engage in a simulated adventure fantasy.[6] The creation of a social space within the machine provides a fantasy world where individuals may formulate imaginary personas and enact alternative lives. Traditional perceptions of identity are complicated when the distinctions between virtual and real environments collapse and the player's 'real' life is affected by their actions in virtual space (Turkle 1996: 357). An instance of this is the phenomena of gender swapping in virtual reality environments. Turkle interprets the practice of virtual gender swapping, enacting a persona of the opposite gender within a MUD, as serving multiple purposes. Firstly, it facilitates consciousness-raising about gender issues (Turkle 1997: 214). By virtually engaging with the concerns faced by individuals of the opposite gender, the user may attain an awareness of gender issues that may subsequently translate to real life situations. Secondly, a female playing a male character, or vice-versa, exposes gender as a construct. Turkle's interviews with participants who play a character of a different gender further suggest that the act of gender swapping serves as a 'vehicle for self-reflection' (Turkle 1997: 219) and gives 'people greater emotional range in the real' (Turkle 1997: 222).

Despite the evident crossover between virtual and real domains in a MUD scenario, Turkle retains the notion that MUDers perceive their engagement with virtual reality (VR) as a means to gain a greater truth regarding the real (Turkle 1997: 216). The theoretical perspective offered by Turkle encourages us to question the relationships between the real and virtual, nature/machine and human/non-human. Yet in distinguishing between real life and life on the screen, Turkle fundamentally maintains the categorical distinction between the two, albeit complicating the status of each.

In this digital era, another means of configuring self and identity is required—one that questions the very status of real and virtual, machine and organism, self and Other. This is because our engagements with the world around us take the form of simulated realities. That is, the categories of embodied existence collide with virtual experience so that the two are no longer separable. Instead of approaching the posthuman through a study of 'real life', as Turkle does, or through Hayles' lens of 'material reality', perhaps an interpretation of the posthuman needs to take into account the representational economy of simulation in which images exist and are circulated, and hence reside beyond the codes of signification and their enactments.

I will investigate how simulation culture, as described by Jean Baudrillard, transforms the process of signification and how this may lead to alternative understandings of reality, the body and selfhood. Although this book, like other feminist writings on this topic, sees the posthuman as useful for women, it differs from them by focusing on the context in which the posthuman circulates and the implications that an economy of simulation might have for how the self, the body and gender are understood. It is Baudrillard's idea of the simulation economy that I will now turn to in order to explore the usefulness of images of a posthuman, post-gender existence.

2

Ways of Looking and Ways of Being

In the last chapter, we began mapping the terrain of the posthuman: a world where digital media, biotechnologies and electronic communications merge and intersect. A number of things were made apparent in this discussion. Firstly, that our experiences of society, the self, representation and reality are increasingly becoming virtual. And secondly, that despite considerable focus on the changing state of the subject in an era of posthumanism, there is little corresponding emphasis on the shifting status of reality. For these reasons, the writings of Jean Baudrillard are of particular interest to posthuman debates because their emphasis on 'tracking the increasingly fundamental role of signs and images in our life' (Kellner 1989: 188) can help us reflect on the nature of reality in a cybernetic age. His theory of simulation, especially, 'creates a space to wonder about the real' (Grace 2000: 25). As products of the digital revolution, I think that posthuman images do a similar thing—they provoke questions about how reality is experienced and understood.

In this respect, the way that the world is conceptualised through images becomes an important aspect of theorising the posthuman. In saying this, I want to make it clear that it is not my intention to read posthuman images and come up with a 'better' or 'truer' interpretation to those that have already been offered or to provide the 'answer' to what posthuman images are depicting. Typically, this is the way that critics approach representations. They analyse them for some significance. They might ask 'What is this picture saying?' or 'What does this advertisement mean?' I'm less interested in making meaning about the posthuman than I am in locating posthuman images as part of an ongoing debate about reality, representation and subjectivity. Although this book takes as its starting point images of the posthuman—representations that depict the fusion of the organic and the informational—its primary concern is with posthuman images. By the term 'posthuman images', I am not referring to images as those things that depict or reference reality, but as performative acts/events/processes in their own right that function to destroy coherent meaning about the human as an originary form. As is the case with this book, in some instances, images of the posthuman can be posthuman images, and vice-versa. By charting the associations between vision and the construction and experience of reality, it becomes apparent that in an era of hyperreality, there is no truth or answer to be revealed about the posthuman through its representation. Rather, the posthuman emerges at the moment where clear distinctions between things collapse. It is an effect of the hyperreal.

This approach is quite different to visions of a posthuman future articulated in science fiction (SF) narratives. Often, these visions of utopian or dystopian fantasies act as a mirror on our world, allowing us to reflect on what humanity is and where it is going. Or as István Csicsery-Ronay puts it 'SF embeds scientific–technological concepts in the sphere of human interest as actions, explaining them and explicitly attributing social value to them' (Csicsery-Ronay 1991: 387). What we find in a simulated reality, as proposed by Baudrillard, is that science fiction is no longer a significant or legitimate mode of explaining the posthuman moment. The reason for this is because the gap between the real and the imaginary is eroding, and along with it, the genre of science fiction founded on fantasy (Baudrillard 1994: 212). The posthuman emerges as 'something else' that cannot be indexically connected to 'real life'.

For Baudrillard, the imaginary of science fiction corresponds to a second order of simulacra (an idea I explain fully later in this chapter), whereby the order of signs is founded on a system of serial production materialised through mechanical and technical means (Baudrillard 1993: 55). In contrast, the posthuman occupies a mode of signification that is founded on hyperreality. As a product of the information or digital age, the posthuman collapses and exceeds the boundaries that once differentiated fact from fiction and illusion from reality. By locating the posthuman in the context of a simulated hyperreality, we can disassociate representations of the posthuman from the realm of science fiction, and accordingly, begin to think about them differently.

There are plenty of books out there devoted to explaining Baudrillard's ideas and charting the progress of his thinking, which are recommended if you are looking for a systematic overview of his oeuvre (see, for example, Butler 1999, Gane 1991b, Grace 2000, Hegarty 2004, Kellner 1989, Levin 1996). What I want to do here is briefly introduce you to his notion of simulation as a way of illuminating our present cultural situation and locating the posthuman within it.

Many writers have used Baudrillard's theory of simulation to make sense of aspects of the contemporary world such as the mass media (Chen 1987), advertising (Kellner 1989), and the Internet (Nunes 1995). His concepts of simulation and hyperreality could almost be considered mainstream these days. They are a standard part of many undergraduate creative arts, visual and cultural studies courses. Perhaps more significantly, they have crossed over into the realm of the popular by way of the blockbuster film *The Matrix* (1999), where clever references are made to Baudrillard throughout the film, especially his book *Simulacra and Simulation*, which the protagonist Neo (played by Keanu Reeves) holds in an early scene.

Likewise, Baudrillard's ideas lend themselves nicely to the phenomenon of the posthuman, and can offer us a way of approaching these images as something other than 'good' or 'bad' representations of the women and technology relationship. The logical question for many scholars, including feminists, is: 'If we can no longer think about images in critical terms—that is, what they can tell us about gender, power, the differences between the sexes and the inequalities that stem from that—then how useful are Baudrillard's theories?' To begin exploring this question, let's turn to the idea of simulation.

The Significance of Simulation

At its heart, simulation is a theory of reality, of how we make sense of the images and objects that inhabit our existence, and in turn, ourselves and our place in the world. When Baudrillard talks about simulation, he is referring to the change in the relationship between objects and signs and the implications of this for how we understand the social order. In an age of mass production, mass media and mass communication, a sign system based in image culture has replaced our old ways of understanding social reality. For Baudrillard, this new reality is to be found in an emerging order of media and information technologies. Simulation occurs when the law of value based on a 'reality principle' folds:

> The reality principle corresponds to a certain stage of the law of value. Today the whole system is swamped by indeterminacy, and even reality is absorbed by the hyperreality of the code and simulation. The principal of simulation governs us now, rather than the outdated reality principle. We *feed* on those forms whose finalities have disappeared. No more ideology, only simulacra (Baudrillard 1993: 2).

It is vital to stress that when Baudrillard speaks of simulation, he does not see it as signalling the end of the real, but as bringing about a shift in our idea of what reality is. This is a valuable distinction to make. Simulation does not reproduce reality, nor does it mask, hide or obscure reality. It produces reality.

In his writing on simulation, Baudrillard distances himself from structural relations between the referent and representation established by laws of exchange value. The principle of simulation that Baudrillard poses questions an understanding of value that relies on a dialectical model of language and commodity exchange. The evolution of Baudrillard's writing on the sign can be traced from a Marxist framework that considers the role of the sign as it relates to the remaking of society via capitalist modes of consumption (Baudrillard 1981, 1998a).[1] According to Baudrillard, the system of meaning that has come to typify our current age is no longer the operations of consumption and production of the industrial era, but the circulation of signifiers with no referent in reality. By showing us how Ferdinand de Saussure's linguistic model of signification and Karl Marx's theories of production depend on systems of reference, Baudrillard exposes the limitations of both of these ways of making sense of the world in an age of hyperreality where there is no point of reference anymore (Baudrillard 1993: 6–7).

In a postmodern culture that is widely influenced by media, new technologies and mass communications, objects are freed from their material base to exist in a network of signs. The process is described by Baudrillard as:

> ...a gigantic simulacrum—not unreal, but a simulacrum, that is to say never exchanged for the real, but exchanged for itself, in an uninterrupted circuit without reference or circumference. Such is simulation, insofar as it is opposed to representation (Baudrillard 1994: 6).

He rejects traditional theories of social operations that rely on some sort of relationship between objects and signs. Instead, Baudrillard asserts that the proliferation of signs and images in post-industrial society ensures that signs are no longer exchanged against a real, but may only be exchanged against each other (Baudrillard 1993: 7). In short, signs can be understood through their relation to other signs. They exist independently of the actual objects 'out there' in the 'real' world that they are supposed to represent. In this sense, it would be wrong to suggest that images and signs operate as reflections of reality, because for Baudrillard, no definitive connection can be made between reality and its representation. This process whereby signs become disassociated from any material referent is what Baudrillard calls the 'emancipation of the sign' (Baudrillard 1993: 7). But this is not to say that signs don't have material effects. If, as it has already been noted, images generate our reality, then they *should* act on us. For example, the purpose of advertising is to encourage us to buy products, which in turn has genuine economic implications. The content of the advertisement may not be traceable to a 'real' object in the 'real' world, but the cultural reach of the image, the sites and spaces in which it circulates, forges what we come to know and experience as reality.

When meaning is liberated from the sign so that it no longer refers to an external reality, then reality and representation can't strictly be understood as opposite terms anymore. If we cannot distinguish between once distinct entities such as sign/object or reality/representation, then dialectics as a mode of understanding self, society and identity is rendered ineffectual. In turn, the fixed nature of signifying practice is replaced by a far more uncertain system. To paraphrase Baudrillard, a representational economy of simulation is 'swamped by indeterminacy' (Baudrillard 1993: 2). In this context, any attempt at making meaning is irrelevant, as we can't distinguish between objects and signs with any confidence. It is the 'forms whose finalities have disappeared' (Baudrillard 1993: 2) that now constitute the value system of a postmodern technosociety and inform our visual experiences.

In effect, Baudrillard questions a material critique of representation, offering instead the post-material mode of simulation that denies meaning as derived from an origin or referent. He explains it this way:

> ...all forms change from the moment that they are no longer mechanically reproduced, but *conceived according to their very reproducibility*, their diffraction from a generative core called a "model". We are dealing with third-order simulacra here (Baudrillard 1993: 56).

This shift from the experience of the image as a reproduction of the real world towards the generation of the real through simulation is called 'hyperreality'—a mode of experiencing contemporary life as *more real than real.* As Baudrillard articulates in his keynote text on the theory of the simulacra, *Simulacra and Simulation*, 'simulation is no longer that of a territory, a referential being or a substance. It is the generation by models of a real without origin or reality: a hyperreal' (Baudrillard 1994: 1). My understanding of the hyperreal is consistent with Paul Rodaway's assertion that 'it is important to not treat the hyperreal as specific places or situations, but as a potential way (or limits?) of experiencing an associated mode of signification found in contemporary spaces' (Rodaway 1995: 244–5).

The simulation model or hyperreal, then, acts as a circuit breaker in conventional understandings of meaning-production and sign value by disempowering the signifier. When the image 'has no relation to any reality whatsoever', it comes to exceed signification (Baudrillard 1994: 6). Its signals are free-floating and illegible, and deny the possibility of coherent interpretation (Baudrillard 1993: 57–8). If the posthuman is an effect of the hyperreal, as I am suggesting, then simulation affords another way of approaching the posthuman, a way that exceeds structural equations between a referent and reality.

In all of this talk about the implosion of dichotomous values and the collapse of the sign/origin relationship, it is worth reiterating Baudrillard's central point about simulation—that reality is a production. It is an effect of the sign. As Rex Butler has noted, this interpretation is quite different to popular claims that Baudrillard erases the real. Butler observes that:

> There are thus two different senses in which the real is used in Baudrillard's work: there is the real which is brought about by the system and that real which is the absolute limit to the system. Baudrillard's work, therefore, is not simply to be understood as the celebration of simulation, the end of the real, as so many of his commentators would have it. Rather, his problem is how to think the real when all is simulation, how to use the real against the attempts by various systems of rationality to account for it (Butler 1999: 17).

The idea that simulation both exceeds and upholds the illusion of reality is explored by Baudrillard across a number of his texts. One of the consequences of simulation, Baudrillard tells us, is that we can't speak about the real outside of simulation because it is simulation that makes the real possible. Simulation therefore operates to maintain the illusion of reality. Baudrillard calls this a strategy of deterrence; a strategy whose primary function is to conceal that there is no real outside of simulation (Baudrillard 1994: 7). This is the power and paradox of simulation: its potential to approximate reality, while maintaining no referent in reality. So while simulation undermines origins, it also operates to perpetuate myths of origins and authenticity by upholding the appearance of a real. As Baudrillard explains:

> For reality is but a concept, or a principle, and by reality I mean the whole system of values connected with this principle. The Real as such implies an origin, an end, a past and a future, a chain of causes and effects, a continuity and a rationality. No real without these elements, without an objective configuration of discourse. And its disappearing is the dislocation of this whole constellation (Baudrillard 2000: 63).

Reality is no longer a case of location in a referential signifier, but has become, as Baudrillard argues, '*an effect of the sign*' (Gane 1993: 141, emphasis in text). The reality principle is thus maintained by the approximation of the appearance of the real. As a result, the difference between the order of the real and the order of simulation become indistinguishable.[2] In the book, *The Vital Illusion* (2000), Baudrillard even goes as far as to suggest that we have gone past the point of merely upholding the illusion of reality toward an 'excess of reality' (Baudrillard 2000: 81), whereby science and technology have rationalised every facet of our lives.

Another consequence of simulation is that it complicates our ability to speak about history in definitive terms. This idea has considerable appeal to posthuman debates, where the future is often spoken about as if it has arrived (Fukuyama 2002). When the future is today, there is no longer any distance from which to effectively reflect on the future or the past. This collapse between things is indicative of an era of simulation, and in the article 'The Year 2000 Will Not Take Place' (1986), Baudrillard associates the disappearance of history with the beginning of a culture of simulation. To quote Sean Cubitt, '(u)nder simulation, no distinctions are possible, and therefore no history' (Cubitt 2001: 51). Baudrillard pursues three hypotheses about the disappearance of history. The first suggests that the acceleration of forms of communication in a culture of information and the hyperreal propels the subject 'beyond a certain space–time, a certain horizon where the real is possible' (Baudrillard 1986: 18). As events get sped up, the body is detached from the referential locus of history and the real (Baudrillard 1986: 18).

The second hypothesis Baudrillard proposes inverts the first, by claiming that history disappears via the 'deceleration of processes' (Baudrillard 1986: 20). As opposed to the acceleration of society to a point of 'no-return', Baudrillard interprets the saturation of the 'masses' by information and media as causing a form of inertia. Historical events are made meaningless as 'the masses neutralize history and function as a screen of absorption' (Baudrillard 1986: 20). Rather than projecting into hyperspace, as suggested by the acceleration of history, inertia relies on societal indifference that occasions the end of history. In the third scenario, history disappears not because we are denying it, but because there is too much of it. Baudrillard uses music as an analogy to explain how this excess brings us so close to our reality that we can no longer see it:

> ...we can no longer discover history as it was before information and the media. The original essence (of music, of the social...), the original concept (of the unconscious, of history...) have disappeared because we can never again isolate them from their model of perfection, which at the same time is their model of simulation, of their forced assumption in an excessive truth, which at once is their point

> of inertia and their point of no-return. We will never know what was the social, or what was music before their present exacerbation in useful perfection. We will never know what history was before its exacerbation in the technical perfection of information or its disappearance in the profusion of commentary—we will never know what anything was before its disappearance in the completion of its model...Such is the era of simulation (Baudrillard 1986: 23).

And it is at this moment of excess that Baudrillard argues we inhabit a culture of simulation. For as history and meaning disappear, we can no longer return to an understanding of history or the subject that is located in an original or essential reality. This is the posthuman moment.

It would appear that posthuman figurations can offer us a way to consider what is at stake for notions of identity when the reality principle is abolished, along with all other traditional dialectical value systems. The death of the real does not imply that there can be no meaning inasmuch as it acknowledges that there is no pre-existing real through which we might secure meaning. Approached through the framework of Baudrillard's theory of simulation, posthuman figurations may provide a means for feminism to think beyond critical interrogations about the meaning of 'female identity' toward a mode of thinking whereby we can begin to 'question our presuppositions about the subject and the role of subjectivity as it is modified—or metamorphosed—in contemporary experience' (Rodaway 1995: 242). In the context of simulation, as it will be made evident in the following chapters, subjectivity becomes a process not of identification but of transformation, metamorphosis and catastrophe.

Technologies of Vision and Simulated Worlds

Amidst these discussions, it's worth recognising that simulation is not something that is unique to a digital era. For as long as there has been representation, there has been simulation.[3] And Baudrillard is quite aware of this, having written about three stages of simulation in his 1970s text, *Symbolic Exchange and Death*. Each of the stages Baudrillard identifies corresponds with a particular technique or technology used for the reproduction of objects in different historical periods. For Baudrillard, it is not so much the object that is being produced that is important to our understanding of reality, but the *way* that it is produced.

According to Baudrillard, the first-order simulacrum corresponds to the period from the Renaissance to the Industrial Revolution. During this time, reproduction strived for the '*imitation of nature*' (Baudrillard 1993: 52, emphasis in text). Baudrillard cites the elaborate stucco angels that adorn

Baroque décor as an example of this type of overt copying. Baudrillard likens this to counterfeiting, whereby the copy circulates as a 'corrupt symbol' that can be distinguished from an original (Genosko 1994: 42). The relationship between the counterfeit and the original is one of analogy, whereby the difference between origin and referent, artifice and nature remains clear to the viewer.

The second order of signs sees the original referent abolished by a process of infinite reproduction, made possible during the era of industrial mechanisation. A simple example of this would be any mass-produced product that can be found on the supermarket shelf, such as a bottle of fizzy drink. As each bottle is made by a machine, it is uniformly like every other, which means that not only is it impossible to distinguish between one object and another, but there is no 'original' bottle of drink from which the rest have been copied. Because each product can stand in for or be replaced by another, they are understood to be equivalent to one another. In Baudrillard's words, the second order is dominated by 'a technical principle where the machine has the upper hand, and where, with the machine, *equivalence* is established' (Baudrillard 1993: 53). For Baudrillard, exchange value is the defining feature of the commodity stage. So while there is a difference between the first and second orders—in that the first stage creates an analogy between the original and fake, while in the second order they are equivalent—both are orders of artifice that fundamentally maintain a notion of the real.

It is in the third schema—the age of hyperreality—that our idea of reality begins to change radically. While both the first and second orders maintain the reality principle by assuming a relation between the object and its representation as sign, simulation dissolves the distinction between the two. The equivalence of serial production is superseded by an order of structural value. Third-order simulacrum sees the code as the 'new *operational* configuration' of the production of the image (Baudrillard 1993: 57). As mentioned in my overview of simulation, the only point of reference in the third phase is the model, from which all forms manifest. Since then, Baudrillard has identified a fourth order of signs; the order of the fractal or virus. This stage of value is typified by the abolition of all points of reference. As he states:

> At the fourth, the fractal (or viral, or radiant) stage of value, there is no point of reference at all, and value radiates in all directions, occupying all interstices, without reference to anything whatsoever, by virtue of pure contiguity (Baudrillard 1999: 5).

And since identifying the fractal stage he has spoken of 'integral reality', which like the third and fourth orders operates as a 'kind of ultra reality that puts an end to both reality and to illusion' (Baudrillard 2005: 2).[4] This raises the question: 'What is the significance of visual images in a context where no point of reference exists?'

In order to think through this question, it is useful to explore the connection between the circulation and operation of the sign and the role images have played in culture. Because simulation is, as Sean Cubitt notes, 'a philosophy of reality and our changing relations within it' (Cubitt 2001: 1), it is important to consider how our realities are made and their impact on how we perceive ourselves and others. As technologies have emerged over time, they have had a significant influence on modes of representation and accordingly, how visuality and reality are understood and experienced. With the advent of digital media, there has been renewed intellectual discussion about the nature of visual representation, ranging from the Renaissance, through modernity and the advent of photography, and beyond. Visual technologies—the way that we 'look' at the world—have been intimately tied to these debates about the 'original' and the 'copy'.

To explore these connections further I'd like to draw parallels between Baudrillard's orders of the sign and the shifts in viewing experience which span pre-modern times, through modernity and postmodernity. Part of this process of putting images into context involves investigating the role of visual technologies both in contemporary times and historically, and how they inform our engagements with the posthuman. Baudrillard's interrogation of the reality/representation divide can be seen as part of an ongoing critical tradition, along with writers like Charles Baudelaire, Walter Benjamin and Anne Friedberg, who have explored the role of representation in culture and how the experience of vision impacts on understandings of subjectivity, particularly with respect to the era of modernity.

Much has been written about the virtual dimension of the digital age creating a different mode of being for the subject. And while the rhetoric of transformation, speed and newness is often associated with contemporary and futurist digital technologies, debates surrounding the subject of modernity suggest this has long been the case. Although current narratives of digitisation suggest new modes of being, seeing and experiencing the world, technologies such as virtual reality are perhaps as Geoffrey Batchen claims, 'not something peculiar to a particular technology or to postmodern discourse but...rather one of the fundamental conditions of modernity itself' (Batchen 1996: 28). This is a viewpoint shared by a number of visual theorists like Jay Bolter and Richard Grusin who propose that new and old technologies 'remake themselves and each other' (Bolter and Grusin 2000: 5), and

Barbara Maria Stafford who claims that 'the emergence and convergence of media is simultaneously a wholly ancient and utterly modern phenomenon' (Stafford 1996: 14). Keeping these connections in mind, it appears desirable, then, to explore the interconnections between modern and postmodern theories of representation as a way of approaching the posthuman from within a continuum of technological representation, beginning with the viewing technologies of the Renaissance.

The refiguration of the subject associated with the advent of electronic networks is preceded by a history of representation and viewing dating back to Renaissance times. In its attempts to break from the flatness and surface of Medieval imagery, Renaissance vision championed a realism and solidity of form that was radically different to the metaphysical and quasi-iconic images of the Middle Ages. According to Stephen Heath, technologies of visualisation like cinema and photography are informed by codes of perspective established in the Quattrocento that aimed toward 'the immediate translation of reality in itself' (Heath 1981: 30).

Fundamental to this new style of depicting the world was the implementation of a geometrical perspective that privileged a central vanishing point. By drawing the eye toward the centre of the image, one-point perspective created a balanced, harmonious, homogenous and unchanging space. The Renaissance rendering of the image was not so much a mirror or reflection of reality, but a space constructed to reproduce the dimensions that a single, unmoving eye might see (Panofsky 1991: 29). In this sense, any attempt to translate reality is revealed as a flawed one, as the experience of viewing is determined by the psycho-physiological space of the subject, coupled with the fact that the world is seen through two moving eyes (Panofsky 1991: 31).

What Renaissance perspectival space created for the subject was, according to Erwin Panofsky, 'an objectifying sense of the real'; an image of the world as ordered, solid, grounded and rational, through the use of mathematical principles (Panofsky 1991: 67). Accordingly, the self was positioned as a coherent, unified entity in this systemised visual world. Simultaneously, perspective functioned as 'an extension of the domain of the self' by creating a sense of continuity between the self and the representation of the external world (Panofsky 1991: 68). These dual aspects worked to *create* the illusion of a rational world-view grounded in the objective lens of the all-seeing eye, rather than to *reflect* a given reality.

What we find is that despite the ahistorical tendencies of Panofsky's theories about perspective, technologies of visualisation constituted by geometrical formulae and various perspectival machines contributed to the emergence of a rational view of space in the Renaissance. The visual experience was based on re-creating human perception and constructing a one-to-one correspondence between the real world and the representation of space (Manovich 1996: 230, Veltman 1996: 220). Indeed, the technical apparatuses used by artists of the Quattrocento were precursors to the viewing technologies that emerged during nineteenth-century modernity and those preceding photography such as the camera obscura, stereoscope and phenakistiscope (Crary 1992: 16).[5]

The emergence of modernism in the nineteenth century marked a significant cultural and social shift in the experience of vision and the relationship between representation and the subject.[6] The specific conditions of the nineteenth-century urban metropolis (the architecture of shopping malls and arcades, and the advent of transport such as trains and cars) caused a transformation in the subjective experience of temporality and spatiality and the experience of vision. In the context of new urban technologies and industrialisation, the rational world-view and one-point perspective of the Renaissance was replaced by a mobility of vision suited to modern city life and its ensuing characteristics of uncertainty, flux and movement.

The experience of modernity, as argued by Marshall Berman, emerges from an environment that promises both 'adventure, power, joy, growth, transformation of ourselves and the world—and, at the same time…threatens to destroy everything we have, everything we know, everything we are' (Berman 1982: 15). While for the modern subject this offered new and exciting possibilities, the consequences were the erosion of a coherent notion of selfhood, identity and place in the world. This modernist sensibility is not dissimilar to the debates about the subject of electronic networks discussed in the previous chapter.

The subjective experience of modernity is typified in the figure of the *flâneur* (Baudelaire 1964). The *flâneur* embodied a panoramic style of observation that relied on the movement of an (inherently male) viewer through public space. This moving subject was intimately associated with the transformation of public life and modern consumer culture (Buck Morss 1986: 105). By walking through urban space, the *flâneur* dismantled the harmonious configuration of Renaissance one-point perspective and the immobility of the subject. In its place was a modern experience of vision suited to the flux of urban life and a fluid and mutable subject. What the *flâneur* figure of the urban nineteenth century shows is the impact of cultural and technological shifts on the aesthetics of reception. It also offered a vision of the subject and the world as destabilised, uncertain and ambivalent.[7]

While urban technologies contributed to the modern experience of vision, they also played a significant role in the construction of gender. For example, while the *flâneur* signalled an active, masculine style of observing modern life, women occupied public space primarily as objects of consumption for a male viewing subject—namely as prostitutes (Buck Morss 1986: 119). Women were denied the viewing status of the male *flâneur* largely because of the gender divide between public and private space.[8] However, as Gillian Swanson points out in her article '"Drunk with Glitter": Consuming Spaces and Sexual Geographies' (1995), women such as prostitutes and female shoppers moved out of the feminised, private space to occupy the public, masculinsed spaces of modernity. But this move was largely considered to be a transgressive act, and as a result, women who invaded the public, masculine domain were construed as deviant and pathological for illegitimately occupying male terrain. Swanson argues:

> ...in the second half of the nineteenth century an exchange develops between the meanings of prostitution—embodying working-class urban femininity—and those of the middle-class female consumer, establishing the two ends of a spectrum of pathological sexuality whereby women in general become identified as a disturbance to public life (Swanson 1995: 82).

The idea that the female consumer of modernity comes to signify urban pathology is one I return to in my discussions of Barbie in chapter three.

Yet 'it was as a consumer that the *flâneuse* was born', claims Friedberg (Friedberg 1993: 34). And it was predominantly the aesthetic experience of the mall that Friedberg argues produced of a new kind of gendered observer intimately tied to consumption and a commodified form of looking. Friedberg's study of the *flâneuse* suggests that women could legitimately occupy public space as consumers. Her analysis grants women the position of viewing subjects. A commodified form of looking, whereby women moved materially through space and time, offered one mode by which the female visual experience was sanctioned. The other mode of female mobility proposed by Friedberg involved the consumption of technologically mediated visual experiences.

As the survey of the streets conducted by the *flâneur* mobilised the virtual gaze, 'machines of virtual transport (the panorama, the diorama, and later, the cinema) extended the virtual gaze of photography to provide virtual mobility' (Friedberg 1993: 4). And it was through these 'machines of virtual transport' that women could become mobile viewers. This mobilisation of vision is crucial to understanding the changing experience of perspective and space with the advent of new technologies and their impact on the female subject. Just as the consumption of contemporary digital and electronic media challenges the status and boundaries of the body,[9] the gendered subject of modernism experienced a transformation in both the processes of viewing and subsequent experiences of corporeality. In noting that women's encounters with viewing technologies enable new conceptions of the body, space and identity, Friedberg disrupts traditional formulations of the subject that deny the specificities of gendered experience. In terms of the subjectivity of the observer, the *flâneuse* exists as a modernist precedent of how women negotiate spatiality and temporality in the context of consumer, mass culture.[10]

Photography was another technology of visualisation that promoted a different engagement between the spectator and the image. While the panoramic vision of the moving *flâneur* mobilised the gaze so that the spectator actively and physically participated in the shaping of visual surrounds, the advent of photography saw the spectator become increasing immobile (Friedberg 1993: 28). The camera transformed the visual by creating an image independent of the spectator. By distancing the spectator from the active viewing process, photography encouraged the proliferation of both technology and the image, a proliferation equated with the 'triumph of a *mass* culture' (Sekula 1986: 4). Photography signals a shift in visual experience from notions of an 'original' toward mass reproduction and the copy.

This concept has been explored by Walter Benjamin in his often-cited essay 'The Work of Art in the Age of Mechanical Reproduction' (1968b). Here, Benjamin explains how the mechanical means of production opened up, for the first time, a way of imitating an original through a copying process. The potential for infinite reproduction of an object by mechanical reproduction offers a democratising corrective to what Benjamin decrees are the outmoded and elitist concepts of authenticity, essence and aura associated with the myth of origins. For Benjamin, reproduction is a positive thing, offering an egalitarian mode of liberation from the tyranny of tradition and authenticity and authority (Benjamin 1968b: 220). Clearly, Baudrillard's concept of the industrial simulacrum is indebted to Benjamin's writings on reproduction. Indeed, Baudrillard acknowledges the centrality of Benjamin's work to his own model of serial reproduction as the dominant system of value of the second order. Where Baudrillard's thinking diverges considerably from Benjamin's is in his formulation of a third order of the image where the very notion of a real and its artificial reproduction collide and implode.

To return to photography, the idea that the photograph is a copy of something in the 'real world' means that it can be interpreted as a form of vision that challenges the concept of authenticity by displacing the 'aura', or uniqueness, of the original form. At the same time, as a copy of an original, photography still upholds the distinction between what is real and what is artifice. Whereas the authority of the original is undermined by mass reproduction, it nonetheless retains its status as an original in Benjamin's schema, although 'the quality of its presence is always depreciated' (Benjamin 1968b: 223).

This distinction between the real and the copy can only be maintained if photography is interpreted as a mechanical means of providing a direct, unmediated image of an external reality. Photography, in this context, is conceived as complementary to empirical, scientific notions of truth and objectivity. When considered as a triumph over realism, photography allows for an accurate recording of reality by mechanical means that permanently fixes an image. The empirical and objective eye of the camera thus ensures 'photography's privileged connection to the world' (Krauss and Livingston 1985: 28).[11] In *Camera Lucida*, Roland Barthes concurs, observing that regardless of the construction or physical manipulation of the image, photography's status as an image resides in an indexical relation to the real (Barthes 2000).

In his explanation of how the photograph affects the viewing subject, Barthes discerns two orders of the photographic image, the *studium* and the *punctum*. He describes the punctum as the 'element which rises from the scene, shoots out of it like an arrow, and pierces me' (Barthes 2000: 26). While studium relies on established codes and modes of reading and identification with the image, it is the notion of the punctum that interests me here, as it signals a shift away from structural interpretations of the relationship between reality and its representation to disrupt the unity of the photograph. Although photography maintains an indexical relation to the real, Barthes does not configure this in terms of structural relations, but as a 'kind of subtle *beyond*', where the image 'pricks' the viewer (Barthes 2000: 59). From this perspective, the punctum reclaims some element of an essence or real, even thought this essence is found in the fleeting and transitory existence of the image at one moment in space and time, rather than a concrete indexical relation between image and referent.

Despite acknowledging that the photograph is a mechanical copy, Barthes tries to reclaim an 'aura' for the photograph through this idea of the punctum. One could argue that Barthes wants to reinstate the photographic image with value in an era of simulation and mass production, particularly when compared to digital image making. Martin Lister astutely notes that the 'newness' of digital imaging risks creating a false dichotomy between 'new' and 'old' forms of lens based media (Lister 1995: 8). Thus, the mechanically reproduced copy, proposed by Benjamin to liberate the image from the tyranny of origins, regains its status as 'image' via its connection to the real, over and above the inauthenticity of digital data that cannot ever represent reality. Indeed, Baudrillard attests to the strategy of simulation to generate the illusion of the real, as opposed to the representation of reality.

This brings me back to the current stage of the image where the posthuman resides. The contemporary experience of the visual is no longer locatable via a link between the original object and its reproduction, but functions in terms of the simulation model and fractal pattern. New forms of visual culture such as computer games, digital photography and computer-generated imagery (CGI) films ask for another kind of engagement with the real because digitisation undermines a representational economy predicated on an original and a copy. So where does this leave the subject and what is their relation to images and society? It would appear that at the point of the collapse of signification, today's subject of mass media and communications networks experiences the world quite differently to the subject of modernity. While the modernist subject of nineteenth-century lifestyle and technologies was a subject in flux, a protean precursor to the contemporary fragmented figurations of identity, the subject of hyperreality disappears as the distance between things erodes, including the distance between objects and subjects. Following Baudrillard's trajectory, the explosive characteristics of modernity have been substituted for a culture of postmodern implosion. The ensuing collapse of signification liberates the object, rupturing the subject/object dichotomy from which traditional ideas of subjectivity are forged. If at this stage you are feeling uncertain about your place in a simulated world, you are not the only one. Baudrillard's challenge to the integrity of the subject and the status of the real has caused much consternation among scholars.

Critiquing Baudrillard

The most prominent criticism levelled at Baudrillard reiterates a broader claim against postmodernism—that the collapse of all divisions tends toward the erasure of political, social and cultural meaning. To what extent, then, are Baudrillard's theories useful and relevant to an examination of contemporary cultural and political life and the place of the subject within it? Not very, says Douglas Kellner, for whom Baudrillard's collapse of 'social phenomena into one another' creates a 'bleak picture' whereby 'Baudrillard no longer poses *any* social alternative, resistance, struggle and refusal' (Kellner 1989: 214).

Sean Cubitt also takes a negative view of simulation, calling it a 'pessimistic theory, a theory of the endless reduplication of the same' (Cubitt 2001: 5). Although it is not only Baudrillard's theory of simulation Cubitt is directing his comments at, but simulation theory in general. The main problem Cubitt identifies with simulation theory is its emphasis on the relationship between representation and reality. He argues that by making reality its major cause for concern, simulation theory ultimately 'seems to lay claim to a universal account of everything, including the supposedly abandoned completion of grand narratives' (Cubitt 2001: 150).

For Cubitt, it is wrong to understand simulation as a universal order of social relations. Rather he sees it is 'geographically specific, and does not seem to illuminate the relentless reality of Third World exploitation' (Cubitt 2001: 138). It's likely that he is referring to simulation theory as geographically specific to the First World, which is itself a troubling assertion in that it assumes that non-Western 'Others' are somehow outside of, or excluded from, global technologies and market forces when clearly they are not. The idea that Third World exploitation is somehow outside of simulation subscribes to what Arjun Appadurai critiques as an inadequate model of centre–periphery relations in explaining contemporary global interactions (Appadurai 1990).

The indeterminacy that informs Baudrillard's thinking has been criticised for erasing the potential for agency in the subject. By suggesting that simulation somehow trivialises the inequities and hardships marginalised groups experience, Cubitt, like Kellner, is fearful that we will lose the ability to critique power relations based on the differences between categories such as the Left and the Right, First World and Third World, male and female, and deny the subject the agency of resistance. Although she is not commenting on Baudrillard per se, Rosi Braidotti's concern with articulating subjectivity is typical of the view that the 'disappearance' of the subject is incompatible with a feminist political project:

> ...one cannot deconstruct a subjectivity one has never been fully granted; one cannot diffuse a sexuality which has historically been defined as dark and mysterious. In order to announce the death of the subject one must first have gained the right to speak as one; in order to demystify meta-discourse one must first gain access to a place of enunciation (Braidotti 1991: 122).

Likewise, on conceptualising Baudrilliard's writing on the code as deterministic, Sara Schoonmaker cautions that 'any form of determinism makes it difficult for a theory to analyze the complexities of social reality' (Schoonmaker 1994: 72).

Yet, according to Rex Butler, there is a fundamental problem with many of Baudrillard's critics and commentators. He claims that they fail to read Baudrillard 'first of all *in his own terms*' (Butler 1999: 13). For example, evaluating Baudrillard from a Marxist perspective (as Kellner does) is 'already to predetermine the answer the analyst will arrive at: that Baudrillard's work is inadequate' (Butler 1999: 14). Butler suggests that part of the project of reading Baudrillard 'in his own terms' must involve suspending pre-existing frameworks through which to compare or examine his work in order to:

> ...try to grasp the internal logic of Baudrillard's work, what it is already saying about its relationship to the external world, the possibility of applying theory to examples, its affinity to that of other thinkers, how the sign works and whether it can even be represented. It is not definitively to stop the possibility of such things, but it is to think how it is a problem—a problem that Baudrillard himself might be addressing (Butler 1999: 15).

As I refer to images throughout this book, I am to a degree drawn into the realm of representation that Baudrillard argues is impossible. Despite this, I do think that there is scope to undertake the task of analysis beyond a critical theory framework, or as Butler suggests, 'think how it is a problem' (Butler 1999: 15). This is what differentiates my book from a number of feminist critiques of Baudrillard that tend toward this external, or critical, approach.

Despite Baudrillard's considerable contribution to discursive fields such as visual, cultural and media studies, feminist theory has largely dismissed Baudrillard's ideas. The one notable exception has been Victoria Grace's germinal feminist exploration of his oeuvre, *Baudrillard's Challenge: A Feminist Reading* (2000). Despite this recent intervention, there have been few points of engagement, or attempts to negotiate common ground between feminist theoretical strategies and Baudrillard's work. It is impossible not to acknowledge that feminist political projects and Baudrillard's theories are not always complementary. Many have found Baudrillard's antagonistic statements directed toward a feminist politic in texts such as *Seduction* (1990a) and *America* (1988a) to be particularly troubling. Indeed, some of the most vehement criticism of Baudrillard's attitude to women manifests from male theorists' critiques of these texts (Gane 1991b: 57–65, Kellner 1989: 143–150). My use of Baudrillard differs from other feminist engagements with his scholarship that predominantly take the form of critical response to his theories on seduction (Gallop 1987, Plant 1993). Baudrillard's falling out with feminism over his writings on seduction and attitude toward women has resulted in little productive engagement with his work from within feminist analyses of image culture.

Jane Gallop's engagements with Baudrillard's writings on seduction in 'French Theory and the Seduction of Feminism' (1987) are indicative of feminism's rightful unease with his provocative and often radical assertions regarding the nature of subject relations. In this article, Gallop denounces Baudrillard for 'seeing feminism as stupid, wrong, mistaken' (Gallop 1987: 114). Alongside her critique of his theory of seduction as maintained within a contradictory logic, Gallop is particularly apprehensive about the way that Baudrillard speaks to women from a position of superiority 'that knows the truth of the feminine and the masculine and can thus, from this privileged position beyond sexual difference, advise women how best to combat masculine power' (Gallop 1987: 114). By criticising Baudrillard for being a male theorist who claims to know what is best for feminism, Gallop dismisses the possibility of a productive exchange or dialogue between feminism and his work.

Along with Gallop's initial critique, perhaps another reason for the lack of dialogue between feminism and Baudrillard's scholarship can be found in the relative inaccessibility of Baudrillard's texts to an English-speaking public during the 1970s and the 1980s. Gallop acknowledged in her analysis that very few Anglo–American theorists were familiar with Baudrillard's work, and at that time only a small selection of his writings were available in English (Gallop 1987: 111). But my purpose here isn't to defend Baudrillard on the topic of seduction. Although the seduction debates constitute an important aspect of Baudrillard's theoretical output, they are explored in significant detail by both Keith Goshorn and Victoria Grace (1994: 257–91, 2000: 158–64 respectively). Rather, I look elsewhere in his body of work, using his theory of simulation to make sense of posthuman images in a climate characterised by the abundance of signs and the implosion of meaning.

Although recent trends have seen Baudrillard's contribution to identity debates bypassed by feminism in favour of Deleuze's productive spin on desire, bodies and becoming,[12] some writers have considered the possibility of alliances between feminism and the theories of Baudrillard (Goshorn 1994, Grace 2000, Morris 1988). And despite many feminists expressing uneasiness with his ideas, Baudrillard's theories do show some affinity with the agenda of poststructural feminisms that interrogate how subjectivity has conventionally been determined. For Baudrillard, it is the challenge to representation brought about by the displacement of the real as the reference point of all meaning that disturbs traditional formations of subjectivity.

What feminism stands to gain from exposing the operations of the reality principle is the possibility for new imaginings of subjectivity that exceed traditional formulations of the body and identity. By contesting the value system inherent to dialectical thinking through the tropes of implosion, systematic reversals and fatality, Baudrillard collapses gender systems based on a hierarchical order of difference. These issues are taken up more fully in chapter four of this book. In the context of third-order simulacra, posthuman figurations operate as sites of unstable signification that disrupt the fixity of meaning and an unchanging notion of being. By challenging oppositional thinking, Baudrillard's theory of simulation may enable a theory of posthuman figurations outside of the current feminist dialogue that situates technology as either good or bad for women.

Feminism and Representation

Having looked at the simulation model, technologies of vision and some of the feminist and broader critiques of Baudrillard's theories, it's time to return to the question I posed at the outset of this chapter: 'If we can no longer think about images in critical terms—that is, what they can tell us about gender, power, the differences between the sexes and the inequalities that stem from that—then how useful are Baudrillard's theories?' En route to answering this question, what has become apparent is that critical thinking about images locks us into a dialectic of selves and Others, subjects and objects, representation and reality, identity and difference. This is the way that feminist theory has conventionally approached images. As the following section will show, both structural and poststructural feminist approaches are still caught up in a debate about 'the nature of meaning' (Grace 2000: 4). If we read images of the posthuman in this way, then the tendency is to interpret these images as either 'good' or 'bad' representations for women, or, as images which allow multiple and complex associations to be forged about women's subjectivity and identity relative to new technologies. Either way, the image has currency or meaning relative to something outside of it, a proposition that sustains a dialectical style of thinking.

To conclude, I want to reiterate my suggestion to approach images of the posthuman in fatal terms, that is, not in order to explain what the image might mean, but how it acts. Barbara Bolt has spoken about the ability of the artwork to escape representation by performing, rather than representing:

> In the fury of painting, rules give way to tactics and the pragmatics of action. The painting takes on a life of its own. It breathes, vibrates, pulsates, shimmers and generally runs away from me. The painting no longer merely represents or illustrates reading. Instead, it performs. In the performativity of imaging, life gets into the image (Bolt 2004: 1).

Bolt suggests that images can operate in another register, beyond referencing reality. Similarly Baudrillard asks us to consider representations as having a life of their own. Baudrillard uses the example of a fake holdup to show how this type of representation of a 'real' event has effects and consequences that act to produce the reality principle:

> This is how all the holdups, airplane hijackings, etc. are now in some sense simulation holdups in that they are already inscribed in the decoding and orchestration rituals of the media, anticipated in their presentation and their possible consequences (Baudrillard 1994: 21).

These ideas about how representations work are very different to established feminist approaches to visual forms such as film, advertising, television and artwork. Starting from the body of feminist film analysis of the 1970s and early 1980s, feminist thinking has influenced significantly how we decipher media images of women.

Arising from the urgent political climate of second-wave feminism, feminist film aesthetics questioned how women had been depicted in film. It argued that women often occupied peripheral roles to the male protagonist of the film, as 'secondary subjects'—wives, lovers, daughters, victims—but rarely fully-fledged, complex characters in their own right. In addition, feminists working in this field claim that these images both reflected and constructed women's subordination in society. By interrogating the masculinist depiction of women in cinema, they brought to the fore previously unchallenged assumptions about the role of spectatorship and the gaze in gendered subject constitution (Mulvey 1989a); stereotyping and constructions of femininity in visual representation (Kuhn 1985); as well as debates about the material effects of representational systems on women's lived realities (Creed 1987, Gledhill 1984).

Likewise, the pornography debates spearheaded by Andrea Dworkin and Catharine MacKinnon in the 1980s were fundamentally concerned with the connection between a practice of representation and its effects on the status of women within a phallocentric cultural, social and political economy (Dworkin 1981, MacKinnon 1979). Louis Althusser's theory on ideology was instrumental to these debates because it helped explain how women were positioned as objects of masculinist consumption; recruited into the social order by the hail of ideology (Althusser 1984: 48). In accordance with an Althusserian schema, the victim status of women did not reflect a pre-given reality, but actively constituted their existence as secondary subjects. The way that women were represented produced their status as subordinate in patriarchal society. For early feminists writing about the depiction of women in areas like film, advertising and pornography, many images of women were considered to be 'bad' representations because they depicted a 'false' reality that did not reflect what 'real' women were like. The assumption here is that there is a 'truth' about women that exists behind the image.

One of the strategies proposed by feminism to remedy ideology-effects was to create positive depictions of women—images that would show what women were 'really' like. To counteract the construction of women as objects of oppression by a masculine visual economy, feminist film theory encouraged women to create their own images of themselves as a way of promoting better, more truthful, and realistic reflections of female experience. Another strategy, typified by Mary Kelly's multimedia artwork *Post-Partum Document* (1973–9), was to refuse to depict women altogether (Kelly 1983). Kate Linker explains the rationale behind this as 'a protest against the body's use as an object, and against its appropriation to the sexist doctrine of essential femininity' (Linker 1984: 403).

Clearly, the body of feminist theory described here maintains an understanding of the social order in terms of Baudrillard's second-order simulation, whereby there is a direct link between what is represented and an outside reality. Mike Gane reminds us of Baudrillard's agenda to 'show that no adequate analysis of systems of representation can, simply, refer to the "real" world (the referent), as if this was unproblematic' (Gane 1991a: 95), yet this is precisely what is occurring in these debates. Likewise, I take issue with the distinction that sees representation as something that is 'like reality' or 'not like reality'. While the notion of a real located in the material reality of women's experience is the basis for this feminist political project, the real also operates as its limit point by presuming that there is a direct link between reality and images, and these are distinct spheres. When images are only understood as references for reality, we obscure their role in generating our reality, or in this case how they act to generate an illusion of what a woman is.

Despite the polemical interventions of feminist film theoreticians, by the late 1980s a shift occurred in feminist thinking about images. Exposure to French poststructuralism in the areas of literary deconstruction typified by Jacques Derrida and the later writings of Roland Barthes, the psychoanalysis of Jacques Lacan and Julia Kristeva, and Michel Foucault's politics of power/knowledge, inspired feminist reconfigurations of subjectivity and meaning as multiple, unfixed and fluid. In light of engagements with a poststructuralist critique of the unified subject, feminist aesthetics has undergone a radical shift away from psychoanalytic, ideological and material–realist concerns with the meaning of representation toward a focus upon the discursive constructs and practices shaping the text, the reader and modes of production.

Feminists working in this vein are critical of earlier approaches to the representation of women because they pay little attention to how audiences construct meaning or consider affective responses to the text.[13] Early feminist film criticism neglected to consider the role of the female spectator as a 'resistant reader' who can intervene in the naturalisation of an ideological stance within a particular cultural text (Dolan 1998: 289). Rather than existing as oppressed victims of masculinist representational practice, women can act as agents of resistance. Examples of this include performance critic Elin Diamond's suggestion that the female performer 'look back' at the spectator in an attempt to disrupt the Oedipal construction of woman as fetish object of the gaze (Diamond 1997: 54); the multiple positions of identification for both the female and male viewer of the filmic text offered by Laura Mulvey in her later scholarship (Mulvey 1989b); as well as the body of lesbian film criticism that recasts the practices of viewing in terms of same-sex desire (De Lauretis 1994).

Along with recognising that women have the power to resist, feminist interventions into the relationship between women and images positioned women in the role of active participants in making meaning, as sophisticated consumers and producers of visual texts. Foucault's view of power as dispersed and accessible has been central to challenging established paradigms of women's relationship to consumer capital (Foucault 1980: 186–7, 1984c). Typical of this kind of approach is the writing of Australian media studies scholar Catharine Lumby, who suggests that feminist critiques of mass media that determine images as 'sexist', 'degrading' and 'insulting' to women have themselves become a dominant point of view that 'is out of touch with the way people consume images' (Lumby 1997: xxv). In her project to 'take issue with feminist readings of media images and offer alternative accounts' (Lumby 1997: xxiv), she carves out a space for women to partake in a more critical relationship with images. Lumby believes that reading images is a subjective endeavour that may result in the construction of multiple and diverse meanings, depending on the viewing position occupied by the subject.

Although no direct reference is made in her text to the writings of Baudrillard, she shares with him the belief that the proliferation of signs in contemporary image culture registers as a significant shift in social operations. So while her argument is consistent with Baudrillard's claim that the meaning of an image can't be traced definitively back to a referent in reality, she differs from him by claiming that multiple meanings can be found in images. Now the problem with arguing that meaning is multiple and fluid is that it still maintains a relationship between a thing in the real world and how it might be read or interpreted. Explaining this in terms of Baudrillard's critique of the signifier (Sr) and signified (Sd) relationship, Victoria Grace argues that a poststructural analysis:

> ...simply shifts the code from one of equivalence to one of polyvalence and leaves the fundamental structure intact. The fundamental structure is the dichotomous separation of the Sr and the Sd, and the codified nature of the construction of meaning according to a *polyvalent* logic of identity/difference (identities/differences). The structural assumptions about the construction of the meaning of 'objects' remain the same whether our meaning is assumed to be the same as, or different from, that of 'others'; assumed to be fixed or floating and fluid. Equivalent or polyvalent, meaning is still 'valent', that is, has the propensity to register a positive identity on a single scale of value; whether this is a single point or multiple points is irrelevant. It remains within a binary construct of identity/difference, Sr/Sd (Grace 2000: 9–10).

Not only does Baudrillard's thinking about the image complicate the post-structural turn toward a multiplicity of meanings, but also proves troubling for feminist theorisations of representational practice that are based on strategies of identification or resistance. This is because the content of the message delivered by ideology is of little concern to Baudrillard. As the image doesn't have any connection to reality in a hyperreal system, the question of meaning becomes one of media form rather than content. Or as Richard Smith argues, 'there is nothing behind the representation to be exposed, rather truly critical or radical thought should turn its attention to the performativity of the representation itself and its effects and consequences' (Smith 2005: 5).

In many ways, the photographs of Cindy Sherman take a step toward the idea that the image acts as something other than an index of the real by challenging realist assumptions about women and representation in popular culture. For example, by invoking the politics of the masquerade in *Untitled Film Stills* (1977), Sherman denies the fixity of woman's identity, instead opting for an indeterminate and often ominous critique of how femininity is constructed by Hollywood filmmaking. Sherman reassesses the politics of a feminist materialist production of imagery that stands as a totalising reality of women's experience. Rather, she creates what Mulvey describes as 'a re-representation, a making strange' of representations of femininity (Mulvey 1996: 67). Positioned concurrently as producer and object of consumption, Sherman collapses the distinctions between subject and object, referent and real. In this regard, Sherman's tactic of representing woman as an appearance or an illusion shares with Baudrillard's agenda a disruption of the association between an image and its referent.

When the relationship between feminism, representation and reality is questioned, it becomes apparent that traditional approaches to identity politics are no longer adequate to figure subjectivity in an era of hyperreality. This discussion has made it clear that posthuman figurations manifest at the point where the distinctions between the virtual and the real collapse. This dissolution of values occurs within the specific temporal and spatial context of the hyperreal, opening up another way of thinking about virtuality and reality that does not see them as separate categories. While traditionally, representation functions to uphold the distinction between what is considered fantasy and what is valued as real, by interrogating the real we might encourage a transformation in how the self is experienced within contemporary cultural conditions. Baudrillard's order of simulation alerts us to the failure of identity based on self/Other relations. As a process of exceeding signification, simulation requires us to rethink the distance between bodies and representation. The following chapters are devoted to critically assessing the modes by which this transformation has enabled the rupture of the signification process.

3

Barbie: A Posthuman Prototype

Every Sunday morning in a suburban shopping-centre car park, people can be found buying and selling their pre-loved goods. Like its counterparts in London and Amsterdam, this open-air market in the inner suburbs of Melbourne is made up of a mix of professional sellers and locals clearing out the unwanted contents of their wardrobes and garages. Young girls often split the cost of a stall and spend the morning together selling their 'junk'. Other stallholders can be found week after week at the same site, making a living from second-hand clothing and antiques. Angela McRobbie writes of the flea market as 'an oasis of cheapness, where every market day is a "sale"' (McRobbie 1997: 193). And it is the potential pleasure of finding a bargain that encourages me to trawl through aisle upon aisle of clothing, bric-a-brac, trinkets and records.

I approach a stall. Carelessly laid out on the asphalt is a line of Barbie dolls in various states of undress (see figure 1). They appear unkempt and unloved, stripped of their glamorous ensembles and petite shoes. The dolls are surrounded by old household items, keeping company with empty chocolate boxes, sunglasses, a pair of secateurs, a silver goblet. Each of the objects waits to be purchased, taken and used in another context. Barbie, too, waits to be transformed again. I want to photograph the Barbies among this array of discarded forms. I adjust the lens of my camera and frame my shot. The stallholder jokes about charging a photographer's fee. After all, my engagement with the dolls is a form of consumption.

Barbie is so pervasive in contemporary popular culture that she hardly requires description. At a glance, you could sum her up as blonde and busty. There is little doubt that when she emerges from her plastic box she is far more stylish and well-attired than the dolls in the photo. Launched onto the market by Mattel in 1959, Barbie was originally designed as a fashion doll for adults to buy. It was only later that she became popular as a toy for little girls (Peers 2004). It is from her beginnings as a fashion plate that Barbie came to stand for glamour, beauty and style (Billyboy 1987, Lord 1994).

But take away her fancy clothes and she is somewhat ominous. Her taut rubbery limbs extend out from a compact torso. Like armour, her plastic shell is rock-hard, forming a distinctive configuration of the body as contained and controlled—defended against the possibility of rupture. A synthetic sheen radiates from her surface, evoking a sense of smoothness and fluidity, despite the awkward joins noticeable between her plastic core and her waist, her head and neck, and her limbs. Something else resides beyond the rigidity of the mould. Barbie inhabits a form that is neither entirely inflexible, nor prone to dissolution. Instead, a feeling of tension is created by the tautness of her body; like a build up of energy with the potential to mutate, metamorphose and reformulate. All the while, the possibility of rupture is denied by the elastic and malleable properties of her plastic frame. Barbie is neither unitary, nor fragmented. She is a transformer.

For those who grew up in the 1980s, the term 'transformer' is likely to evoke memories of those 'robots in disguise'—the action figures produced by toy company Hasbro that switched from vehicles into robots. I will get to these Transformers later. For others, the word might prompt different associations with persons or objects that have the ability to transform. A few things that immediately come to my mind are the television shows about plastic surgery like *The Swan* and *Extreme Makeover*, where individuals are physically remade over the length of a program. Although this is one example of a transformative act, it is not the kind of transformation I am promoting here. Perhaps closer to the mark is the technological instrument used for the control of an alternating current by increasing or decreasing the voltage. Like the transformer of electronics, Barbie may be perceived as a sign-switcher in constant process, a voltage converter that circulates ad infinitum.

As a 'transformer'—an in-between phenomenon constantly circulating in the ambivalent space between the image and its referent, between illusion and the real—Barbie calls established categories into question. Part of the purpose of rethinking Barbie as a transformative, plastic figuration is to highlight some of the difficulties of constructing a politics of subjectivity grounded in identity. What is offered in place of identity is an alternative modality of subjectivity that is not aligned with a process of identification or a practice of resistance. Perceiving the subject as transformative offers a figuration more suited to a social imaginary, in which ideas of self, truth and reality are complicated by our immersion in technology.

Given the ingrained associations between Barbie dolls and female glamour, pitching her as a transformer might appear to be a hard sell. Add to this the hostility directed toward Barbie for being a bad role model for girls, and

Figure 1. *Barbies at the Flea Market.* Photo: Kim Toffoletti.

one is bound to wonder what is so transformative about a doll whose unrealistic and unattainable bodily proportions make women feel inadequate? If the model of female success and beauty has a tiny waist, long blonde hair and wears couture, then what does that tell us about how women are valued in society? Questions like these have dominated contemporary understandings of Barbie, whose iconic status as the perfect model of femininity has been largely criticised by academics as being detrimental to women and girls. I want to move past these familiar arguments to look at Barbie in a different light.

Building on my arguments regarding the representational economy of simulation, I suggest that new forms of visual culture change not only the way we approach images, but our understandings of bodily modalities and experiences. As Jean Baudrillard tells us, simulation culture transforms the process of signification by destabilising a coherent association between the real and the image. Figurations such as Barbie function to encourage alternative understandings of the body and self as transformative, rather than bound to an established system of meaning. She is a precursor to the posthuman; a type of plastic transformer who embodies the potential for identity to be mutable and unfixed.

In my mind, Barbie acts as a 'bridging' figure between debates surrounding gender and representation, and posthuman, post-gender figurations because she displays aspects of both the modern and postmodern cultural condition. Like the modern mannequin in the shop window, she symbolises a 'type' of female consumer, as well as an object of consumption. But the ambivalence of Barbie's plastic body also anticipates a posthuman form that displaces signs of the body to a space outside of a fixed signifying practice, so that they may circulate as pleasures, possibilities and potentialities.

Feminist Interpretations of Barbie

For the most part, Barbie exists simultaneously as an object of fascination, conflict and rancour for a generation of second-wave feminists. Early semiotic and sociological critiques of Mattel's famous doll position her as a 'perfect icon of late capitalist constructions of femininity' (Urla and Swedlund 1995: 281). Interpreted in this framework, Barbie signifies fixed gender roles, heterosexual norms and consumerist values to which women must strive. Barbie is said to teach girls the codes of femininity through standards of dress, bodily ideas and modes of behaviour. She is rigid and slender, always smiling and immaculately groomed and attired, mostly in pink. By playing with Barbie dolls girls learn that in order to be successful and popular women, just like Barbie, they must look good. Importantly, this fashioning of the self relies on buying clothes, make-up, and material luxuries.

The body of literature that portrays Barbie as a mainstream cultural commodity marketed toward the white, heterosexual girl argues that Barbie encourages women to be consumers (Motz 1983, O'Sickey 1994, Rogers 1999). Marilyn Ferris Motz says that 'Barbie is a consumer. She demands product after product, and the packaging and advertising imply that Barbie, as well as her owner, can be made happy if only she wear the right clothes and owns the right products' (Motz 1983: 128). At the same time, Barbie is said to embody the idea that women in capitalist culture are themselves commodities to be purchased, consumed and manipulated. This idea has been around for far longer than Barbie has existed, and I will return to it when I discuss Barbie's relationship to that other static, plastic clotheshorse; the shop window mannequin.

Ann du Cille's writing on multicultural Barbie extends this proposition to suggest that not only gender but racial difference is commodified in the form of Barbie. In her influential 1995 study on the merchandising of racial difference, du Cille exposes multicultural Barbies as essentially all the same in form and features, bar some slight gradations in skin colour. This is despite Mattel's attempts at marketing each as unique through clothing and branding devices. The circulation of a plethora of diverse yet identical Barbies collapses difference into a pluralism of 'sameness' that fails to displace the hierarchy of the white self versus the non-white Other (du Cille 1995: 556).

In this argument, Barbie is troubling because her marketability relies on both the consumption and negation of cultural difference. This can be seen in the development and marketing of a range of black Barbie dolls, given the names Shani, Asha and Nichelle. For du Cille, the cultural currency of these dolls is explained in terms of their difference to Barbie, while maintaining the key attributes and features that make Barbie desirable—her long thick hair, small waist and petite facial features (du Cille 1995: 559–60). As the exotic Other, these dolls can never displace the primacy of Barbie. They will always signal a deviation from the original and authentic blonde doll. When interpreted as the epitome of racial and gender commodification, Barbie can offer little more than a harmful and exploitative image of femininity.

Emblematic of the trend toward theorising the relationship between women and consumption as largely detrimental is the depiction of Barbie as an icon of the cultural plastic that women's bodies have become in a technological age—as objects to be manipulated, controlled and dominated (Rogers 1999: 125). These sentiments echo, and are informed by, the strand of materialist feminism that associates technology with the masculine desire to control and manipulate nature, and in effect, women (Cockburn 1985, Wajcman 1991).

Writing on the plasticity of Barbie, Mary Rogers maintains that Barbie symbolises a type of contemporary body associated with the consumption of 'new technologies of the flesh' (Rogers 1999: 112). Barbie is indicative of the plastic body of endless transformations and eternal youth, manifested via the consumption of mechanisms of control such as cosmetic surgery, fitness clubs and health retreats. In this schema, Barbie functions as 'an icon of an emergent, consumerist "somatics"—a technology of the body driven by the idea that our bodies can be whatever we like if we devote enough money and attention to them' (Rogers 1999: 112). The manifestation of the self as 'plastic', as Rogers conceives it, deems plasticity as not only elastic and variable but as a mould casting a fixed bodily ideal.

One of the best-known examples of a woman who has refashioned the self through plastic surgery is Cindy Jackson, who has undergone extensive operations to transform herself into a Barbie look-a-like. In Jackson's case, Barbie doesn't simply exist as a symbolic representation of a female ideal. Jackson, in becoming a simulation of Barbie, destroys the distinction between the real and its representation. As suggested by the title of her autobiography *Living Doll*, Jackson is 'realer' than a Barbie doll. The connection between dolls and the feminine are not lost on Jackson. She is the lead singer of a rock band called The Dollz and throughout her website (www.cindyjackson.com) she refers to herself as a 'doll' (Jackson 2006).

So is Cindy Jackson the living embodiment of the manipulated and controlled female body, as symbolised by Barbie? From Mary Roger's perspective, Jackson can only be a victim of a consumer society that promotes the normative ideal of womanhood as youthful, firm and slender. Although plasticity may offer unlimited potential for the body, it seems that only certain kinds of bodily transformations, based on desired models of femininity, are accepted and encouraged. Paradoxically, technologies of the body are marketed as offering multiple modes of transformation and regeneration, yet Rogers suggests that the plastic body reinscribes a rigid feminine ideal. The final section of this chapter delves into these ideas further to rethink women's relationships with technology in a posthuman age where the body and identity are malleable and transformative.

Although one strand of feminist commentary argues that Barbie's white, hairless and slender form symbolises an unrealistic female ideal driven by a system of commodity exchange, poststructural feminist and queer theories of the body have promoted an alternative view of Barbie as empowering. Erica Rand's study of Barbie play and queer identity (1995) and Lynne Spigel's writing on Barbie collectors (2001) move away from an interpretation of Barbie as a negative female stereotype. By exploring how people actually interact with and respond to Barbie, their research complicates traditional definitions of Barbie as a symbol of women's oppression under capitalism and patriarchy.

Spigel looks to the actions of Barbie collectors, both heterosexual women and gay men, to suggest that the 'value' of Barbie shifts according to the various groups who ascribe her with meaning (Spigel 2001: 321). For many adult Barbie collectors, it is through craft practices such as making doll clothes that they begin to formulate their own stories about Barbie. These stories provide a medium for self-disclosure that allows the subject to explore the difficulties of conforming to socially sanctioned models of womanhood. Instead of blindly complying with the ideals of femininity that Barbie is supposed to represent, female collectors negotiate 'the contradictions entailed in actualizing the kind of ideal womanhood that the classic white Barbie so vividly embodies'. In particular, Barbie offers 'a vehicle through which collectors investigate the problems of growing up female in our culture' (Spigel 2001: 326).

Another instance of this reworking of the dominant Barbie narrative takes the form of her reappropriation by queer culture. In her study of Barbie consumption by gay men and women, titled *Barbie's Queer Accessories* (1995), Rand exposes the limitations to interpreting Barbie as an ideological tool of white patriarchy. Taking to task Gramscian theories of ideological hegemony and counter-hegemony in the context of Barbie play, Rand questions the seamlessness of an identity politics based on self/Other identification. For Rand, Barbie play is a far more complex practice. In her interviews with queer adults, their memories of playing with Barbie reveal the complexities and contradictions of this act to the formation of sexual identity. Particularly illuminating are the questions she raises concerning queerness in relation to mainstream and marginal discourse and the practices of cultural subversion employed as a political strategy by queer Barbie play (Rand 1995: chapter two).

For Rand and others, Barbie offers a site for queer identity and pleasure through resistance to the heteronormative ideals she is said to represent. For example, Barbie's stereotyped representation of femininity is parodied by drag queens, while her male counterpart Ken is reinscribed with a gay identity in order to challenge the associations between masculinity and heterosexuality (Urla and Swedlund 1995: 304). Barbie's subversive potential has also been recognised by groups like the Barbie Liberation Organization (BLO), who, in 1989, switched the voiceboxes of a range of talking Barbie dolls with those of the boy's action figurine GI Joe prior to sale (Brillo Magazine 1996). This act of culture jamming aimed to challenge gender stereotypes that the toys were believed to perpetuate. Interviews with young girls also indicate that instead of reinforcing ideals of women as passive and objectified, Barbie can act as a site for girls to resist and reject the stereotypes of femininity she embodies (Rakow and Rakow 1999).

These examples suggest that people who collect and play with Barbie don't simply accept the prescribed or dominant cultural meaning that she is supposed to represent. Instead of emulating the particular brand of femininity that Barbie embodies, according to this mode of thinking, individuals may subvert or resist what Barbie stands for in the process of forging their own gendered and sexual identities. Although Erica Rand acknowledges the 'unfixed place of resistance' (Rand 1995: 101) in her stories of subversive Barbie play, the act of resisting the dominant order is the primary means by which queer identity is differentiated as Other to a heterosexual norm.

Yet as the boundaries erode between centre and periphery, consumption and production, figuring identity in terms of a self/Other dichotomy becomes increasingly problematic. Barbie inhabits a hyperreal space that confuses these once distinct spheres. The consumption of Barbie by marginal groups (such as black women, gay men and lesbians), as well as Barbie's appropriation in non-commercial activities (as in the handsewing of Barbie clothes), is indicative of the growing ambivalence undermining the stability of the subject as categorical distinctions collapse. This confused cultural space demands an understanding of subjectivity beyond identity politics. As Baudrillard reminds us, the failure of self/Other relations in our contemporary cultural climate is based upon the impossibility of resistance in an era of hyperreality where all categories—political, sexual and aesthetic—become liberated 'after the orgy' of modernity (Baudrillard 1999: 3).

When the value system based upon the relations of subject and object, real and virtual is confused, Baudrillard's observations lead to the conclusion that there is no Other to resist. Subjects don't always simply 'identify' or 'resist identifying' with popular icons such as Barbie and the multiple meanings she evokes. Instead, there is less and less distance between the subject and the object from which the subject might resist, which is brought about, to some extent, by the range and scope of media experiences. In the third order of simulation that abolishes the real as a coherent category of analysis, Barbie is a sign that inhabits multiple spaces and forms, as indicated by the pervasiveness of the Barbie brand across different media. The proliferation of media and communication sees Barbie occupy the world of advertising, Internet culture (she has numerous websites devoted to her), marketing and movies, as well as the female body, as with the case of Cindy Jackson. Not only is the Barbie doll marketed for consumption, but there is a range of merchandise displaying her brand name, including magazines, stationery and clothing. The recognition of the Barbie brand attests to her cultural reach beyond her status as a doll.

Barbie's status as both consumer and object of consumption can be further understood by looking at the relationship forged between consumption and femininity during modernity. Critiques of Barbie as a bad role model for girls may also be located in the critical discourses surrounding femininity, consumerism and bodily violence, as evidenced by the historical construction of the mannequin in the nineteenth century.

Model Consumers

The mannequin may be considered as the quintessential modern emblem of consumerism, femininity and artifice, prior to the advent of Barbie. Deriving from the dressmaker's dummy, by the mid-1920s the mannequin was a common fixture in the shop window and department store. It functioned as a '"role model" inviting women to identify with feminine spectacle. It stood for the belief among retailers and advertisers that women would respond to the suggestion that they use goods in order to appear modern' (Conor 2004: 108). Although the mannequin was a lifeless replica of the female body, it was also life-like, emulating the style, looks and sensibility of the modern woman.

The ambivalence in the mannequin's status as real and unreal is in keeping with the psychoanalytic interpretation of the mannequin as an uncanny form, which Freud describes as 'that class of the frightening which leads back to what is known of old and long familiar' (Freud 1955b: 220). As machine and commodity, the mannequin emerges as a kind of deathly double that is simultaneously mechanistic and vitalistic. The industrial origins of the mannequin are also noted by Jean Baudrillard, who distinguishes the mass production of the automaton by its location in a productivist mode of the second order (Baudrillard 1993: 53). That said, there is a rich history of life-like automatons prior to the advent of mass production techniques (Daston and Park 1998, Hanafi 2000). By definition, automatons of the Renaissance moved of their own accord, making them quite different to today's static fashion mannequin. According to Zakiya Hanafi, 'matter formed by artificial means and moving of its own volition would seem to be endowed with spirit' and it is this apparent spirit that made early moving statues equally wondrous and disturbing (Hanafi 2000: 54). Although sharing with many other automatons the status of being both alive and not alive, what is specific to the mannequin is its explicit purpose as a simulacrum of the female form for the purposes of commodity capitalism.[1]

Conventional accounts of Barbie echo Hal Foster's observation that 'the mannequin evokes the remaking of the body (especially the female body) as commodity' (Foster 1993: 126). The mannequin represents a modernised form of femininity, typified by consumerism. Like the female *flâneuse* of nineteenth-century modernity identified by Friedberg (1993), and discussed in the previous chapter, the mannequin inhabits modern spaces of consumption, such as the mall and the shop. While the mannequin helped legitimate women's presence in public spaces as active consumers and spectators, it also positioned them as part of the public spectacle. According to Liz Conor, being on public display encouraged women to consume products in order to present an ideal version of the feminine (Conor 2004: 114).

The equation of the mannequin with a woman is complicated, however, by Tag Gronberg (1997), who suggests that the specific characteristics of the modern mannequin can function to *de-emphasise* feminine qualities. The modern mannequin is differentiated from more traditional 'realist' wax forms by stylised limbs, the erasure of facial characteristics, and the use of textured gold and other metallic substances on its surface. By emphasising these non-human qualities, the mannequin doesn't attempt to represent an actual woman, but functions as a 'cancellation of the conventional signs of feminine beauty' (Gronberg 1997: 379).

Although mannequins were made to look less like women through the use of metallic paints and textured skin, this erasure of femininity on the body of the mannequin had troubling consequences. It created a 'disturbing violence, an evocation of woman suffocated through representation of the female body as "gilt" in silver or gold' (Gronberg 1997: 386). This violation of the female body is accentuated by the mannequin's status as fetish object of the male gaze. Her featureless face is unable to return the gaze of the male spectator. Gronberg understands this violence to be tied to the mechanisation of the female consuming body, as a mode of policing or controlling the threat of the consuming female.[2] She states:

> These mannequins substitute…for the female consumer in particular: a 'légion d'idoles' stands in for the crowds of women shoppers on the urban street enabling the circumscribed and demure gaze of the non-Western woman to be fantasized as a (reassuring) alternative to the active and desiring look of the woman shopper. The woman shopper—the woman who 'wants'—was an ambivalent and threatening figure (Gronberg 1997: 391).

Foster notes that the ambivalent status of both the commodity and machine in the popular psyche is primarily understood 'in terms of feminine allure *and* threat, of the woman as erotic *and* castrative, even deathly' (Foster 1993: 134). These remarks are consistent with the body of literature (from Martin Heidegger (1977) through to Andreas Huyssen (1986) and the work of feminist scholars such as Judy Wajcman (1991)) that equates technology with destruction, and subsequently a threatening femininity that requires control. The form of the mannequin thus embodies the equivalence constructed between woman as consumer, and mass reproduction and mechanisation.

This association is also well-documented throughout surrealist art practice, which often represents the mannequin as a fragmented and fractured female body. Rosalind Krauss and Jane Livingston argue that the surrealist break-up of the female form signals that the category of 'woman' is a construct rather than a natural state. This is in keeping with the surrealist project of the *informe* that aimed to dissolve the formal categories organising reality, such as sexual difference (Krauss and Livingston 1985: 19–20). In his interpretation of Hans Bellmer's *Poupée* works of 1934–5, Foster also suggests that Bellmer's dismembered dolls stand for something more than an example of the mannequin as a fetishistic and voyeuristic image of woman. By considering Bellmer's distorted mannequins in light of fascism, Foster locates something beyond the fetishisation of woman, whereby the masculine subject confronts the possibility of his own dissolution in an act of identification with, or becoming of, the fragmented female form (Foster 1991: 94).[3] Although Krauss, Livingston and Foster attempt to rethink the mannequin beyond its associations with the fetishisation and objectification of women within the context of the surrealist project, many feminist critiques of Barbie simply replicate the deep-seated associations that link the mannequin, femininity, consumerism and bodily violence.

The equivalence constructed between the white woman as consumer, mass reproduction and mechanisation embodied by the mannequin pervades cultural understandings of Barbie, and subsequently, her construction as a symbol of sexist and racist values. In an attempt to enable alternative engagements between gender, cultural consumption and subject constitution, I want to pose another way of understanding Barbie that circumvents an approach to the female body as violated by technology, mass reproduction and consumerism. Rethinking Barbie in this way serves to counter theories of the subject that are confined to the biological limits of the body. It also allows us to re-evaluate how images and objects are consumed in a technological age.

When photographing the collection of Barbies at the flea market, I am struck by their 'objectness'. It is not the notion of Barbie as a passive object or model of the feminine that I am implying by this. Nor do I think that the dishevelled and trashed Barbies, half-naked with hair unkempt, indicate some sort of resistance to an ideal of feminine beauty. What fascinates me is the very erasure of specificity that distinguishes them from the surrounding assortment of items. In *The Transparency of Evil* (1999), Baudrillard proposes that categorical distinctions between things become contaminated in a culture of simulation, so that:

> Each category is generalized to the greatest possible extent, so that it eventually loses all specificity and is reabsorbed by all the other categories. When everything is political, nothing is political any more, the word itself is meaningless. When everything is sexual, nothing is sexual any more, and sex loses its determinants. When everything is aesthetic, nothing is beautiful or ugly any more, and art itself disappears. This paradoxical state of affairs, which is simultaneously the complete actualization of an idea, the perfect realization of the whole tendency of modernity, and the negation of that idea and that tendency, their annihilation by virtue of their very success, by virtue of their extension beyond their own bounds—this state of affairs is epitomized by a single figure: the transpolitical, the transexual, the transaesthetic (Baudrillard 1999: 9–10).

Barbie, too, erases the specificity of the category of 'woman' by operating as an endlessly proliferating sign of the body that explodes any possibility of articulating the 'truth' about female identity. Even when stripped bare of her frilly, feminine accoutrements, Barbie reveals nothing about 'real' women because her longer-than-long legs, masses of blonde hair, and pneumatic breasts exceed the limits of phallogocentric signification by virtue of their hyperfemininity. The way that the markers of the feminine are exaggerated on her form confounds the category of 'woman' because it can no longer be contained to a fixed set of attributes. Barbie comes to occupy what Baudrillard calls the 'fractal', or fourth order of the sign, whereby the proliferation of the unbound signifier incites a viral mode of replication that liberates value from any point of reference (Baudrillard 1999: 5). In the case of Barbie, her exaggerated styling and the relentless proliferation of her form in media and popular culture characterise her as an 'unbound signifier' that prompts us to consider whether there can be any definitive truth to the term 'woman' at all when the characteristics of what counts as a woman cannot be contained within a binary logic of male versus female, or real versus representation. The Barbie look-a-like, Cindy Jackson, is a case in point. She is not a realer or truer version of womanhood than Barbie, inasmuch as she is a simulation of a doll, which itself is a simulation of the feminine. Her meaning has disappeared in the ongoing propagation of signs. By advocating the dissolution of all values, Baudrillard eschews a productivist logic of modernism grounded in the grand narratives of identity, reality, knowledge and truth. As simulation disrupts value systems through which meaning is inscribed, it allows us to think of Barbie differently to a representation of a 'real' woman.

If we are to agree with Baudrillard that our present cultural situation is typified by contagion and contamination, or the invasion of all categories by each other, then Barbie does not simply reflect an ideal image of femininity. Instead, the indeterminacy caused by the collapse of absolute value systems refracts meaning from her plastic body. Plasticity implies instability and process, and like its definition, the many forms plastic may take are ambiguous and contradictory. The generative potential of plastic resides in its ability to become any shape. It is transformative, contaminating the distinctions between natural and artificial, subject and object.

Plastic Fantastic

Central to my narrative of Barbie as a transformative figuration is the notion of plasticity. As a product whose 'substance is very much her essence' (Lord 1994: 73), plasticity lies at the heart of refiguring Barbie. It is Barbie's very plasticity that ensures the body's disappearance and allows us to rethink the paradigm that equates Barbie with real women. The history and theory of plastics divulges an ambivalence inherent in its formulation, use and meaning. In this context, Barbie's plastic form may be interpreted as an unstable referent that functions to disable, rather than determine meaning.

The confused cultural space that plastic inhabits is suggested by the multiple definitions it is given in the *Oxford Concise Dictionary* (1995), which include 'artificial' and 'insincere', as well as 'formative' and 'creative'. And while plastic is primarily defined as 'any number of synthetic polymeric substances that can be given any required shape', its derivative term 'plasticity', suggests a mode or element of being that emulates plastic's variable qualities.

Plastic is the definitive symbol of the mid-twentieth century, a period characterised by 'artificiality, disposability, and synthesis' (Fenichell 1996: 5). Its indeterminacy also situates it within the territory of the postmodern, marked by the destabilisation of hierarchies such as authenticity versus reproduction, and high versus low culture (Jameson 1991). While the materiality of plastic is rapidly being extended by the virtuality of the microchip, plastic's importance in the information age is noted by Stephen Fenichell, who argues that the definition of post-industrial, postmodern society as the information age could equally be termed the plastic age:

> Plastic provides us with the material prerequisite for information storage and retrieval, both analog and digital. From photographic film to audio- and videotape, from computer discs to CD-ROMs and CDs, plastic not only imitates natural materials, it allows us to recreate an entirely new world of the visual and aural imagination and record it for instant replay, as well as for posterity (Fenichell 1996: 5).

Furthermore, plastic has penetrated the human body in the form of prosthetics, artificial joints and valves, raising the kinds of concerns expressed over cyborg and posthuman bodies as unnatural (Fenichell 1996: 5). The way that it has seamlessly replaced organic components, both within and outside of the anatomical body, makes us question what it is we value as 'real' and 'human'. This new world of simulated phenomena that plastic inhabits and, in part creates, challenges notions of authenticity by destabilising a modernist paradigm and undermining the ideals of autonomy and origins that structure an identity politics of the subject.

Given plastic's dominance in contemporary consumer society, its associations with modern, industrial society invite consideration. Initially conceived in the nineteenth century as a miraculous substance offering limitless possibility, plastic's appeal resided in its ability to imitate the material world (Meikle 1995: 12). As plastics boomed in the post-war period, its reputation as a wonder material was accompanied by its growing status in the vernacular. Almost anything could be made from plastic, and it was. With the mass production of goods plastic came to permeate our lives and especially our homes—from chairs to drinking cups to the clothes on the washing line. According to Jeffrey Meikle, because it is so common and available, plastic has come to represent the ideals of equality, democracy and accessibility (Meikle 1995: chapter six).

So, while on the one hand, plastic was celebrated as a material with endless potential, on the other it was stigmatised for being *un*real. It was derided as vulgar and inauthentic because of its commonality and transience in a throwaway culture. For these reasons, plastic became associated with everything that was fake, dehumanised, inauthentic and valueless (Hebdige 1988: 50, Meikle 1995: 7). Even today, to call someone 'plastic' is to demean them by questioning the very core of their 'real' self. The writing of Roland Barthes is emblematic of this hostility toward plastic, which he fears undermines a value system that is based on origin stories. For Barthes, plastic marks our turn away from all things original and natural in preference for imitation and artifice. As a result, the primacy and wonder of nature is not only displaced by plastic's prosaic characteristics of artifice and inauthenticity but risks being lost to us (Barthes 1973: 97–8).

It is the very material and symbolic ambiguity of plastic that allows us to generate an alternative understanding of the relationship between the body, technology and representation as transformative. Instead of replaying gendered assumptions that associate mass culture and production with the feminine and inauthentic, I suggest that Barbie's plasticity embodies a generative tension. Her promise lies in her plasticity. The plastic constituting Barbie's frame is hard in places and rubbery in others. A lightness, or synthetic sheen radiates from her smooth form, evoking a sense of mutability or a state of flux. Like the stretched rubber band of a catapult, her elongated limbs are taut and filled with potential energy. Barbie is ready to metamorphose. Yet tension is a volatile state. The risk of snapping accompanies the potential to be flung into another place or become another form. An uncertainty is created by a plasticity that threatens to transform into something else.

It is the instability of value systems that allows for this play in form. Barbie, like her plastic body, is a shifting referent. 'Against the differential play of value', Baudrillard observes, is a 'dual play of form: reversibility and metamorphosis' (Baudrillard 1998b: 4). Metamorphosis is explained by Baudrillard as:

> ...a happy catastrophe: it is the ceaseless changing of the one sex into the other, of ideas one into the other, of tones, words and colours. It is the changing of the human into the inhuman and on through the total cycle of appearances, forms and substances respectively: vegetable, mineral, animal and human. And why not of other superhuman forms once the human is no longer the be-all and end-all? (Baudrillard 1998b: 4).

One of the central propositions to emerge from Baudrillard's critique of value systems is the destabilisation of meaning. But the dissolution of established systems of meaning does not have to mean that the subject and the body are abolished entirely. As Julia Kristeva reminds us in *Powers of Horror* (1982), the tensions between the multiple and dynamic self and a coherent sense of self need to be sustained to avoid the dissolution of the subject. This state of tension is reflected in Kristeva's 'subject in process', whose unresolved and discontinuous state disrupts systems of meaning, ordering and understanding.

The unresolved state of the subject may be likened to the unresolved status of Barbie's plastic body. It is as an object of potentially endless transformation inhabiting the space between rupture and rigidity that Barbie may challenge the limits of both. Looking again at my photograph, I am struck by the trio of dolls on the left of the picture—a headless male doll and two Barbies. They bask in the full sun, cut off from the rest of the group by a shadow that envelops the remaining dolls. Arranged neatly above the Barbies are three pairs of sunglasses. Above and to the right are three lipstick cases. As evidenced by this haphazard collection of junk, the generative potential of plastic resides in its ability to become any shape. Each of the objects is plastic, differentiated only by their degree of malleability and the mould in which they have been cast. The primacy of one object above another is made redundant when configured in terms of process. Plasticity, as Barthes reminds us, erases the value difference between things. Valuation is made impossible. Meaning disappears in the endless propagation of signs:

> The hierarchy of substances is abolished: a single one replaces them all: the whole world *can* be plasticized, and even life itself since, we are told, they are beginning to make plastic aortas (Barthes 1973: 99).

Neither do the objects made from 'natural' substances—the glass bottles, the wooden bowl or the metal seceteurs—have greater value than the plastic Barbie, by virtue of their organic composition. They are no more or less real than the plastic toy. No greater economic value is given to any one object in this random arrangement of mechanically reproduced goods at the flea market, with each object a simulacra contaminating the distinction between what is authentic and what is fake. In this respect, plastic does not function as an imitator of nature, as Barthes proposes. Plastic does not strive for equivalence with the real, rather the simulacra is reality. As a substance of simulation, plastic dissolves the opposition between the real and what it represents. Likewise, there is no 'truth' to the meaning of Barbie. Barbie's place on the asphalt, among the array of knick-knacks, can be regarded as outside a rigid category of signification. She is neither a real nor unreal representation of the female body, but an appearance that challenges the reality principle.

In claiming that '(o)nce I used to analyse things in critical terms, of revolution; now I do it in terms of mutation' (Gane 1993: 43), Baudrillard locates an alternative strategy for the subject to deploy in an age of media networks and communications. Likewise, by offering Barbie as an example of a transformative figuration of subjectivity, I do not intend to position her as a literal embodiment of the plastic subject. Neither is it my intention to deny the material conditions of existence but to suggest that as the distance between ourselves and our cultural objects falls away, the place of the subject at the centre of the world is destabilised, creating the potential to rethink subjectivity as always in process. Reconfiguring the idea of plastic in the cultural psyche is an attempt to disturb the unity of the subject in favour of a more fluid conception of self. As Fenichell states: 'We mould plastic. And plastic moulds us' (Fenichell 1996: 9). Interpreting the posthuman as plastic, as a potentially transformative entity, is a process of recognising the necessity for new engagements with cultural conditions that confuse hierarchical binaries of self/Other, mainstream/marginal and real/virtual.

Toward Transformation: Revisiting Children's Toys

Barbie is certainly not the only toy that has come under scrutiny for constructing and reflecting gender relations and identities in the 'real' world. By taking some time to look at how the idea of transformation, particularly gender transformation, has been understood in literature on children's toys and child's play, we can further explore and complicate the idea that images and objects 'fix' meaning. Given that this chapter began with a vision of Barbie as a transformer, I think it's necessary to return to those other well-known toy transformers. In pop culture parlance, the trademarked term 'Transformers' refers to the 1980s animated television series and the toys that 'transform' from cars/trucks/boats into towering robot machine–men, or cyborg entities.

Transformers are not exclusively for boys, but are marketed to them, and appeal to the traditional associations between masculinity and technologies of warfare, industry and automotive machinery (Wajcman 1991). Playing with toys like Transformers explicitly encourages and legitimises the idea of transforming the self in male culture. Cultural studies scholar Marsha Kindler has written about this link between transformation and masculinity in her article 'From Mutation to Morphing: Cultural Transformations in Greek Myth to Children's Media Culture' (2000). Kindler highlights the importance of masculinity in Greek mythic narratives of transformation, and the continued association of men with transformative capabilities in popular cultural contexts, such as *Teenage Mutant Ninja Turtles* and *Mighty Morphin' Power Rangers*.

The active engagement required in the process of 'transforming' the toy from its vehicle state to a machine–man and vice versa reinforces the alignment of man/culture/activity in opposition to woman/nature/passivity. If we are to maintain the dichotomous positioning of women with nature and passivity, Barbie, as a standard object of girls' doll play, fails as a transformative entity. Judy Attfield identifies the prevalence of such dichotomous thinking in her examination of the different types of joints in the design of Barbie compared with those of the boys' toy Action Man. Her study illustrates how Barbie's limited and simplistic joints render her more suited to posing than motility (Attfield 1996: 82). Comparing Barbie with Action Man's moveable parts and complex ball and swivel joints, Attfield concludes that the 'cliché of "feminine" as passive and "masculine" as active is literally embodied in the design of the toys' (Attfield 1996: 85).

Susan Willis promotes a similar view in her account of child's play and gender formation. Arguing that the construction of gender is intimately tied to commodity consumption, she concludes that Barbie as well as He-Man 'do not offer the child the possibility of prolonging polymorphous sexuality or developing an open notion about gendering. Instead they define the rigid separation of the sexes; and what is more, a narrow conceptualisation of gender' (Willis 1991: 27). Like Attfield and Kindler, Willis recognises the associations between transformation and masculinity, viewing this as a limitation to how we understand identity, change and social relationships (Willis 1991: 39).

Another approach to gender and transformation is offered by Mattel, who market Barbie's transformative capabilities in terms of the endless range of clothes and accessories available to both Barbie and the consumer. According to Kindler, Mattel's advertising techniques represent Barbie as permanent and unchanging 'hardware', which is supplemented by a range of prolific, high-turnover and constantly changing accessories or 'software'. Similarly, multiple versions of Barbie are available to the consumer, making it possible (and likely) to own a number of different Barbies that nonetheless maintain a common identity as Barbie. Kindler concludes that Mattel's portrayal of Barbie as fixed ultimately functions to restrict her shape-shifting capabilities (Kindler 2000: 77).

For example, a recent visit to a local toy store revealed Barbie's latest incarnations as a photographer's model, as well as the fairytale characters Snow White and Cinderella. In the past, Barbie's careers have included being an astronaut and a female president. From this perspective, Barbie displays a malleability in the multiple personas and roles she enacts, while retaining a coherent identity. This interpretation of Barbie finds its theoretical complement in Judith Butler's (1993) notion of performativity. For Butler, gender roles are performative enactments that ensure the materialisation of female bodies through the reiteration and citation of the discursive codes of feminine ideals. Interpreting gender as something that is enacted serves as a strategy to counter the notion of femininity as an essential and inherent quality. Indeed, Barbie's hyperfeminine qualities imply that gender itself is a simulation; an artifice that is reproducible, rather than a natural characteristic. The transformations Barbie may undergo, however, are limited to the changing of accessories, careers and roles. Despite the multiple, changeable and often empowering roles that Barbie dolls offer to young girls, in conventional accounts, Barbie's identity and bodily boundaries remain intact.

What we can conclude from each of the studies referenced above is that while the gendered assumptions associated with child's play are questioned, these analyses uncritically presuppose that toys prefigure an adult word. The imaginary world of the child is seen as shaping an adult reality. This is in keeping with Barthes' perception that toys are fixed within a universal system of meaning, thus allowing us to make sense of the 'real' world. He laments the inability of toys to 'offer dynamic forms' through which the subject may transform the self, particularly in the case of plastic toys (Barthes 1973: 53). Barthes equates plasticity to a deathly stasis. It destroys nature, threatens humanity and denies the pleasure of child's play (Barthes 1973: 54–5).

These arguments make it difficult to imagine Barbie as transformative. When interpreted in terms of Barthes' structural analysis, the marketing and design of toys, and feminist critiques of cultural consumption, the limited motility in Barbie's plastic limbs and her plastered on smile seem as fixed as her meaning. Both Attfield and Kindler's studies take the material parameters of Barbie's body to be the limit point to thinking beyond established interpretations. In adopting an approach to Barbie through Baudrillard's idea of the trans state, I want to move beyond these ways of thinking to suggest that the plasticity of Barbie's form disturbs conventional understandings of Barbie as passive and static. In doing so, the perception that the body is the contained and unchanging site of subjectivity becomes complicated.

Consistent with my approach to rethinking established perceptions of Barbie as representative of reality is Carol Ockman's suggestion that Barbie functions as a fantasmic body. Ockman complicates Barbie's status as an ideal figure of femininity through Kenneth Clark's definition of the nude. Her argument hinges on the notion that Barbie's ability to represent an ideal without representing the nude creates a productive tension between the real and the ideal. For Ockman, Barbie's static body is timeless. She exists in a 'physical state outside of time' (Ockman 1999: 83). Simultaneously, 'Barbie's accessories...produce a kind of "reality effect" that naturalises Barbie's body, rendering it paradoxically both authentic and timeless' (Ockman 1999: 85). Ockman concludes that the tension created by Barbie's fantasmic status culminates in acts of resistance against the ideals of womanhood that Barbie is said to represent. An example of this oppositional strategy can be found in the work of artists who have used Barbie to critique feminine stereotypes. The tendency of some art practitioners to actually mutilate Barbie's form in their work critiques the violence experienced by real bodies, particularly the violation of the female corpus. In Ockman's argument, what is useful about the confusion between ideal and real is that it opens up new strategies for resistance.

While this study is of value to the extent that it locates a site of productive tension between the ideal and the real, Ockman maintains, and fails to problematise, the categories of real and ideal, which sustain an interpretation of Barbie within practices of signification. As a result, the potential of this tension is denied; a tension that would allow Barbie to be reconfigured as 'something else'. In my mind, this tension doesn't sustain the real and the ideal in a dichotomous relationship, but instead creates the possibility for infinite transformation at the point of the collapse between reality and representation. When the dissolution of the real and ideal abolishes the basis of meaning, Barbie demands another mode of interpretation.

Feminist Responses to 'Cultural Plastic'

Not all feminists are convinced of the liberatory potential of a displaced and diffuse subject. The plastic potential of the transformative subject doesn't always sit well with a feminist political project that aims to reclaim for women the subject position denied to them by the ethos of modernism. Prevalent within a dialogue of gendered subject constitution is a concern with reinstating elements of modernist values of autonomy, unity and essence, albeit in the process of attempting to undermine the privileged status of the white, Western male subject of antiquity. Indicative of this anxiety regarding the subject in crisis is what Susan Bordo (1991) has termed the 'cultural plastic' of bodies and identities.

In a rigorous attack on plasticity as a postmodern paradigm, Bordo accuses popular culture of falsely espousing 'the rhetoric of choice and self-determination', and suggests that postmodern theories of subjectivity operate to efface the material and social realities of lived bodies (Bordo 1991: 109). According to Bordo, the cultural practices of shaping or constructing the body through plastic surgery or attending the gym are symptomatic of the postmodern tendency toward homogenisation and normalisation. In speaking of the plastic postmodern subject as capable of endless transformations, Bordo is concerned about the integrity and status of the human body and the erasure of gender and race difference. It is the normalising power of cultural imagery that Bordo argues perpetuates 'a construction of life as plastic possibility and weightless choice, undetermined by history, social location, or even individual biography' (Bordo 1991: 110).

For Bordo, the celebration of the plastic body is part of a broader 'postmodern conversation' that has come to typify many aspects of cultural life. Television in particular is singled out for promoting an 'anything goes' mentality that presents a 'grab bag' of undifferentiated and homogenising notions of difference, where '(a)ll sense of history and all ability (or inclination) to sustain cultural criticism, to make the distinctions and discriminations which would permit such criticism, have disappeared' (Bordo 1991: 115). Postmodern feminism's endeavours to deconstruct the hierarchical dualisms structuring difference and the unified subject are rejected by Bordo. New constructions of subjectivity are dismissed as plastic, artificial multiplicities that can never acknowledge the reality of women's lived experience (Bordo 1991: 117).

Bordo is also critical of postmodern theories that interpret bodies as sites through which individuals actively produce themselves as subjects. The notion of liberation and autonomy in an age of consumption and capitalism is closely aligned with the cultural constitution of plastic as a metaphor for liberation, accessibility, democracy and the cult of the individual, as noted earlier in this chapter. The idea that transforming the self is simply a matter of individual choice denies what Bordo considers to be larger social inequities that allow only certain subjects particular freedoms. Bordo considers this problematic for feminist reform because a focus on the micro politics of the individual can obscure the bigger structural inequalities that need to be addressed in order to improve the cultural, social, political and economic position of women as a social category.

So plastic surgery procedures, for example, are not seen as potentially empowering for women who choose to transform the self, but dismissed as control mechanisms that produce passive and idealised bodies, even though women might think themselves to be active and knowing subjects. While acknowledging that individuals are informed by and 'act' in the context of institutions such as the media and patriarchy, what is troubling about this mindset is that it leaves little scope for individual agency. Here Bordo is drawing on Foucauldian notions of the body as produced through power-effects to argue that postmodern theory erases the 'disciplinary reality' of the normalisation of the subject/body through the rhetoric of free choice (Bordo 1991: 112–3). Echoing these sentiments is Nancy Hartsock, who asserts that Foucault's 'stress on heterogeneity and the specificity of each situation leads him to lose track of social structures and instead to focus on how individuals experience and exercise power' (Hartsock 1990: 168–9).

Anne Balsamo also uses Foucauldian theory, in particular the notion of biopower, in her analysis of cosmetic surgeries. Her primary criticism is that the viewing technologies used in medical and scientific discourse exercise control upon the female body. The specifically technological nature of the plastic body is emphasised by Balsamo, who asserts that the technological gaze has transformed the body into a site where the physical transformation of the material body (cosmetic surgery) becomes a sign of culture (the cultural ideas of Western beauty) (Balsamo 1996: 56–79). No longer are representations such as Barbie key signifiers of the female technobody of consumer capital, but instead material bodies themselves become the sites for cultural ideals of female beauty. Yet by positioning women as objects of medical–technological discourse, Balsamo assumes women have limited access to, and knowledge of, the technologies impacting on their bodies. As a result, women are accorded little or no power to refigure the self in an active relationship to technoculture. This is in keeping with the strand of feminism that considers technology as detrimental to the social, cultural and political position of women in society, as discussed in chapter one.

The influential notion of 'technologies of gender', coined by Teresa De Lauretis, underwrites the commentaries of Bordo and Balsamo. The phrase speaks of the construction of gender difference by regulatory discourses of techno-social and biomedical technologies (De Lauretis 1987). So while the plastic body can be understood in Foucauldian terms as a product of power/knowledge relations (Foucault 1977: 27–9), for these feminist materialists, power is never conceived beyond a top-down dynamic that situates the female subject as the victim of power-effects. Foucault's body is disciplined and controlled by an abstract power that is primarily linked to institutions such as the clinic, the school and the prison (Foucault 1977). In this schema, the body is produced by disciplinary mechanisms, such as observation and examination, whereby power resides outside of the body.

Yet for other feminists writing about women's agency in undergoing plastic surgery, Foucault's writing suggests that women can exercise power (Covino 2004, Davis 2003). For example, in *Discipline and Punish*, Foucault questions the myth of a totalitarian monopoly of power in preference of a consideration of the diffuse and unstable nature of power relations. Foucault states:

> …power is exercised rather than possessed; it is not the 'privilege', acquired or preserved, of the dominant class, but the overall effect of its strategic positions—an effect that is manifested and sometimes

> extended by the position of those who are dominated (Foucault 1977: 26–7).

In the search for new formulations for feminist understandings of the techno–human relationship, the interrogations of Bordo and Balsamo prove limiting to a study of posthuman figurations. Their use of Foucault's theory of power to claim that particular groups hold more power than others configures social inequality and bodily control as an effect of rigid power networks. This is indicated by Balsamo's self-stated aim to 'describe how certain technologies are...ideologically shaped by the operation of gender interests and, consequently, how they serve to reinforce traditional gendered patterns of power and authority' (Balsamo 1996: 10).

In my analysis of Barbie, I want to think about plasticity in a different sense to the liberalist paradigm of self-determination and free choice, and to argue for Barbie as an appearance of the feminine that confounds the 'truth' or 'meaning' of woman. Plasticity doesn't have to signal identity as either fixed in a rigid form, or fragmented, but may offer a mode of inaugurating the transformative subject. In response to Bordo's perception of the postmodern project as lacking historical and social grounding, I claim that the discursive practices arising from postmodern understandings of subjects are contextual. Recognising the proliferation of experiences available to the subject in any given context and at any particular moment may allow for new approaches to subjectivity that are not grounded in a 'truth' about the self, but consider how representations like Barbie act on us and the effect of this on our perceptions of self and reality.

Like the plural and decentred subject of postmodern discourse, the concept of the transformative or plastic subject allows for an exploration of the cultural and social contexts in which new figurations of subjectivity emerge. Closely aligned and in conjunction with the confusion of boundaries between marginal and mainstream in the millennial landscape is a disruption of the distinctions between self and Other, organic and machinic, nature and artifice; a disruption instigated by the increasing proliferation of mechanical, technical and digital technologies in everyday life. Tiziana Terranova (1996) pinpoints this as an ontological shift in both human society and how the body is perceived and experienced within a high-tech world. Underlying this shift, she claims, is an increased exposure to the simulated image in popular media, in conjunction with the increased use of technology in daily life (Terranova 1996: 167).

Baudrillard recognises that 'all these formulas are reductive, in so far as they always revolve around the real—the problem being to exorcise or appropriate it' (Baudrillard 1998b: 97). Configuring Barbie as plastic offers one attempt at avoiding reductive interpretations, providing instead an example of a transformative object that challenges the reality principle. The plasticity, artifice and malleability of her form contest signification and elude a fixed interpretation. In this transformative state, it is the degree to which the subject shifts between and within unstable markers such as sex, race and gender that matters. In this regard, Barbie serves as a tool to think through the transformation of bodies and identity in a 'trans' state after the orgy of liberation. Technologies of the body and mass media influence the body in ways that open up possibilities for figuring subjectivity that depart from a unified notion of identity. I agree with Erica Rand's suggestion that Barbie does not solely exist as an ideal of womanhood that women identify with or reject. The transformative subject doesn't exist as a point of identification. In the techno age of plastic bodies, Barbie invalidates a notion of the material body as the limit point of subjectivity. Conceiving of the subject in terms of transformation can help us decode the mindset that writes the plastic body as a technology of control and containment, or as fixed in the real. It can serve as a strategy to hack into the phallogocentric codes that structure ideals of femininity, and scramble interpretations of embodiment that reinscribe an unchanging and essentialised myth of woman as tied to nature.

4

Posthuman Monsters: The Erasure of Marilyn Manson

I scan the spines of hundreds of plastic cases lining my shelves. Each holds a silver disc where music is etched as a digital code. Transformed from the live sounds of the recording studio into the 0:1 co-ordinates of the information grid, the music on each CD must be decoded by the machines of digital technology in order to be heard. Unlike the musical trace contained in the analogue system of phonography, digital recording re-presents, stores and transmits music as data (Rothenbuhler and Peters 1997: 245). To access this code, I need to enter the musical matrix, which in this case is my labyrinthine CD collection. The process of selecting, sorting and playing CDs seems antiquated when compared to the digital downloading of songs. Lacking the speed and accuracy of such technologies, my eyes skim the titles numerous times. Clumsy, frustrated, I search the files again for a particular disc. Read: error. I can't see the title. I know it is in here somewhere. My eyes lock on the CD's clear blue spine and I struggle to retrieve it from my disorderly classifying system.

INTD-90273 MAR1LYN MAN5ON MECHANICAL ANIMALS NOTHING RECORDS

Turning it in my hand, my eyes fix on the cover. CD art can't be found on my iPod. I want an image to hold in my hand and I'm going about it the old-fashioned way. Specifically, I want this picture. It depicts goth rocker Marilyn Manson, circa 1998. His face is lean and vampiric, framed by a mass of iridescent red hair flecked through with yellow and blue streaks. His infra-red stare radiates out at the viewer in a way that is unsettled and unsettling. There is also something awkward about the contours of Manson's body. Against a slate–grey backdrop his shape seems to jump out of the page, evoking the potential to bend and contort. The texture of his distended form could be likened to a composite of pasty flesh and rubber. Although his skin is the colour of plaster, it displays a plasticity that stretches over his frame to cover and contain his interior elements. This artificial skin, like plasticine, begs to be moulded, disrupted and reformed.

Both troubling and fascinating are the small mounds on Manson's chest and his indeterminate genital bulge, which are emphasised by his pose. With his shoulders pulled back and flanked by a pair of disturbingly long arms, Manson accentuates his ambiguous genitalia. Like a malleable sheath, his skin stretches firmly, yet comfortably, over a body that is neither male nor female. Despite clearly suggesting sex organs, these body parts show no trace of the inversions and extensions that typify the human body. The characteristics of the abject self are absent—protruding nipples, coarse hair, the vaginal cut, the eye of the penis, or the umbilical remnant of birth. No such markers rupture the seamlessness of the skin's surface.

I wonder about this confused depiction of sexual difference. How can we explain bodies that exist outside of the distinct categories of 'male' and 'female'? Queer and transgender theorists have provided one framework through which to make sense of bodies that go beyond culturally prescribed norms of gender and sexuality, and in the process have challenged the notion that the socially constructed category of 'gender' is the enactment of a person's biological 'sex', or indeed that 'sex' itself is a biological given (Bornstein 1994, Butler 1990, 2004, Halberstam 1998, 2005, Stone 1995).[1] What I want to examine here goes beyond critical understandings of gender and sex toward the realm of simulated realities. While sharing the vision of queer and transgender thinkers to destabilise a two-category system of gender difference, I want to focus on a different site where gender identity is contested—that of the posthuman body—and situate this analysis in a climate where digital technologies inform how images are made and understood.

Can posthuman, post-gender images, like queer, bisexual and transgender bodies, encourage us to move beyond a dialectical way of thinking about, not only gender, but other social categories of difference? What can novel depictions of gender identity reveal about the circulation of categories of sexual difference? How might we speak about differences when the markers that once distinguished categories of gender and race are no longer distinct or definable? On what level can individuals identify with such images? Using the images from *Mechanical Animals*, this chapter reflects on these questions, and in the process of doing so, makes the argument that the posthuman is a monster for the digital age; a boundary form that calls into question ontological configurations of difference. In particular, it considers the implications of digital image making for understanding sexual difference and its accordant power-effects in the context of virtual worlds and biotech breakthroughs.

Figure 2. Marilyn Manson, *Mechanical Animals* album centrefold image.

But it is not only the difference between the sexes that Manson contests. Opening the cover sleeve reveals a centrefold image of Manson languidly stretched out on a sofa made of grey tubing (see figure 2). What this picture shows that the front cover doesn't is Manson's metamorphosis into a hybrid of animal, human and machine. Most striking is the transformation of Manson's feet into pincer-like hoofs that define him as the 'mechanical animal' of the CD title. Rendered like a cartoon character's, there is a comic element to his clumsy, oversized hoofs. These bovine appendages challenge the integrity of the organic body, teasing and taunting the viewer to make something of Manson's morphogenesis into an animal.

As neither male nor female, organism nor machine, human nor animal, Manson confuses the role of the image as either reflecting the self or representing an Other. He displaces this logic for the ambiguity of a transitional state that defies a natural order. Part feline, part bovine, part hominid, Manson is the mutant product of a perverted genetic code. Resplendent with red glowing eyes, a metallic sheen and elongated fingers, he invokes the terror and fascination of the alien–vampire–monster. Accordingly, Manson may be located in what Braidotti has observed as late postmodern, postindustrial society's fascination with 'borderline figures' (Braidotti 2000: 157). The popular cultural trend toward the freakish, vampiric, alien and mutant has been theorised by Braidotti in the context of an increasingly technologised cultural climate where 'classical iconographic representations of monstrous others' cross-over and mutate with contemporary technocultural artefacts (Braidotti 2000: 157).

As a boundary figure that resists being classified in the natural order of things, Manson's posthuman is also closely aligned with the field of teratology—the scientific discourse of monsters. Various theorists have observed that the monster functions as both Other to the normalised self, and a third state or hybrid entity that disrupts subject constitution understood in terms of hierarchical binary dualisms (Braidotti 1996: 141, Cohen 1996b: 7, Shildrick 1999: 78). The monster occupies potentially contradictory discourses and signifies 'potentially contradictory meanings' (Braidotti 1996: 135). Ambiguity typifies these figures, eliciting anxieties concerning the boundaries and borders of the body, subjectivity and the human. Monsters simultaneously threaten and uphold the integrity of the human, serving as a deviant category, or marginal extreme through which the limits of normal, natural, human identity are defined and secured (Cohen 1996a: ix). Or, as Hanafi puts it, 'the monster is a concept that we need in order to tell ourselves what we are *not*' (Hanafi 2000: 218).

The posthuman shares with the monster a confusion of boundaries that challenges what it means to be human. Both act as boundary figures, and it is this ambiguity that has been strategically used by feminists who analyse monster discourse, to disrupt a humanist version of being. But digital images of the posthuman monster can't be interpreted in the same way as the hybrid creatures of old. Manson and other posthuman forms like him belong to an age of 'cybernetic teratology', typified by the techno–human hybrids, digital mutants and genetically modified freaks of popular culture (Braidotti 1996: 141). In order to approach this image of Marilyn Manson we first need to take into account the context in which contemporary images are produced, how they are consumed by viewers, and what this means for theories of the subject in the posthuman landscape.

Simulation and the Implosion of Meaning: Questioning Categories of Difference

At the beginning of the 1980s, Jean Baudrillard's reflections on the human condition led him to observe that Otherness disappears in a culture of simulation, 'when all becomes transparence and immediate visibility, when everything is exposed to the harsh and inexorable light of information and communication' (Baudrillard 1983: 130). This moment—when electronic media and communication proliferate and accelerate to the point where the individual is subsumed by the relay of information—creates what Baudrillard refers to as the 'transparency of the subject'. Not only does the subject disappear in the hyperreal cacophony of visual signs and information, but the social system is said to exceed its maximum capacity to circulate such data. Society approaches an ecstatic state, overloaded by the positive accumulation and endless proliferation of knowledge, data, facts and signs. He observes:

> Things have found a way of avoiding a dialectics of meaning that was beginning to bore them: by proliferating indefinitely, increasing their potential, outbidding themselves in an ascension to the limit, an obscenity that henceforth becomes their immanent finality and senseless reason (Baudrillard 1990b: 7).

By exploring what resides beyond the extremities of the social, Baudrillard attempts to pass from a dialectical system of interpretation into a space where referential values are impossible. It is at this point of saturation by simulacra that the social is pushed beyond its limits to 'the point where it inverts its finalities and reaches its point of inertia and extermination' (Baudrillard 1990b: 10–11). This form of inertia, however, is not an empty void that is drained of all meaning, but a fatal site of excessive multiplication that causes a reversion or implosion of traditional value systems.

Baudrillard likens this accelerated growth of the world pushed beyond its limit to a cancer. Termed 'hypertely', it is a process of proliferation without beginning or end. Moreover, it is deemed impossible to locate the original source of this state of excess, or to predict its conclusion (Baudrillard 1990b: 13). Our experience of the world has become, using Baudrillard's parlance, 'overdetermined'. This overdetermination is of the order of the hyperreal, where real is no longer opposed to false, but accumulates to become something that is more real than reality. Accordingly, Baudrillard maintains:

> To the truer than true we will oppose the falser than false. We will not oppose the beautiful to the ugly, but will look for the uglier than ugly: the monstrous. We will not oppose the visible to the hidden, but will look for the more hidden than hidden: the secret (Baudrillard 1990b: 7).

This excess of positivity is radically different to the struggle of dialectics that sees the beautiful oppose the ugly and the true oppose the false. Meaning is no longer a question of opposites, but of excesses that destroy stable oppositions by collapsing inward. Manson acts out this proliferation and disappearance by exceeding the boundaries of the natural body.

The centre spread of the *Mechanical Animals* CD sleeve notes sees Manson stretched out on a sofa. The piece of furniture is grey and synthetic with a metallic sheen that reflects off its surface. Its tubular shape and long frame appear distorted and artificial. In this regard, the sofa complements Manson's own plastic form. Both surfaces look technologically produced, they appear almost to be merging into one other. The plasticity of the two forms creates the sense that they are in motion, engaged in the process of stretching beyond their individual boundaries. There is a palpable sense of tension, of process, at the liminal border where the forms touch. Their shared artificiality makes it hard to think about Manson as an autonomous, free and coherent subject that is entirely distinct from an inanimate, fixed object such as the sofa. Rather, both of these forms display a fluidity that works against an interpretation that positions them as animate and inanimate opposites. In the context of this relationship, Manson appears as 'more mobile than mobile', engaged in an act of metamorphosis (Baudrillard 1990b: 7).

Through this play of surfaces, the distinction between the subject and the object is disturbed. Manson's metamorphosis into a mechanical animal is made possible through the process of reversion, whereby his skin pushes beyond its limits, imploding in on itself to annihilate the difference between subject and object, and the structure of signification that differentiates the two. But the paradox of simulation is at play here, whereby 'if two things resemble each other too closely they no longer resemble each other at all' (Butler 1999: 35). This paradox arises because the purpose of simulation is to make the real possible, and in order to maintain an illusion of reality, Manson and the couch can't become the same thing, even though their distinctiveness is increasingly blurred in a hyperreal world. Hence, it is at the point where the subject and object become too much like each other that Manson's plastic body reverses in on itself in a fatal gesture that preserves the reality principle. Like the Barbie doll discussed previously, Marilyn Manson's taut, plastic mould indicates both containment and flexibility. His elongated limbs and distended fingers further signal an elasticity that threatens to morph, mutate and shift into something else, yet never rupture. Absolute annihilation of the subject is made impossible by fatality because the subject disappears at its limit point when its semblance to the Other is too close. The subject does not fragment, but disappears; its form reverses inward in an act of metamorphosis that produces *something else*.

This reversion can be located at the site of Manson's skin. It fails to act as a definitive boundary distinguishing the inside from the outside, the individual from the others, or the organic from the artificial. Instead, his skin signals a Baudrillardian play with categories, a point of liminality where self becomes Other, nature fuses with technology and the organic cannot be discerned from artifice. Judith Halberstam has written of skin as 'at once the most fragile of boundaries and the most stable of signifiers; it is the site of entry for the vampire, the signifier of race for the nineteenth-century monster. Skin is precisely what does not fit' (Halberstam 1995: 163). In a discussion of Jonathan Demme's 1991 film *The Silence of the Lambs*, she argues that contemporary images of the monster locate horror at the level of the skin, thereby disrupting the established gothic model of horror as one of surface and depth. Referring to several scenes in the film, Halberstam illustrates how skin functions to confuse boundaries such as interior and exterior, consumption and being consumed, male and female. What ensues, she argues, is a construction of a posthuman gender founded on mis-identity that remakes gender and the humanistic assumptions upon which identity is forged (Halberstam 1995: 176–7).

Similarly, Manson's emphasis on his plasticity of form suggests that he exists only as a surface, as a simulation without any relation in the real. By digitally manipulating Manson's synthetic flesh so that it looks like moulded plasticine, the function of skin as a boundary between biological interiorities and externalised technologies is complicated. No longer is the technological/human interaction configured in terms of a prosthetic extension or invasion of the unified and organic self by technology. Instead, posthuman configurations play with the boundaries separating the organic and machinic, the human and non-human, interiorities and exteriorities, self and Other. As Manson proliferates, both in terms of digital image reproduction, and the elasticity and endless possibilities of the body, he confounds the finalities of binary oppositions to contest the fixity of signifying practice. Indeed, Manson is that which Halberstam says 'does not fit'; that which annihilates established identity categories.

Manson's artificial skin also makes us question the idea that race categories, like gender, can determine a person's identity. Traditional interpretations of the skin as a 'reflection of the inside' or 'a mirror of the soul' creates the perception that an individual's inner character and identity can be made visible on the skin's surface (Benthien 2002: ix). Skin that was not white immediately located someone as a racialised or ethnic 'type' and accordingly, in opposition to the universal, unmarked norm (Gilman 1985). Although Manson glows with a ghostly pallor, this shade of white is not human. It is more like paint or plaster, with a fake and shiny patina that can't be mistaken for organic, fleshy tones. This plasticised surface does not secure whiteness as the normal human state. Rather, Manson's white skin is overtly visible in a way that ruptures the deep-seated associations between 'whiteness' and the universal, unspecified subject. It exposes the 'slippage between white as a colour and white as colourlessness' which 'forms part of a system of thought and affect whereby white people are both particular and nothing in particular, and both something and non-existent' (Dyer 1997: 47). This display of artifice demonstrates how cultural, not biological, categories construct difference based on skin colour.

In this respect, Manson challenges the reality principle. On certain parts of his body, his skin gleams with a disturbing incandescence that highlights whiteness as a constructed rather than given state, and complicates the ability to locate the 'truth' about racial identities. The metallic sheen that radiates off the grey, shaded, areas of his body also evokes the artifice of the machine. This suggests to me that the surface of his body is a product of technological intervention, and in turn, this highlights that race is a historically contingent and culturally determined category. The vision of whiteness that we are being asked to consume in this picture is not necessarily an endorsement of the technobody that has absorbed the range of human differences. Rather than implying that Manson erases racial specificity, he circulates as an imagining that casts speculation on the role of information and biotechnologies in forging both our raced and gendered identities.

As noted at the outset of this chapter, Manson also defies the natural order because he displays both male and female attributes. Even his name is an amalgam of arguably the most famous female sex siren of Hollywood cinema, Marilyn Monroe, and one of the most notorious male monsters of recent times, cult leader Charles Manson. He is depicted with barely-discernible breasts and an ambiguous genital bulge. These amorphous grey lumps suggest that Manson is no androgyne, but a more complex figuration than either male or female. Manson's sexually indeterminate status complicates an identity based on the oppositional categories of 'man' or 'woman'. These genital lumps and bumps suggest that Manson's sexual status is not denied, but becomes a proliferation of possibilities opened up by the posthuman condition. Anatomical being is no longer a stable referent as Manson's sexual markers exceed the limits of the natural body. By blurring the corporeal signs of sex difference through digital manipulation, Manson leads us to not only question these categories, but the very status of the body and embodied reality as the sites where identity resides. Sexual difference, like skin, is a surface effect, rather than an emblem of identity locatable in the body. By confusing his status as man or woman, machine or organism, Manson refuses to be categorised in traditional terms. Difference, as a marker of sexual, racial and ethnic identity, is under attack.

To suggest that Manson ignores sexual difference, however, is to bypass the key dimension of the technological in reshaping the very status of the human. I think that Manson's image here can be useful in helping us forge a new feminist politics of the subject because he exceeds the categories of woman and man, not because he denies or negates the specificities of difference. This move toward a proliferation of subjectivities and bodily experiences is generated by the social and symbolic interactions between things that confuse the limits of where once autonomous elements begin and end, such as those relations between organic and technological forms. No longer the source of the authentic or natural, the shifting boundaries of the corporeal in turn refigure sexuality, race and gender as fluid and displaced terms. Manson opts for a skin that is neither male nor female, neither organic nor technological, but something mutable that confuses essentialist notions of the body and the natural, occasioning a range of possibilities for what might constitute subjectivity beyond the limits of the body and identity.

In this respect, Manson's is a fatal image, a place of unstable signification that can't be contained in an economy of exchange that relies on a dual and hierarchical model of difference. Manson's ambiguous, yet obvious, sexual markers offer an example of an excessive proliferation of the signs of sex in popular culture. Baudrillard tells us that crossing over into the space beyond signification sees hypertelic growth paralleled by an implosion or reversion where that which is prolific also disappears. Sex, by virtue of its visibility, too, has disappeared. For Baudrillard, sexual indifference is about a 'lack of differentiation between the sexual poles, and on indifference to sex *qua* pleasure' (Baudrillard 1999: 20). In speaking about this phenomenon, he cites Andy Warhol, Michael Jackson and the porn star La Cicciolina as examples of a sexual ambiguity; a lack of gender specificity 'where sexuality is lost in the theatrical excess of its ambiguity' (Baudrillard 1999: 22). Sexual indifference is everywhere. The proliferation of sex has ensured its disappearance. The sexual ambivalence displayed by Manson ruptures semiotic order, so that coherent meaning is not only challenged, but made impossible. For Baudrillard, this fatal strategy is a catastrophic process.

The Subject and the Image in a Posthuman Landscape

In a culture overrun by the speed and proliferation of digital technology, Baudrillard makes the point that our experience of being a subject is fundamentally altered. Postmodernism's fractured and dispersed subject in crisis isn't sufficient to explain our contemporary experience. Instead for Baudrillard, the subject is understood more appropriately in terms of catastrophe. So, too, does Manson circulate as a catastrophic subject rather than a coherent sign or carrier of meaning. Catastrophe is the excess, acceleration and precipitation typified by the information age. Unlike Gilles Deleuze and Felix Guattari's productive possibilities for the subject, catastrophe is a fatal strategy whose potency resides in the unmaking of the subject and the triumph of the object.

Baudrillard's idea of catastrophe allows us to reconceive the relations of reality against representation, and subject versus object, on which a politics of identity depends. Subjectivity eludes definition in a self/Other dichotomy, becoming instead a process of disappearance. Moreover, configuring the subject as catastrophic contests a Marxist-inspired model of the resisting subject. Understanding the subject in terms of his/her defiance of dominant ideologies has been a way of securing identity in resistance to particular aspects of culture and society. In this framework, subjects and objects remain firmly opposed. Catastrophe, on the other hand, makes identity disappear in the acceleration and proliferation of popular cultural signs and artefacts.

Rather than focusing on the centrality of the subject, Manson's catastrophic posthuman form encourages a decentralised model of subjectivity. In this sense, posthuman figurations do not pose as objects or subjects unto themselves, but act as fatal sites that displace the value system on which subjects and objects are constructed in relation to one another. In the process of reversion, the possibility of making meaning is denied. The potential of this mode of theorising for feminism may be located at the point where the logic of dialectical thinking is exceeded, where disappearance problematises coherent meaning. Following this schema, a subjectivity forged on identification with the posthuman is made impossible. Rather, subjectivity is understood as a series of displacements, as identity cannot be secured in relation to popular images in terms of identification or resistance. Identity is abolished by posthuman figurations in favour of a model of the subject that is unstable, transformative and catastrophic.

While Manson embodies the idea of the catastrophic subject who can't be pinned down, he also encourages us to rethink the idea that images are interpreted through distinct and discrete systems of meaning. As the site of confusion between both the species-divide and the categorical distinctions between specialist discourse and popular culture, Manson's posthuman hybrid of animal, machine and human transforms and recodes highly specialist and often complex knowledges such as biotechnology and information technology. Manson gives the impression that he has been moulded into shape, yet can morph, implode or turn against the meanings inscribed on the body through culture. In effect, posthuman figurations like Manson in this image act as mediators between high and low; between the specialist discourses of biotechnology and popular cultural representations. According to Katherine Hayles, the posthuman can be understood as unfolding along the axis of multiple cultural and technical locations, emerging from complex, highly specialised discourses such as artificial intelligence, virtual reality and biotechnology, as well as popular culture sites including science fiction literature and popular film (Hayles 1999: 247). This confusion of categories through which the posthuman emerges reflects the postmodern breakdown of the divide between high art and low or mass culture, by signaling the intermixing of biotechnological narratives with science fiction fantasy. This, of course, is the order of the hyperreal; a Baudrillardian concept explained in chapter two as the point where fact and fantasy are no longer distinguishable. The function of the once-separate disciplines of advertising, art, politics and science to stabilise meaning is abolished in the context of the hyperreal. As the distinctions between autonomous spheres no longer hold, the production of meaning in particular categories and genres is made impossible. Meaning, instead, is everywhere and nowhere, existing beyond any one definitive order of interpretation.

By collapsing the distinction between scientific fact and science fiction fantasy, we are encouraged to engage with contemporary images in a new way. For when highly specific fields of knowledge and specialised discursive practices, such as biotechnology, converge and intermix with popular cultural sites, the images that result from these exchanges need to be negotiated differently. As discussed previously in this book, understanding the role of the image in simulation culture leads us to focus on the image as an object that acts on us, rather than asking 'what does this image mean?' By contesting a value system predicated on binary difference, simulation complicates a model of the self as either entirely resisting or complying with particular aspects of culture. In order to further explore the idea that we need new frameworks to understand how posthuman images act, I want to return to the monster that predates the simulation age to compare how past images of hybrid forms have been approached.

We have already established that the posthuman is the latest borderline figure in a long line of monsters, mutants and hybrids throughout ancient mythology, literature, science fiction and the biological sciences. In a representational economy of simulation culture, however, Manson's posthuman image should be treated differently from earlier representations of the monster. As has been emphasised throughout this book, digital images provoke alternative approaches to the process of analysis and interpretation because the experience of the visual is altered in a simulation society. In the context of digital image making, the real and the imaginary aren't separate spheres but merge to create a hyperreal experience.

In the history of Western painting, the posthuman is preceded by a rich and varied genealogy of freaks and monstrous entities such as the devilish creatures inhabiting Hieronymus Bosch's *Garden of Earthly Delights* (1500–10) or the fantasy figures of surrealism, typified in the work of Salvador Dali and Max Ernst. An example like Francisco Goya's oil painting *Saturn*

Devouring One of His Children (1820–3) shows how the categories of the real and the imaginary are maintained in an order of simulacra that depends on the idea of the natural. Goya's painting depicts the monstrous image of Saturn emerging from a murky darkness. There are no other forms or figures in the painting to situate the narrative historically or culturally. Saturn fills the frame, illuminated against the dark background by a pool of light. His angular and muscular form grips a small, limp body. With mouth agape, Saturn is caught in the act of devouring his victim. His wild hair and bulging eyes radiate with a white luminescence that accentuates his unnatural monstrosity.

Saturn is depicted by Goya as the crazed antithesis of a humanity whose natural order is that of civility and rationality. This is in keeping with the understanding of the monster as a figure through which the human is defined as natural and normal, as well as a hybrid form that threatens this category. As a figure of the uncanny, that which is like yet unlike the human, Saturn provides a means of understanding our place in the world. For in the logocentric order, humanness is defined against what it is not. As noted in Braidotti's study of monster discourse, a unitary and singular notion of selfhood is reinforced and legitimated in the forms and images of the Other; the feminine, the racialised, the monstrous and the technological Other. Taking another approach, Sigmund Freud argues that the myth of the gods acts as a cultural ideal on which man projects his fantasies and 'attributed everything that seemed unattainable to his wishes, or that was forbidden to him' (Freud 1969: 28). As a phenomenon that is more and less than human, this mythical figure is both ideal and abhorrent.

In the act of cannibalism and infanticide, the subject of ancient myth is depicted here as horrendous and unnatural, displaying the magical and mythical powers of ancient gods,[2] while evoking the terror of humanity's own consumption and violence. As a frightening echo of what humanity has become, or the self's Other, Saturn is an assemblage of multiple meanings in the context of the barbarism of nineteenth-century revolutionary society and the gore and terror of ancient myth. In keeping with his renditions of the stark violence and suffering of humanity, depicted in such works as *Executions of the Third of May* (1808), Goya takes an inert and unreal figure from ancient myth and imbues it with a sense of the violence of which society is capable. Functioning simultaneously as a rendition of the real and the unreal, or reflection of the self in the form of an inhuman Other, Saturn acts as a boundary figure who upholds the natural world as reality.

Contemporary images of the posthuman rupture the distinction between the human as the site of a unified, coherent self and the non-human Other of technology. While Goya's Other remains locked in a dialectical relationship with the self, I believe that the posthuman can't be contained in such terms. As a product of simulation culture, it has no Other; no referent from which to constitute the self. Manson's image on the CD is not a representation of Manson in 'real life'. Rather, Manson is himself a simulacrum, unhinging the dichotomy between self and Other, original and representation. The image itself suggests that there is no original Manson to be located outside of the image.

Through the mechanisms of production and circulation, posthuman representations in popular culture are different to the monstrous and inhuman imagery of earlier times, as typified by *Saturn Devouring One of His Children.* Goya's work was painted before the industrial revolution and the advent of technologies such as the camera. By way of its production, it maintains a commitment to the notions of origins and nature. Goya upholds an unproblematic relationship with the real in his image. The real and the natural are what the representational and the artificial are not. His image of the monster operates as a mirror that allows us to know ourselves as that which is not monstrous, but human. *Saturn Devouring One of His Children* also reminds us that mutant creatures have long been a part of the Western cultural and visual landscape. This artwork, along with other depictions of monsters and freaks, is part of a genealogy of mutant and mythical forms that illuminates the precursors to contemporary hybrids like the posthuman. But I'm wary of simply juxtaposing early visual forms against new modes of representing the monstrous. On its own, this strategy doesn't allow us to consider how the image may be understood in a context where the difference between the real and the imaginary is blurred. Contemporary representations of the posthuman allow for engagements with the subject that reside beyond an understanding of the fantastical and transformative images represented throughout earlier imaging practices such as painting, photography and cinema. Moreover, it is crucial for a feminist engagement with contemporary figurations of posthuman, post-gender entities, to examine the impact of technology on the limits of the body, and the accompanying shift in relations between the real and representation in the economy of simulation. In order to do this, we need to consider how feminism has understood the monster so far and the extent to which such ideas are applicable to the posthuman.

The Monsters of Feminism

The question of the monstrous and its relationship to the feminine shares similarities with the debates about women and technology discussed earlier in this book. Like the monster and the human, women and technology are simultaneously compatible *and* incompatible. This seemingly paradoxical and ambivalent approach to technology forged the basis of my argument that posthuman images are neither good nor bad for women, but demand a more complex understanding. Like these debates, an analysis of the monstrous is preoccupied with the ambiguity that surrounds notions of the natural, the technological and the feminine.

Feminist thinkers have identified that difference, deviance and monstrosity are often conflated. And the ontological grounding of this difference is an oppositional structure where women, ethnic, racialised and non-human Others are devalued relative to a unified, positive, masculine model of the self (Braidotti 1994a, 1996, 2000, Shildrick 2000). In a system of binary dualisms, the monster comes to stand for something that is different to the established norm, and this difference is construed as negative. That is, '(t)he freak, not unlike the feminine and ethnic "others", signifies devalued difference' (Braidotti 2000: 164). The monster's ability to simultaneously secure and destablilise our perceptions of selfhood is explained by Braidotti as:

> The peculiarity of the organic monster is that s/he is both same and Other. The monster is neither a total stranger or completely familiar; s/he exists in an in-between zone. I would express this as a paradox: the monstrous other is both liminal and structurally central to our perception of normal human subjectivity. The monster helps us understand the paradox of 'difference' as a ubiquitous but perennially negative preoccupation (Braidotti 1996: 141).

One example of the monster's liminal status in the cultural psyche is the phenomenon of conjoined twins. In her discussion of conjoined twins, Margrit Shildrick sees the monster as unnatural yet not outside nature, functioning as an 'instance of nature's startling capacity to produce alien forms within' (Shildrick 1999: 80). The monster is aligned with nature along the dichotomised gender divisions that associate femininity with (among other things) the body, nature, objectivity and Otherness. So even though conjoined twins are not thought of as the natural human state of existence, they are 'a product of nature's deficiency' (Hanafi 2000: 61). As supposed monstrous, therefore *not* normal bodies, conjoined twins act as a benchmark against which we establish and legitimate what is considered to be properly human.

This example also suggests that reproduction is a key site where women, technology and monstrosity are aligned. In *Nomadic Subjects: Embodiment and Difference in Contemporary Feminist Theory* (1994a), Braidotti also establishes a link between monsters, mothers and machines in contemporary reproductive technology, which she argues 'displaces women by making procreation a high-tech affair' (Braidotti 1994a: 79). She charts the shift in perceptions of the monster, from pre-Enlightenment discourse that views the monstrous as 'something wonderful, fantastic, rare, and precious' (Braidotti 1994a: 85), toward a scientific paradigm where the monstrous is something to escape, control and suppress. Along with this denial of the monstrous in scientific discourse is the rejection of the monstrous power of maternal desire and imagination (Braidotti 1994a: 84–6).

The status of the monster as the anomalous Other to the human, masculine norm, is shared by the feminine. Braidotti argues that the advent of biological sciences in the sixteenth century marked the beginning of a flight from the feminine and a control of the monstrous and maternal, leading to a diminished wonder in the monster (Braidotti 1994a: 89). In claiming that modern science is a male domain that controls the natural, maternal and feminine, Braidotti implies that the new monsters of contemporary technoscience are harmful to women. For Braidotti, the medicalisation of the body denies women the agency and power of maternal reproduction.[3]

Braidotti claims that today's science strives to make the abnormal perfect in order to contain the unruly and unquantifiable elements of the monstrous. As she explains:

> Ever since the mid-nineteenth century, the abnormal monstrous beings, which had been objects of wonder, have fallen prey to the massive medicalization of scientific discourse. The marvelous, imaginary dimension of the monster is forgotten in the light of the new technologies of the body (Braidotti 1994a: 88).

Yet by distinguishing the 'old' monsters of pre-Enlightenment times from the 'new' monsters formed through the technologisation of the body and reproductive technologies, Braidotti creates a new hierarchy. The monsters that preceded scientific and medical institutions are valorised for their affinity with nature and the feminine over those man-made monsters. Not only is nature's monster celebrated for its association with maternal power, but as a figure of wonder and awe it challenges the scientific, masculine way of constructing the world as rational and knowable.

In expressing a nostalgia for the maternal and feminine untainted by the invasion of masculinist technologies of control and classification, Braidotti perpetuates the idea that women are incompatible with technology, and that technology is unproductive for women; a position I have questioned. By aligning the monster with the organic Other, she reinforces the monster and human as mutually constitutive. Yet, there are a number of feminist scholars who have contested this division. Rather than separate the natural from the artificial, Donna Haraway has suggested that the monsters of technoscientific worlds offer the promise of new and productive affiliations between the feminine, the non-human and the technological (Haraway 1992: 327). Even *Frankenstein*, the ultimate scare-story about the dangers of technology, has been put to use by feminist thinking to challenge the separation of categories like nature and technology, the self and the Other (Waldby 2002).

Gail Weiss has been particularly critical of Braidotti's use of the monster metaphor as a feminist tactic to challenge the social order. Whereas Braidotti is wary of biotechnologies because they repress and control the subversive elements of the monster, Weiss argues that new technologies do not attempt to deny their monstrous tendencies. Rather, biotechnologies 'replicate, rather than efface, the horror and fascination that has always accompanied the interpellation of the monster' (Weiss 1999: 173). And, according to Weiss, it is through this process of replication that biotechnology takes away much of the monster's potency as a feminist metaphor for a difference that threatens to disrupt phallogocentric models of selfhood (Weiss 1999: 174).

Significantly, it is through the body that the feminine and the monstrous are associated in terms of the horror and fascination of abjection (Kristeva 1982). For Kristeva, there is a kind of power in abjection, in that it disturbs the secure boundaries of the body. Particularly because of the associations between the feminine and the body, the abject has been used by many feminists to revalue and re-empower the female subject, and especially the maternal body and the birth process (Creed 1993, O'Connell 2005, Shildrick 2000). So without the wound of abjection and, notably, without a belly button, does Manson diminish the positive associations between the feminine, the monster and the maternal?

In a backlash against Shulamith Firestone's suggestion that women's liberation would be achieved when they were freed from the reproductive burden though technological advances (Firestone 1970), a number of feminists have been largely critical of the effects of reproductive technologies on women's social power and status. One feminist position sees the control of human life and creation accorded to the male scientist, hence positioning woman as the passive, exploited subject of a masculinist medical and scientific establishment (Arditti, Klein and Minden 1984, Corea 1985, Spallone and Steinberg 1987). Such arguments have been complicated and extended to explore how technology displaces the symbolic power of the maternal (Braidotti 1994a, Sofia 1992).

I resist an interpretation that reinscribes the myths of technology as erasing the body in favour of the abstract information of the machine, or as signaling a flight from the material and maternal conditions of bodily experience. Rather than reading Manson's missing umbilical hole as an explicit rejection of the maternal, his image provokes us to question the notion of origins, or indeed, a 'natural' in an age where the involvements of medical technologies in the birthing and reproductive processes are commonplace. Like the cyborg before him, Manson reminds us that a state of nature contra the artificial is fast collapsing.

The Power of Myth: New Conceptions of Difference

Contemporary myths associated with biotechnologies, particularly those informed by feminist debates around who controls reproduction, tend to construct these technologies as dangerous for women. From Mary Shelley's *Frankenstein* (1969, originally published in 1818) to Dolly the cloned sheep, tampering with the genesis of life has been intimately associated with the monstrous and that which threatens human integrity. At the same time, these feminist critiques have rightly exposed that scientific narratives obscure the monstrosity of new reproductive technologies, promoting the myth that biotechnologies protect women from the uncertainties of natural reproduction. I want to move beyond this way of thinking to consider instead the ways that popular culture images act to disrupt and make ambivalent complex and highly specialised discourses such as biotechnology and digital technologies.

Importantly, it is the posthuman image *as simulation* that can challenge myths of biotechnology that uphold established constructions of the body and identity. Popular perceptions of biotechnology often operate along the lines of myth-making as it is understood by Roland Barthes, whereby myths serve to naturalise elements of culture so that they appear to be a normal part of our everyday life. In the case of biotechnology, the way this is done is to obscure or gloss over its potential dangers, to allay the fear that is associated with technologies controlling us and perhaps ultimately threatening what it means to be a human being. Meaghan Morris offers another view of the operations of contemporary culture in her observation that 'commercial culture today proclaims and advertises, rather than "naturalizes", its powers of artifice, myth invention, simulation' (Morris 1993: 306). It is this approach, whereby artifice is exposed rather than obscured, that in my mind better explains how images of the posthuman such as Manson operate in popular culture.

According to Barthes, myth functions to naturalise mass culture in the popular psyche. Barthes makes this claim in his keynote text *Mythologies* (1957), where he argues that ideology is reproduced and expressed in the objects we encounter in our day-to-day activities. Myth becomes the common language through which the products of mass consumerism are accepted into our lives (Barthes 1973: 11). In the series of short essays that make up the volume, Barthes reveals how popular cultural objects such as cars, soap powder and steak and chips become normalised through semiotic and ideological mechanisms.

As a signifying practice, myth operates as a communicative form that makes meaning (Barthes 1973: 109). Barthes draws heavily here on Saussure's theories of language as a system of signs through which the world is constructed. While Barthes differs from Saussure by firmly locating myth within a historically determined sign system, Barthes nonetheless maintains a commitment to understanding the structure, rather than the content, of the text founded on an underlying system of meaning (Barthes 1973: 111). As ideological tools, myths are cultural constructs that function to mask systems of power. Myth, in Barthes' terms, is '*depoliticized speech*' (Barthes 1973: 143, emphasis in text). In keeping with Althusser's understanding of ideology as the reproduction of dominant systems through the imaginary relation of individuals to the world in which they live, Barthes says that '(w)hat the world supplies to myth is an historical reality…and what myth gives in return is a *natural* image of this reality' (Barthes 1973: 142). The purpose of myth, then, is to empty everyday objects of any political significance and in doing so render them powerless and banal.

Although Barthes' concept of myth relies on the collapse of the artificial and the natural as separate categories and exposes such terms as cultural constructs, myth is said to operate as an ideological practice that produces reality. Compare this to the current sign order of simulation, where artifice and nature collapse in an act that simultaneously secures and displaces the real. I would like to pursue, then, the culture of simulation that Baudrillard advocates as a model of figuring signification that challenges Barthes' notion of myth as a production of ideology and semiotics. I argue that a biotechnological, informational and digital age requires a different approach to myth that takes into account how visual images are experienced. In reconsidering the established idea of myth as something that naturalises culture, as Morris does, I favour an interpretation of myth as a simulation effect that can disrupt the seamlessness of signifying practice. To further explore the changing nature of signification and its implications for popular cultural engagements, the face of Greta Garbo as described by Barthes in *Mythologies* is compared to that of Marilyn Manson. It is because they emerge from two different economies of representation—the cinematic and the digital respectively—that this juxtaposition is useful for rethinking the concept of myth.

Describing Garbo in the film *Queen Christina*, Barthes asserts that her 'make-up has the snowy thickness of a mask: it is not a painted face, but one set in plaster' (Barthes 1973: 56). In likening Garbo's skin to a plaster cast, Barthes reveals the function of myth as that which obscures reality. Garbo's face–mask is the myth, unchanging and perfect; forever upholding the 'Platonic Idea of the human creature' (Barthes 1973: 56). The mask never cracks and never deteriorates. Artifice is made natural through the constancy of Garbo's face as an 'absolute mask' (Barthes 1973: 56). Fixed as the ideal woman, her face is an archetype that never changes. This mythic woman is upheld and legitimated by representation; what resides behind the mask is never exposed but ever present.

The cinematic face is Garbo's mask; her copy that confuses yet relies on an original in order to function as myth. As Walter Benjamin has discussed, while mechanical reproduction displaces the aura of the original, there remains an original nonetheless (Benjamin 1968b). For cinema, like photography, is an analogue reproduction of the second order, locked in a relationship between an image and its reality. Upholding the distinction between the image and the real is crucial to the function of myth in Barthes' terms, whereby myth is the false representation of a reality that resides behind the sign. Without a distinction between the real and representation, there can be no myth. Hence, myth must maintain a differentiation between the image and its referent, illusion and truth. Accordingly, the face of Garbo operates as myth on the cinematic screen by sustaining the relationship between sign and referent. For myth to mask reality, our understanding of what is real cannot be disturbed.

Unlike Manson, whose fluidity of surface disrupts the categories of gender, the fixity of Garbo's face ensures that gender distinctions are secured. Although Barthes describes Garbo's face as 'almost sexually undefined' (Barthes 1973: 56), he never challenges her status as a woman. The female 'face–object' is of the order of the patriarchal imaginary. The gendered boundaries between male and female, self and Other are maintained by the unmoving surface of her skin. Compare this to the plasticity of Manson's skin. Like Garbo, Manson displays the fragility of a plaster cast, yet will not break. His skin is more like plasticine than plaster. Skin, like gender, is viewed by Manson as a malleable and fluid surface phenomenon. The posthuman hides no truths about gender beyond what is represented. Rather, in an economy of simulation where the relationship between the image and its referent collapse, simulation becomes reality. There is no falsity to be revealed by the simulated image. The myth of origins cannot be upheld. In accordance with Baudrillard's understanding of the shifting status of the image, Manson does not reflect, mask, pervert or obscure the absence of reality (Baudrillard 1994: 6). In a world of simulation, the sign *is* real.

For Barthes, Garbo represents the 'fragile moment when the cinema is about to draw an existential from an essential beauty, when the archetype leans towards the fascination of mortal faces, when the clarity of the flesh as essence yields its place to a lyricism of Woman' (Barthes 1973: 57). Here Barthes exposes the naturalisation of the cultural construct 'woman'. Garbo is revealed as an archetype, an essence of woman constructed on the cinema screen. As myth, her face is deployed by ideology to present a truth about woman. Yet as Barthes claims, this myth of the woman-ideal, in fact, masks a truth. The historical, social and cultural contexts that allow for the differences between women are transformed by myth into an unchanging ideal. In much the same manner, second-wave feminist film theorists approached the representation of women in cinema as untruthful and distorted accounts of women's lived experience. Like Barthes' theory of myth, early feminist analyses of representation were founded on theories of ideology and semiology, and advocated material existence and experience as the true site of women's reality. Feminist critiques of patriarchal systems of power and knowledge have also exposed the function of binary thinking on the construction of the subject. Woman, it was revealed, was positioned as object in opposition to a male subject, thus accorded non-existence in the paradigm of binary thought (see Cixous 1980, Grosz 1987, Jay 1991). In Barthes' schema, Garbo is positioned in a predetermined regime of signs that negotiates difference in a binary dialectic.

By signifying the archetypal woman, Garbo's face both affirms and *masks* difference. As Barthes' exemplar of the female form, Garbo denies the differences between women in a process of representing difference *as* sameness, while also being positioned vis-à-vis man as radical alterity, the representation of difference *as* difference. Camilla Griggers has spoken about the female face as the site of a coded system actively produced and fixed by the dominant phallogocentric regime. In deploying the Deleuzian notion of faciality to make her argument, she points out that faciality is not a process of identification but 'a question of technology, of a machinic operation of signs' (Griggers 1997: 3), whereby the mechanical gaze of both cinema and the digital structures how the viewer sees and constructs a face in this mechanism of signification.[4]

According to Griggers, the face of white woman, embodied by the Hollywood screen icon, is contained by the mechanical gaze of the cinematic apparatus. This face is made to neutralise, contain and police 'minoritarian forms', otherwise described as all forms of Otherness that do not comply with a model of white, bourgeois, feminised and democratised identity (Griggers 1997: 5). Griggers thus accords a dual function to woman in the Hollywood system. The threat or difference of white woman is accommodated by Hollywood cinema so the Other of race and class is subsumed by the white woman who comes to signify 'the consumable face of democratized and feminized bourgeois identity' (Griggers 1997: 17). Garbo, as the archetypal face of white woman, operates very much in line with Griggers' mode of thinking. In both instances, difference is acknowledged, but rendered meaningless and non-threatening by the representation of race, class, sexual and ethnic difference inherent in the category Woman, as the same.

Unlike Garbo's mask-like face, Manson's plastic skin suggests a reversibility and fluidity of form akin to the virtual morph generated in digital space. While it is impossible to witness Manson change over time on a CD cover, the potential for Manson to morph resides in his status as a digital image. Vivian Sobchack considers 'implied reversibility' a key feature of the morph, stating that '(w)hether or not one actually sees the reversal is irrelevant to the "lived" knowledge of its possibility' (Sobchack 1994: 44). It is according to these terms that I want to think about Manson as a new monster for the virtual era, as an example of a digital image that confuses the categories of difference.

The Digital Morph: Same or Other?

Sobchack's edited collection on digital morphing, titled *Meta-Morphing: Visual Transformation and the Culture of Quick Change* (2000a), provides a contemporary point of engagement to pursue the question of difference in relation to transformative images. By situating the morph in a broader genealogy of mythology, magic, 'trick' films and attractions, Sobchack invites the reader to consider the digital morph's 'continuities and discontinuities with earlier forms and figures of "marvelous" transformation' (Sobchack 2000a: xv). Indeed, the strength of the essays in *Meta-Morphing* resides in their awareness of the historical formation of the transformative figure before the advent of digital technologies. This is consistent with my own examination of the reshaping of perspective in chapter two, which saw the modernist subject of nineteenth-century lifestyle and technologies as a subject in flux, a protean precursor to postmodernism's fragmented figurations of identity.

In her own contribution to *Meta-Morphing*, Sobchack turns her attention to the erasure of difference as a crucial marker of identity in contemporary instances of digital morphing. The essay titled '"At the Still Point of the Turning World": Meta-Morphing and Meta-Stasis' argues that the digital morph circulates in popular culture as a figure that is banal and familiar, but also a site of fascination and impossibility (Sobchack 2000b: 131–2). The widespread practice of digital retouching in magazines, particularly images of models and celebrity photo shoots, is one such example of this making the strange common and the common strange. Sobchack in part celebrates the uncanny and paradoxical qualities of the morph, arguing:

> It calls to the part of us that escapes our perceived sense of our "selves" and partakes in the flux and ceaseless becoming of Being—that is, our bodies at the cellular level ceaselessly forming and reforming and not "ourselves" at all (Sobchack 2000b: 136).

Morphing taps into our own sense of being a subject in flux. Sobchack claims, however, that the material experience of space and time is complicated by the digital morph's 'quick-change' qualities and powers of reversibility. Sobchack is especially critical of the way that the morph assimilates difference and Otherness into a figure of the same. Taking Michael Jackson's *Black or White* video clip as one of her examples, Sobchack argues that its parade of multi-ethnic and racial faces seems to celebrate difference, while denying it through the morphing of one face into another (Sobchack 2000b: 139). And while difference is conventionally understood in terms of binary hierarchies, whereby man is privileged over woman, black over white and self over Other, Sobchack suggests that the reversibility of the morph presents a myth of equality by undoing these structural disparities. This process of reversibility also obscures the spatial and temporal aspects of lived existence in which difference operates (Sobchack 2000b: 141–2).

This homogenisation of the heterogeneity of difference in the space of popular culture is also said to occur in Benetton advertising. As argued by Henry Giroux, mass advertising adopts a legitimising function in order to 'disguise the political nature of everyday life and appropriate the vulnerable new terrain of insurgent differences in the interests of a crass consumerism' (Giroux 1994: 6). The threat of difference risks destabilising the unity of white, Western masculinity, thus difference is diffused into sameness, and denied political efficacy. According to Giroux, Benetton negotiates difference via a 'strategy of containment', whereby the potential antagonisms of difference are marketed in such a way that differences are dissolved into a depoliticised pluralism that invokes a myth of global harmony.

As a 'digital morph' or techno–mediated mutation, it would be easy to analyse Manson in a similar way to these other examples. Barthes' understanding of myth lends itself to a reading of Manson as an image that reinforces or naturalises meaning through a repetitive process of endless signification. If we approach Manson in critical terms, he appears decontexualised; space and time fall away as he hovers against a nondescript grey backdrop that gives no indication of his spatial and temporal co-ordinates. His body denies any definitive markers of sexual difference in a way that negates the power relations between gendered subjects. In this framework, Manson is a 'bad' representation because he does not accurately reflect 'real life'. Yet one of the problems with taking this kind of interpretive approach to the posthuman is that it sustains an oppositional style of thinking, in that the image has currency or meaning relative to something 'outside' of it. In turn, this can tell us little about how images shape our sense of reality. In a simulated world that strives to produce the effect of distinct categories in the wake of their collapse, Manson is what Baudrillard calls a 'fatal object' because he challenges the reality principle. His body is not natural or harmonious, but a surface that radiates a synthetic sheen to prompt a response from the viewer. He engages us because the image is pure spectacle, a surface without any 'deeper' significance. There is no reality outside of this representation, no subject to be defined against an object, no self to be secured relative to an Other. And it is this unintelligibility that complicates an analysis of difference in posthuman images. Outside of signification, difference is dispersed, annihilated and opened up, so that identity is not enforced but destroyed.

Traditionally, the potential threat of difference is contained in a mode of signification based on a self/Other logic whereby radical alterity is denied and negated. Sobchack's study of the digital morph, feminist interrogations of difference, and Giroux's critique of Benetton, all see difference in this way. So even though difference is erased in each of these examples, an oppositional model of thought always needs a latent Other for the self to exist. Each example highlights the inability for difference to be conceptualised outside of a dominant regime of thinking by stressing the way that difference is absorbed and contained in the dialectical model of the self/same. Accordingly, difference within this system allays the threat of the Other, because it may be controlled and knowable. The question I ask, then, is 'can difference be otherwise negotiated in image culture so as to configure the posthuman, not as the denial of difference, but as a catastrophe and illusion?'

It is a difference that exceeds a dialectical logic that threatens how we know the world and make meaning. For this type of difference is no longer understood relative to a dominant term. Rather in Baudrillard's schema, difference is annihilated so that it cannot be interpreted as different to something. As Grace explains:

> These 'differences', which, in Saussurian terms, create the possibility of 'identity', are conceptualised by Baudrillard as *parallel positivities* (my term); they are not differences that have a negative valence relative to a positive, but rather they represent an infinity of positive values that never converge, never engage, that can never transform an 'other' or be transformed, but rather jostle around in an endless, shifting, arbitrary hierarchy. Baudrillard calls this a logic of difference, as did

> Saussure in this theory of signification, but this is a difference that separates and distinguishes positive identities and not a difference that constitutes otherness (Grace 2000: 23).

What Grace is describing is a kind of exponential logic, a proliferation of differences that escape containment and homogenisation by exceeding signification. This focus on difference and its representation is fundamental to understanding what is at stake for women in the age of the posthuman. Refiguring the concept of difference is crucial to a feminist politics of representation as it enables an understanding of how images function in a post-material, post-gender and posthuman landscape. As a sexually indeterminate, technologically mediated entity, Manson destabilises the Cartesian dualisms that underpin the liberal–humanist subject, as well as a notion of female identity based in positive difference. Through his plastic form, Manson dismantles the over coding of signification that structures a coherent identity.

The illuminating red glow of Manson's stare is reminiscent of the penetrating gaze of the disembodied lens of science. With eyes like infra-red lasers, Manson mimics the all-seeing gaze of the visual technologies of science and the military. Science and medicine have been understood by Foucault in terms of biopower, in which their analytical, neutral and objective gaze fixes and regulates knowledges. For Foucault, visual control is a form of power deployed in the service of knowledge making practices (Foucault 1977). Yet like the monster, Manson challenges the scientific rationale of order, classification and naming. There is no system under which he can be categorised. Even an attempt to make Manson conform to a socially sanctioned 'type' through modifications to his body (genetic or otherwise) is hopeless because he is the aberrant product of these technologies. His burning stare 'sees through' an overarching biotechnological narrative of a new world order, refusing to comply with a seamless and controlled vision of a technological future. But he belies any such definitive meaning as he is both the watcher and the watched, confusing the boundaries that traditionally serve as a limit point between self and Other.

Manson's infra-red eyes are no window to the soul. The viewer is not welcome to gaze into them. Confronting the viewer is a laser-like stare that mimics the scanning devices of military technology, or the spaces of consumption—the beep of the supermarket scanner. As perception is made technological, Manson evokes the machine as an aspect of the self (Turkle 1980). He confuses the distinction between bodily interiorities and machinic exteriorities so that the machine becomes an integral dimension to embodiment. Manson cannot become an inert and 'safe' product of biotechnology because he simultaneously occupies the position of the body threatened by the scientific gaze, and a body who exceeds the empiricism of the scientific paradigm. The interconnections and interfaces of the techno–human interaction complicate simplistic distinctions, making it impossible to judge the effects of biotechnology as either good or bad.

Donna Haraway has theorised the 'New World Order, Inc.' as an imaginary configuration, a way of understanding the global tendencies of culture and capital precipitated by information technologies and technoscience (Haraway 1997: 6–7). Haraway's use of the term functions along the lines of ideology-effects, whereby representations both construct and reflect a contemporary cultural landscape. In the instance of posthuman figurations, it is a world of biological, informational and digital technologies in which these representations circulate. Yet an interpretation of posthuman images in terms of semiotic meaning-production and ideology-effects is limited for this study, because posthuman images do not operate to reflect who we are or define what we are not. Rather, they reside in a space of simulation that questions conventional understandings of subjectivity, the body and reality.

Challenging traditional ideas of the subject, language and culture offers the possibility to think about difference in another way. The articulation of difference as an oppositional posturing between self and Other, reality and representation, is rethought. Beyond dialectics, difference functions as an ongoing process of proliferation that can account for the experiences of different bodies to various technologies, recasting how bodies are lived and imagined. Manson encourages a new vision for feminist thinking about the status of the subject in a climate of information technologies. He does this by destabilising difference. This is not the utopian cyberpunk dream of transcending the flesh to enter the virtual. Instead, Manson is a mutant entity that causes a slippage in the formation of meaning. By disrupting the limits of the body, Manson exceeds signification, challenging established notions of identity and difference, and enabling new models of embodied existence beyond dialectical thought.

5

Communicating the Posthuman Way with TDK

CDs again. They surround me as I wander the aisles of my local music mega-store. Having selected my purchases, I make my way to the counter, passing popular music on my left, alternative music to the right. Behind the current darlings of the radio charts, and less conspicuously advertised, is the often-maligned genre of country music, hidden away like an embarrassing older relative. I reach the register and wait to be served, vacantly staring ahead with CDs in hand. Stacks of CDRs—blank, recordable CDs—are piled up along the wall in front of me. These discs contain no information. They have nothing to communicate. Their emptiness is shared by the advertising poster stapled crudely to the wall. It shows a gurgling baby with dumbo-sized ears and square, computer-screen eyes. My impassive stare takes in the poster and wall of CDs. Neither returns my gaze. As I pay for my goods, I ask the shop assistant for the poster.

The 'mutant baby' is one image from the TDK advertising campaign featuring the slogan 'Evolve to TDK' (see figure 3). In a warped twist on the Nazi eugenics project, this blonde-haired, blue-eyed mutation of the 'master race' fantasy has evolved freakish sensory appendages to accommodate the increasing auditory and visual stimuli of the information age. With eyes suited for the computer terminal and ears tuned to signals from the satellite dish, the human species and its evolution are depicted as an inevitable consequence of the heightened consumption of digital and electronic media. As both a product and viewer of the media circuit, the posthuman baby complicates the place of the subject in a culture typified by the acceleration of communication.

The chubby mite adopts a portrait pose, shot from the chest up. Wisps of baby-blonde hair frame a face that radiates an ecstatic smile. Stark and solitary against a white background, the viewer is left to wonder whether the baby is a boy or girl, or where the parents of this naked, vulnerable child might be. It is, however, apparent that the image has been digitally altered.

The baby is a simulation. No child in the 'real' world could possibly be born with the square eyes and oversized ears of the TDK baby. Or could it? It appears as though defining the child's gender is of less concern than the question of whether 'it' is human at all. Perhaps there are no parents. Indeed, why would there need to be if evolution accelerates beyond biological reproduction toward technologically mediated techniques of cloning and replication?

As the basis of electronic media, information has become the privileged term in contemporary culture (Poster 1990: 7). Paul Virilio suggests that this is because time and space are compressed and sped up in a digitally driven environment. As a result, information comes to supersede sensation as the primary mode of experiencing the world (Virilio 1991: 46). New digital forms of communication alter how we understand ourselves and others in the media landscape. When temporal and spatial narratives are replaced with non-linear, accelerated and compressed bundles of information (Lash 2001: 110), is the possibility for meaningful exchange between people lost? Do bodies matter? And what is at stake for women as subjects in the media?

In contrast to analyses that see the body and media flows of information as distinct entities, I want to explore a model of the body as an interface system that is immersed in diverse communication forms. Building on the idea that a society saturated by information risks obliterating the subject, I discuss how communication technologies inaugurate a posthuman body, and what the effects of this are for women in a new media society. By taking the view that a shift to the information age alters our experience of reality, possibilities emerge for different ways of understanding what counts as material existence. When the subject is an interface, speed and information flow through the 'informational pathways connecting the organic body to its prosthetic extensions' (Hayles 1999: 2).

The TDK baby typifies this type of contemporary body—a body that emerges from the eradication of any critical distance between the human subject and information and media systems. The TDK tot becomes another element in the cacophony of media signals. Its glistening eyes and wide smile suggest that it is caught up in experiencing the 'pleasure of an excess of meaning' (Baudrillard 1994: 28). The potential pleasures of the information and entertainment technologies advertised by TDK are located at the site of the body-as-screen, where the acceleration and proliferation of signs and information converge. The sense of anticipation, enjoyment and joy that can be brought about by entertainment technologies, such as stereos and televisions, is literally embodied in the TDK baby.

Many feminists have written about the pleasure women experience from consuming (as well as in some instances producing) communication forms like television, magazines and music (Ang 1985, McRobbie 1978, 1999,

Figure 3. *Evolve to TDK* advertising poster.

Modleski 1982, Stacey 1994). Their focus has often been on feminised genres such as soap opera, women's magazines, chick flicks and romance novels. In discussing the varied ways that women consume culture, they have moved away from Laura Mulvey's idea that women are objects to be looked at, rather than active agents who take pleasure in participation. The concepts of female agency and a revaluing of the feminine have been central to this thinking.

But the pleasure that the TDK baby experiences is different to this. It is not so much about looking at, or identifying with, or fantasising about something, but it is a pleasure that results from the collapse of boundaries in the information age so that the subject encounters the world purely as spectacle. The experience of being immersed in media environments triggers multiple sensations and sensory modalities brought about by the erosion of the boundaries between once disparate components like the subject and the object, the self and the Other, the real and the virtual. Writing about the idea that information media can be another site of pleasure for women, Barbara Creed begins to move away from the bind that structures representation and reality as indexically linked. She proposes that 'the nature of pleasure itself may change. While virtual reality appeals to the visual, of course, it also places prime importance on the tactile. Touch may come to assume the primacy now accorded to the visual. Some players may construct scenarios that displace voyeurism altogether as a dominant source of pleasure' (Creed 2003: 126). When subjects participate in virtual reality experiences, such as those explained by Sherry Turkle in chapter one, they become part of an information network rather than looking in from a place of 'reality' outside the virtual screen. As virtual worlds become sites where sensations and emotions are felt, rather than observed from the outside, our sense of reality is no longer fixed in a diametrical relation to the image. The possibility emerges then, as Creed suggests, for the rapid flow and instantaneous qualities of new communication networks to create new modes of pleasure outside of the reality/representation paradigm.

So it would appear that the baby's joyful grin is not so much a response to an encounter with communication technologies as it is an effect of the implosion of boundaries between the human and the digital. The infant is experiencing what Baudrillard calls an 'ecstatic state'. Another set of social relations has taken over from those that distinguish between the self and the external world. S/he is on another wavelength, occupying the spaces of simulation where the traditions of perspectival space and real time are no longer the dominant frameworks through which we experience and make sense of the world. By 'Evolving to TDK', the TDK baby presents us with a potential refiguring of bodily limits as they are extended and transformed to accommodate the acceleration and heightened consumption of communications and media in the information age. The place of the subject in the media forms one half of the narrative of the posthuman that I pursue here. The other, closely aligned with the issues of species evolution and the fate of humanity, is the question of speed.

The Speed of Technological Life: Space and Time Revisited

The immersion of the TDK baby in multiple sensory modalities represents what a number of cultural critics have identified as a challenge to traditional understandings of space, time, reality and materiality in the wake of media technologies. Writing about the history of science fiction (SF) films produced in post-1950s America, Vivian Sobchack pinpoints a shift in how temporality and spatiality are experienced and perceived in contemporary culture. As Sobchack asserts, science fiction film is intimately bound to questions of technology, the future and the alien Other. Put in her words:

> …as a symbolic medium whose function is representation, the American cinema has also increasingly articulated the new "sense" and "sensibility" generated by this technology and its spatial and temporal transformation of contemporary experience. As might be expected, this articulation is nowhere more evident or given more emphasis than in the SF film—for SF has always taken as its distinctive generic task the cognitive mapping and poetic figuration of social relations as they are constituted and changed by new technological modes of "being-in-the-world" (Sobchack 1987: 224–5).

Clearly, Sobchack is talking about science fiction in terms of a second order simulacra. She encourages a mode of reading images that takes into account the impact of technological artefacts upon 'both our lived experience and our cultural representations' and highlights the importance of interpreting technology in a 'lived' context informed by cultural, social, political and economic conditions that make such technologies possible (Sobchack 1987: 223). In arguing for an altered sense of how we see the world through narratives and the lived experience of technology, Sobchack's study of science fiction cinema maintains a logic whereby images are tied to a reality.

Yet she recognises the shift toward simulated realities in a digital era, where technology has contributed to an alteration in how time and space are experienced by the viewer. In characterising this trend she says:

> The popularization and pervasiveness of electronic technology in the last decade has reformulated the experience of space and time as

> expansive and inclusive. It has recast human being into a myriad of visible and active simulacra, and has generated a semantic equivalency among various formulations and representations of space, time, and being (Sobchack 1987: 229).

Amid the digital communications revolution it is important to remember that earlier media technologies like the photograph, film and painting have influenced the way we come to understand ourselves and the world through space and time, and continue to do so today. What Bolter and Grusin's concept of remediation shows is that new technologies don't simply supersede previous types of media, but that both old and new media forms are refashioned by each other (Bolter and Grusin 2000). In this vein, Allucquere Roseanne Stone recognises the existence of 'proto–cyberspace' technologies, which include the diorama, the botanical garden and the carnival. These products of modernity created a new sense of space and of being in the world just as, for Stone, virtual systems now enable the formation of different kinds of communities and modes of identity (Stone 1992: 610).

Critic Paul Virilio picks up on these themes in his book *The Vision Machine* (1994), where he argues that the effects of technology on how time and space are represented have had a profound impact on the way that images are read and understood. More specifically, he focuses on the technologisation of perception to interrogate the cultural shift toward speed and information precipitated by new technologies. For Virilio, the issue is not so much that temporal and spatial modes are changing, but that speed has come to supersede both as the definitive mode of perception. If, as Virilio suggests, speed is a way of configuring the relation between objects, then what are the consequences when the intense speed of our current information networks essentially erases any relation between things? In the context of electronic communications, the triumph of speed results in a crisis in perception that threatens how we understand the world we inhabit, and crucially, our place within it.

Virilio has spoken about the screen as an example of a technology that embodies the 'instantaneous interface between the here and now' (Virilio 1988: 4). In the past 20 years, the screen that was once found on the television set, the PC or in the movie theatre has gone mobile. The old screen is joined by a range of new 'vision monitors', to use one of Virilio's terms. The mobile phone, the laptop computer and global positioning systems are just a few of the instantaneous and portable communication devices that accompany us everywhere we go. In the world of micro- and nanotechnologies, information 'here and now' is small enough to be carried in our pocket. Increasingly, technologies are converging, as is the case with the mobile phone, which has moved beyond mere auditory communication to become a portal to the Internet, a camera, and a television or movie screen rolled into one (Levinson 2004). Or, as Anne Friedberg postulates:

> Now, a variety of screens—long and wide and square, large and small, composed of grains, composed of pixels—compete for our attention without any (convincing) arguments about hegemony. As screens have multiplied and divided, so has subjectivity. As we spend more and more of our time staring into the frames of television, computer, and hand-held screens—windows full of text, icons, 3-D graphics, streaming images, streaming audio—a new post-perspectival, post-Cartesian subjectivity has emerged. The multi-screen, windowed visuality of Windows software has become an apt figurative trope for this new subjectivity. As the beholder of multiple windows, we receive images—still and moving, large and small, artwork and commodity—in fractured spatial and temporal frames. With this new "windowed" multiplicity of perspectives we can be at two (or more) places at once, in two (or more) time frames in a fractured post-Cartesian cyber-time (Friedberg 2004: 348).

The larger-than-life square eyes of our posthuman progeny are indicative of this alternative way of looking in the digital age that Friedberg talks about. Just as the visual apparatus of the TDK baby is reformulated, changing from round eye sockets to the square space of the screen, so, too, is our understanding of vision challenged in an age of simulation. When vision is distorted by speed, it 'perverts the illusory order of normal perception, the order of arrival of information' (Virilio 1991: 100). In this image, the baby's eyes are also screens, hence serving the dual purpose of looking and being looked at, which effectively become the same thing. The TDK baby is a model that pre-empts the real, embodying this shift in how technologies converge, as well as how the distance between our technologies and ourselves, the subject and the object, is eroding.

By confusing that which looks (the eye), with that which is looked at (the screen), the TDK baby is at the point where there is no longer any temporal delay or spatial distance between objects, data and people. In this case, the speed of information communication has eroded the distance between the baby and the vision monitor, and as a result, a face-to-face meeting of the body and technology is made impossible. The eye cannot look at the screen from a place 'outside of' technology. Rather, the eye and the screen interface to create another kind of configuration of the body and technology that resides between representation and reality. What is pictured on the screen becomes the subject's way of seeing and experiencing and existing in a hyperreal world. What is viewed and what is experienced cannot be differentiated. The TDK image neatly shows the point of collapse between the observer and what they observe, the spectator and the spectacle they consume. In becoming the television set or computer screen, the TDK baby exemplifies the idea that the body has become pure information, abolishing any coherent sense of the relational differences between reality and virtuality, self and Other, past and future.

What has become apparent through the course of writing about the posthuman is that a number of different theories of identity formation exist, resulting in the subject being interpreted in various ways: as a biological entity (Dawkins 1976), a product of psychical processes (Freud 1955a, Lacan 1977), or a cultural construction (Butler 1990). As traditional conceptions of space and time have been replaced by a concern with speed and information, we move beyond these theoretical modes of figuring identity toward an articulation of the self as an information network. Posthuman figurations may be seen as imagining this shift toward something that is beyond biological or sociological theories of what it means to be human. The potential of technology to generate multiple and varied imaginings of the body, beyond established codes that limit what a body might be, transforms how bodies are lived and conceived. This new kind of corporeality is brought about by technologies that position the subject as immersed in techno networks to the point where the body and technology cannot be clearly distinguished. This collapse is explained by Scott Lash in the following way:

> Now the unconscious surfaces into the everyday; as the transcendental of the economy collapses into culture of everyday life; and as art becomes just another mode of communication. Technological forms of life suggest, not positivism, which is the subject–object type thinking of classification, but *empiricism*, in which the observer is in principle not fundamentally different from the observed (Lash 2001: 109).

When speed erases the distinctions between subject and object, observer and observed, representation no longer functions in terms of a practice of signification that upholds the relation between representation and reality. As the nature of time is altered, the visual and the real are experienced in new ways. In Virilio's schema, 'real time' consists in part of both the present and immediate future (Virilio 1994: 66).[1] For the subject to interact in 'real time', the parameters of the body require reformulation.

When the demarcations between subject and object, spectator and scene collapse, a new way of figuring the relationship of the subject to technology emerges. As a digital construct, the TDK baby exhibits the mutability and transformation of the body in technology. This is not to imply that becoming posthuman necessitates square eyes, or growing a larger pair of ears. Rather, simulation transforms how we understand reality, representations and bodies, so that we see them not as fixed terms, but as contested sites. This is because in simulation culture there is no referent for the image in the real. The inability to locate the markers of difference at the site of the body suggests a mutation of form that extends beyond traditional conceptions of bodies, gender and subjectivity. Emerging instead is a proliferation of recombinant and hybrid states of being, instigated by the collapse of differentials between the subject and the media.

The Subject in the Media

In a number of his writings, Baudrillard has attempted to make sense of the technological developments that affect both everyday experience, our speculations on an uncertain future, and the place of the subject in the media circuits of electronic communication. In his essay 'The Ecstasy of Communication', he speaks of a subject in a 'universe of communication', which sees 'our own body and the whole surrounding universe become a control screen' (Baudrillard 1983: 127). Subjectivity in the context of electronic communications, as promoted by Baudrillard, contests a psychoanalytic subject model based on a mirror relationship between subject and object, which privileges the subject. In the contemporary flows of media and communication, Baudrillard claims that individuals no longer identify with, or project their sense of self, onto representations or objects. Rather,

> In place of the reflexive transcendence of the mirror and scene, there is a nonreflecting surface, an immanent surface where operations unfold—the smooth operational surface of communication (Baudrillard 1983: 126–7).

In a context where the real gives way to the hyperreal, Baudrillard seeks to put an end to dialectics, to value systems where identity is forged through differentiation from the Other. The subject is no longer alienated from his/her environment, but experiences the ecstasy of communication. This ecstasy results from the proliferation of signs in a hyperreal world that liberates meaning from its object-referent. Instead of being the locus of knowledge and being, the subject becomes a 'nonreflecting…surface of communication' in the circuit of signification and meaning (Baudrillard 1983: 127). Effectively, Baudrillard aims to displace a Western concept of the self as unified and coherent.

When the subject can no longer be differentiated from media and communication networks, the limits of the subject demand to be rethought. It is at this point of collapse between the subject and the media that Baudrillard's theory of the subject in communications invites comparisons with the TDK advertising campaign. In a circuit where exchange exists only between different media, conceptualising the subject in Baudrillard's terms sees the televisual eyes of the posthuman acting as screens within an auto-referential circuit (Baudrillard 1988b: 8). Douglas Kellner has interpreted Baudrillard's theory of the self as a screen in terms of the sublimation of the subject by the proliferation of media technologies, arguing that Baudrillard denies the subject a dynamic relationship with its technological surrounds. Kellner claims:

> ...for Baudrillard all the media of information and communication neutralize meaning, and involve the audience in a flat, one-dimensional media experience, which he defines in terms of a passive absorption of images or resistance to meaning, rather than an active processing or production of meaning (Kellner 1989: 70).

Paul Virilio also taps into this cultural anxiety concerning the 'free will' and 'usefulness' of the subject in an information age. In an interview published in *Block* magazine in 1988, Virilio speaks about the displacement of the subject by the speed of contemporary technology. When the sensory mechanisms of the human organism cannot 'keep up' with the acceleration of society, people effectively lose their ability to respond to the increasing demands of the communication influx (Virilio 1988: 6). For Virilio, the intensive acceleration of electronic communications limits humanity's response properties, so that we can no longer sustain a sufficient 'real time' dialogue with the information relayed by electronic media. This kind of mass contamination destroys the act of communication as a process of exchange, because the rate at which these messages are disseminated stems any ability for feedback, meaningful engagement, comprehension or response on the part of the subject. Effectively, this results in the violation of the subject by the images and information of a media culture that it cannot meaningfully engage with (Virilio 1988: 5). In the context of media and information systems, 'we get replaced, and we are replaceable' (Virilio 1988: 6).

A linear, one-way model of communication, theorised in terms of an active sender (transmitter) and passive receiver underwrites the approach taken by Virilio. In this schema, audiences are configured as an undifferentiated group that is subject to the hegemonic effects of mass culture (Adorno and Horkheimer 1973). If we are to follow a model of communication that interprets media and culture as the primary determinants in the production of meaning, the only possible relationship for the subject with the products of these technologies is a negative one, where information flows uni-directionally across the passive human receiver. When the self becomes a signal and the body is disassociated from the locus of identity and being, the subject comes across as a victim of media technologies.

There is little doubt that Baudrillard also thinks that the subject is ill-equipped to protect itself from the relentless influx of media (Baudrillard 1983: 132). And even though he denies active agency and meaning to the subject within the digitised spectres of the hyperreal, this does not necessarily mean that there is no hope for individuals in an increasingly media-saturated world. Rather, as Grace observes, in our hyperreal world, understanding the subject is 'not a question of passivity, but the non-distinction between active and passive. It is no longer a matter of who or what is doing what to whom' (Grace 2000: 99). Neither does it mean that Baudrillard is vehemently opposed to technology on the grounds that it threatens the integrity of the human subject. On this point, I argue to the contrary—Baudrillard is more akin to a celebrant of technology for the reason that the techno–human engagement questions the logic of Enlightenment ideas about selfhood.

By rejecting the idea of the subject as an active agent, Baudrillard is questioning the construction of the subject as an individual and separate entity who can choose to resist from a place outside of media culture. The process of being immersed in communication changes the subject so that they become part of the information circuit; the subject is information, they are no longer outside it. By effectively dismissing the possibility of resistance, appropriation or response by the subject to media forms (Fiske 1987, Hall 1995, 1996), Baudrillard creates a new conception of the subject as part of the media circuit. Indeed, any one, fixed response (whether that be passively absorbing or actively resisting the media) in an economy of simulation is impossible for Baudrillard as systems of value are abolished.

As discussed earlier in this book, Baudrillard suggests that the disappearance of the subject is an implosive gesture that radically undermines dichotomous poles of value. Disappearance in the context of techno–human relations may actually work in favour of the subject by refiguring the relationship between the subject and technology traditionally couched in terms of a positive or negative value judgement. Rather than interpret the body as a passive screen that abolishes the subject, Baudrillard contests the idea that there can by *any* sort of relation between the subject and technology. He proposes an alternative experience for the subject in the media that does not function along conventional lines that see communication as a process that occurs between senders and receivers.

Inspired by Marshall McLuhan's catchcry that the medium is the message (1964), Baudrillard makes the following proposition:

> ...*the medium is the message* not only signifies the end of the message, but also the end of the medium. There are no more media in the literal sense of the word (I'm speaking particularly of electronic mass media)—that is, of a mediating power between one reality and another, between one state of the real and another. Neither in content, nor in form. Strictly, this is what implosion signifies. The absorption of one pole into another, the short-circuiting between poles of every differential system of meaning, the erasure of distinct terms and oppositions, including that of the medium and of the real—thus the impossibility of any mediation, of any dialectical intervention between the two or from one to the other (Baudrillard 1994: 82–3).

According to this statement, any relation between dualisms (such as sender and receiver or media and audience) is rendered impossible by a simulation economy that abolishes a dialectical system of meaning. Terms cannot be defined against one another, but collapse into each other, or implode under the weight of an excess of meaning and information. What this implosion creates is the type of non-communication that Virilio and others have identified. Baudrillard takes this a step further than his contemporaries by claiming that this kind of media implosion makes it impossible to analyse the act of communication in terms of active or passive participants. In Kellner's reading of Baudrillard, the subject is subsumed by information; a passive rather than active producer of meaning. Kellner's interpretation relies upon maintaining a relation between the medium and the real. Accordingly, the real and the medium are upheld as coherent categories. This is quite different to the perspective on offer here, which sees the media collapse into the real so that the subject *is* information.

Simulation functions here as a productive irony that simultaneously displaces the subject, while advancing a framework for theorising the subject in technology beyond identity politics. By absorbing meaning, Baudrillard's implosive simulacra occasions alternative forms of subjectivity that reside beyond signification, rather than negating the subject entirely. He offers an alternative to thinking about the subject and object as irreducible terms. When the subject is no longer projected into the image or object, something else occurs that opens up possibilities for thinking about subjects outside of a self/Other dialectic:

> No more fantasies of power, speed and appropriation linked to the

> object itself, but instead a tactic of potentialities linked to usage: mastery, control and command, an optimalization of the play of possibilities offered by the car as vector and vehicle, and no longer as object of psychological sanctuary (Baudrillard 1983: 127).

Lash calls this collapse of dualisms a 'flattening' of ontological and epistemological formations based on binary dualisms, resulting in 'the radical monism of technology' (Lash 2001: 108). In attempting to make sense of contemporary social engagements as they are negotiated through everyday technologies, Lash suggests that as forms of life are flattened, stretched out and sped up, they become '*lifted out*' (Lash 2001: 108, emphasis in text). He explains this in terms of an 'opening out' of traditionally closed systems, such as the individual and the social body. They become externalised systems that are open to the movement of communication and information between each other. Exposed to the world, these once closed systems now function as interfaces (Lash 2001: 108).

Most significantly for the subject, technology's monism implies that the boundaries once alienating the self from the spectacle dissolve when the body as a site of power is absorbed by the matrices of technoculture. This is evidenced in the TDK infant, as the distinctions between observed and observer collapse. The newborn looks at the world, its boxed eyes housing square pupils that stare out to somewhere beyond an engagement with the viewer, with the Other. In this act of 'looking beyond', the TDK baby avoids returning the spectator's gaze. Like Manson's infra-red stare, this refusal to connect is neither a form of active resistance, nor a gesture of identification and engagement. Baudrillard claims that the truth constructed by the gaze of authority—the panoptic vision that locates, controls and creates the Other—is no longer applicable in an age of technological communication. The absolute gaze is abolished by the TV eye (Baudrillard 1994: 29). The gaze is not so much denied by the TDK baby, as made impossible when self becomes Other. There is no one position to take as sender or receiver, observer or observed. We are part of a bigger circuit.

Rather than being 'left out' and undermined in a digital world where media systems accelerate beyond human response times, the TDK baby indicates the bodily modalities that are open to the subject when the self becomes an interface. The increased speed of information and communications in contemporary life does not erase subjectivity per se, but reconfigures it. TDK's posthuman imagines the self as something that moves beyond a politics of identity determined by binary frameworks. As a digital simulation without gender and beyond the human, the posthuman emphasises the necessity for a transformation of subjectivity. Transformation allows us to make sense of the place of the subject in the networks and circuits of contemporary communications. No longer is 'the self' a product of a fixed body and unchanging identity, but emerges through the process of converging with technologies.

The increased surface area of the infant's eyes, mouth and ears imply more than a prosthetic projection of the body. Too much information results in an excess of meaning, a transparency that erodes the distinction between the real and the medium through which it is represented. Oversized and misshapen, the eyes and ears of the TDK baby are 'lifted out', as Lash puts it, to become the flow of information. The real becomes the medium, and the spectator becomes the spectacle, or as Baudrillard would have it, "'YOU are information, you are the social, you are the event'" (Baudrillard 1994: 29). There is no more discrete subject as the distinctions between the real and the medium dissolve. The broad smile of the TDK baby is spread across its face, its ears appear to have been pulled in opposite directions from the lobe and the tip. This stretching of sensory surfaces challenges the limits of the body as it is traditionally coded. Like Barbie and Marilyn Manson, the posthuman TDK baby disappears by exceeding the limits of the natural body.

Women in the Media-ted Circuit

We have previously talked about the concern of some feminists for the gendered body and the female subject who risks 'disappearing' in the information circuit. Much materialist feminism has theorised the technological refashioning of the body as displacing the lived physicality of everyday existence and struggle for women. Vivian Sobchack directs such a critique at Baudrillard specifically in the context of discussing the J.G. Ballard novel *Crash*. Referring to Baudrillard, she says:

> The man is really dangerous. Indeed, as I sit here with a throbbing, vivid "inscription" on my left distal thigh, I might wish Baudrillard a car crash or two. He needs a little pain (maybe a lot) to bring him to his senses, to remind him that he has a body, his body, and that the "moral gaze" begins there—with the lived sense and imagined feeling of the human body not merely as a material object among others, but as a material subject that bleeds and suffers and hurts for others because it can bleed and suffer and hurt for oneself. If we don't keep this subjective kind of bodily sense in mind as we negotiate our technoculture, then we, like Vaughan, like Baudrillard, will objectify ourselves to death (Sobchack 1991: 329).

Much of the talk about women and the media circulates around identity. For example, as discussed at length in chapter one, there has been significant debate around female invisibility in cyberspace, as well as how gender specificity is disappearing and the consequences of that. When we talk about womanhood as something that is grounded in corporeal, socially and culturally prescribed female experience, electronic communications that collapse the distinctions between subject and object, nature and technology, risk undermining the status of the lived body in subject constitution. Others have been more optimistic about the kinds of possibilities for identity afforded by the digitally driven circuits of communication and information. As mentioned in chapter one, cyberfeminists have reclaimed virtual spaces as a way of enabling female identity and securing a female presence in cyberspace. What we find with both of these viewpoints is that they take a critical approach to the issue. What I mean is they are focused on exploring whether interactive media networks can offer a space to forge coherent identities, given the social inequalities experienced by gendered, raced and queered bodies. But, as my position throughout this book would suggest, we reach the limits of these arguments when we get to the question of the real. Debating the question of how women in the 'real' world negotiate a 'virtual' technoculture returns us to an approach to technology as either good or bad for women. Moreover, it assumes a universal and knowable identity category of 'woman', which can be spoken about unproblematically.

Baudrillard prompts us to redirect the debate away from securing a real. If we are to accept Baudrillard's logic, what is at stake here is not the opposition of reality and virtuality, but that it is no longer possible to distinguish between the two. Consequently, this forces us to consider what is at stake for identity politics when the experience of information society remakes our reality. In this context, to try to 'return to the real' is the wrong strategy. One way of moving beyond an idea of female identity located in established definitions of the material and reality is to think about the real and identity in different terms. To interrogate the real, however, is not to say that there is no reality. Like Sobchack and others, I acknowledge that we are situated bodies who feel and experience the world. It is the question of what we come to know and experience as reality that is of concern here. That is, 'reality' is not a given but rather, in a culture of simulation, images such as the posthuman baby perform to make the world as we know it, to generate our sense of what is real.

For example, we can think of the posthuman body as offering a means of exposing the reality principle. As information, the posthuman body can 'disappear' into the information network and confound the very system of simulated realties. Baudrillard says that 'the fact that priority is given to the identity of the network and never to the individuals' identity implies that option of hiding and disappearing into the intangible space of the virtual and thus, the option of not being located anywhere, which resolves all problems of identity, not to mention those of otherness' (Baudrillard 2005: 10). By disappearing into the information network, the posthuman plays the game of simulation.

This strategy of confusing the system on its own terms is not dissimilar to the way a computer virus operates to reproduce, replicate and survive in the information network. The way that the virus contaminates the system is a useful conduit to configuring alternative relationships between the body and technology that moves beyond the coding of technology as either good or bad for women. Contamination, or the viral, as it has been theorised by Vicki Kirby in the context of postmodern feminisms (Kirby 1994), suggests the potential for new fusions between, and combinations of, established codes. The hybridity that ensues from contaminated forms challenges the perception of technology as instigating a loss of subjectivity, identity and corporeality.

Similarly, the TDK baby operates as one such viral or fractal form, occasioning a new understanding of the body and technology. Rather than legitimating the erasure of embodied experience through technology, posthuman figurations reformulate how the subject is constituted in and by its cultural surrounds. Resisting the tendency to interpret the body as erased or negated by technology, I argue instead that a new kind of subjectivity is created in the contamination of biological and information networks. The gendered subject (or for that matter, the queer or raced subject) does not exist outside of technology but is forged by its immersion in information networks. Posthuman figurations, such as the TDK baby, exhibit a protean bodily modality more suited to the collapse between material and informational systems. Fundamental to a rethinking of subjectivity is acknowledging that the range and limits of what constitute humanness and the body are expanding and continually shifting in the context of digital technologies, challenging conventional interpretations of how the world is lived, experienced and perceived.

In an age that Stone has termed 'technosociality' (Stone 1992: 610), subjectivity is no longer understood as aligned with the natural or organic, thus assuming an incompatibility with the machine or non-natural. Instead, Stone argues that we situate ourselves within the context of contemporary technologies, which blur the boundaries between self and technology. For the purposes of this feminist project, such techno–human engagements function strategically to displace conventional identifications and meanings figured in terms of oppositions such as nature/technology, self/Other and human/non-human. Moreover, the importance of Stone's study for a theory of the interface resides in her consideration of how social interactions brought about by technology, such as cyberspace, may function as transformative. This concurs with an understanding of the posthuman as a figuration that calls into question the distinction between reality and the virtual. The TDK baby implies such subjective formulations by interfacing between information networks and the body. What manifests in place of traditional notions of the natural subject, is a radically altered conception of the self as mutable and able to flow between networks, affiliates and matrices of knowledge.

The prosthetic element of electronic media is central to Stone's analysis of the subject in technology. For it is the point of engagement between technology and human that destabilises established notions of the self as locatable in a fixed body. Stone's analysis supports my argument that the economy of the body requires reorganisation to take into account new modalities of being in the technological age. Her example resonates with my insistence that the body is not lost, but experienced differently through technology. TDK's posthuman image encourages us to reflect on how we conceptualise reality when bodies interface with electronic media, and the distinctions between subject and object, spectator and scene become increasingly blurred. I ask for bodies to be re-envisioned as part of a circuit of communications that collapses a dialectical economy. But not so that bodily experience is denied, but reconceived as an interface.

Prostheses and Systems

This idea of the fusion of human and technological components is not entirely new. Prior to the advent of digital information networks, and well before Baudrillard assessed the impact of technology upon the human subject, Freud addressed the changing status of humanity in an age of industrial and technical progress. In *Civilization and its Discontents* (1969), Freud charts a shift from the inhuman qualities of an all-seeing and all-knowing God, toward the human attainment of these God-like ideals through technological advances. As a result of technology, Freud claims that 'man has, as it were, become a kind of prosthetic God. When he puts on all his auxiliary organs he is truly magnificent; but those organs have not grown on to him and they still give him much trouble at times' (Freud 1969: 28–9). Freud's remarks foreground the interdependency of techno–human encounters. On the one hand, technology offers man the possibility to access a power akin to that of nature and the gods. But the flipside to the promise of technology is the trouble it brings; a trouble that threatens to undermine an Enlightenment humanist vision of a self-constitutive and autonomous subject.

Since Freud wrote about the technological prosthesis as both man's potential liberation and burden, the prosthesis has become a popular metaphor for those seeking to explain the place of the subject relative to information and communication technologies. For McLuhan, it is the operations of the media that function as prosthetic extensions of the human. His vision of the subject interprets electronic communications as technological tools used to extend the range and scope of the human body. That is, communication networks function to prosthetically augment the 'natural body', hence overcome its limitations in a mediated world (McLuhan 1964: 30). This idea is more commonly understood by McLuhan's catchphrase, 'the medium is the message'; a term he explains as follows:

> This is merely to say that the personal and social consequences of any medium—that is, of any extension of ourselves—result from the new scale that is introduced into our affairs by each extension of ourselves, or by any new technology (McLuhan 1964: 15).

Fundamentally, what concerns McLuhan is how the medium (in this case, media technologies) affects human relations. Technological mediums for communication, information dissemination and exchange transform the way humans interact, he says, because 'it is the medium that shapes and controls the scale and form of human association and action' (McLuhan 1964: 16).

Although McLuhan argues for an interpretation of the media as an extension of bodily senses, ultimately he upholds the distinction between human and non-human components. Even though Baudrillard is deeply indebted to McLuhan's model of media theory, his theories differ from those of his predecessor by collapsing, rather than upholding, the distinction between self and Other. It is from McLuhan that Baudrillard derives his argument for an understanding of media networks based on an analysis of form, rather than content. Baudrillard maintains that it is the medium itself that manufactures what we know, rather than the message it carries. Instead of technology forming an extension of man, Baudrillard inverts McLuhan's model by locating the subject inside the integrated circuit of unmediated and direct sensory flow. This contravenes a theory of techno–human relations that views the subject as a discrete component that is connected to, but fundamentally separate from, information networks. In the age of digital technology, the prosthesis takes on new meaning as bodies are represented and theorised as seamlessly wedded to technology. What this results in, according to Baudrillard, is the eradication of any relational difference between the subject and information.

The TDK baby invites a reconsideration of McLuhan's formulation of the body/prosthesis relationship, a formulation that interprets the technological as the extension of a unified, corporeal subject. In the digital era, the interaction of the natural with the machine results in something beyond a mere prosthetic extension of an undifferentiated, organic notion of the self. In coupling the organic and technological, the body may be reinterpreted as a boundary site—neither entirely natural nor cultural but a configuration that negotiates the limits of corporeal existence within an increasingly technological environment. In this way, the interface acts as another kind of prosthesis that is not so much a material extension or external projection from a 'natural' body, but a flow of information between biological, digital and media systems.

Running along the bottom of the poster in small print is TDK's prominent advertising slogan 'TDK does amazing things to my system'. Its resonance with the current media generation forges an association between this well-known phrase and the campaign described here. 'What exactly does TDK do?' you might ask. 'And to what system?' The viewer is invited to consider how 'TDK does amazing things to my system' in light of the company's motto of 'Evolve to TDK', which appears in large letters in the lower third of the poster.

In the instance of this particular TDK advertisement, the posthuman is articulated as both product and consumer of the visual image in the context of digital manipulation and communication. In an era of mass marketing hype, potential customers are encouraged to consume the image of the baby, and in turn, TDK products. While the baby is the image we consume, the infant is also advertised as a consumer of TDK's product line of blank video tapes, audio cassettes and CDRs. The body is made over to accommodate the consumption of TDK products. Eyes replace the TV screen and ears become speakers. The infant's thin mouth stretches across its face, providing the ideal size and shape for the insertion of a CD. In this regard, the TDK baby evokes the confluence of media, or multimedia, whereby categorical distinctions between cultural forms collapse. The TDK baby is the body *as* stereo.

In this play of words and images, the distinction between organic bodily systems and mechanical communications systems is rendered increasingly problematic. In the act of consumption of TDK products, the body becomes the stereo, rather than the bodily system and the technological system existing as discrete entities. The consumption of TDK products precipitates this evolution. No longer will an individual need a stereo when the individual becomes a stereo.

The development of an amplified sensory system by the posthuman TDK baby suggests this new kind of engagement with the external environment, where the distinction between the subject and technology is abolished. His/her auditory and visual pathways are depicted as larger than life, offering an increased surface area to interface with its surrounds. In this instance, the prosthetic extension of the body isn't a compensatory mechanism to make up for a perceived corporal incompleteness or inadequacy. It is not brought about by anything that is lacking from the body, but results from an excess, or proliferation, of information in the contemporary age. The relationship between the subject and the technology it uses is superseded by the exchange between different media. In terms of the entertainment technologies TDK advertises, information flows from component to component of the TDK system—from the televisual, to the stereophonic to the interactive. Lash observes that engaging with, socialising in, and making sense of the world around us depends upon interfacing with technological systems, so that 'we operate, less like cyborgs than interfaces' (Lash 2001: 107).

The performances of Australian artist Stelarc offer us another site though which to explore the idea of the interface. He envisions the kinds of formations of the body and the self that can be made possible by the techno–human interface.[2] Stelarc's fascination with challenging the physical parameters of the body and interrogating the limits of its capabilities was evidenced in his early body suspension performances of the seventies. But it is in later performances that Stelarc explores the ideas of bodily extension and enhancement in the context of electronic culture and digital communications networks. Rather than enacting the loss of the body into technology and media systems, Stelarc's performances suggest that a new kind of corporeality is created in the mix of biological and information systems.

In the performance *Handwriting* (1982), Stelarc introduced the world to the now infamous third hand. First conceived as a mechanical structure with limited capabilities that could be attached to his already existing arms, the third hand has 'evolved' to become an integral part of Stelarc's oeuvre. Standing behind a pane of glass, Stelarc holds a pen in each of his three hands. Although attached to his right arm, the third hand works independently to the other hands, with each writing different letters to make up the word EVOLUTION. The third hand is activated by pulse signals that travel from Stelarc's abdominal and leg muscles via electronic wires into the mechanical hand. It becomes part of Stelarc's body circuitry, albeit through external, artificial, neuronal networks that pass from his lower body musculature to power the third hand. As information travels from the neuronal pulses of the biological body into the artificial hand, not only does the third hand become part of the neurological circuitry of the body, but the status of the body as an organic and natural entity is scrambled. Such posthuman configurations suggest a protean bodily modality more suited to the interactions between material and informational systems.

Stelarc speaks of the third hand in the *Handwriting* performance as an addition to, rather than an extension of, the body (Stelarc 2002). And while *Handwriting* is typical of his challenge to fixed notions of bodily identity, later works see Stelarc complicate further the relation between the body and technology. Appendages such as the third hand function less like additions to an inert and unified organic body, and more like insertions that collapse the boundaries between where the self ends and technology begins.

Ping Body, first performed in 1996 in Sydney, and subsequently performed in various locations around the world, sees Stelarc wired up to the Internet. Stelarc stands naked, his body encased in circuitry. This external nervous system functions in a feedback loop with his biological mechanisms. Internet noise, pulsing through the wires connecting the Internet to Stelarc, induces involuntary movements through the body. Body and performance are activated from outside the individual. By locating the stimulus for involuntary movement outside the body, Stelarc inverts conventional interpretations of the relationship between the subject and the Internet. As Stelarc elucidates:

> Instead of collective bodies determining the operation of the Internet, collective Internet activity moves the body. The Internet becomes not merely a mode of information transmission but also a transducer, effecting physical action (Stelarc 2002).

As the body moves in response to the ebb and flow of data, these involuntary movements of the body subsequently activate Stelarc's third hand. A feedback loop is created that extends the limits of the body. Stelarc's posthuman reconfigures the body as part of a circuit of communications that collapses dialectical thinking, so that bodily experience is not denied, but prosthetically extended outwards to interface with the environment and directed internally to invade the body. The physical parameters of corporeality are extended through the interplay between the human body and the flows of the data stream. The performance encourages a reappraisal of the body–technology relationship, highlighting that the range and limits of what constitute humanness and the body are expanding and shifting in the context of digital technologies. By manipulating space and time, Stelarc challenges traditional understandings of how the world is lived, experienced and perceived, particularly with respect to the body and identity. By figuring subjecthood in contemporary mass media as an interface, Stelarc's posthuman figurations serve to undermine oppositional thinking that positions subject and object, technology and nature as irrevocably and diametrically opposed.

While *Ping Body* enacts a body encased by techno networks, Stelarc does not mean to imply that the corporeal is enveloped or erased by media systems. Rather, he envisions the body as a phantom: 'phantom not as in phantasmagorical, but rather phantom as in phantom limb sensation—a kind of visual visceral sensation that is still coupled to a physical body' (Stelarc interviewed in Farnell 1999: 133). In Stelarc's terms the techno–human engagement no longer signals an obsolete body, but an absent body, 'DESIGNED TO INTERFACE WITH ITS ENVIRONMENT' (Stelarc 1998: 117). In rupturing the once incompatible spheres of nature and technology, Stelarc exceeds his understanding of the body as an interface or phantom model. The fusion of the technological environment with the organic body is deployed to theorise the splitting of the species (Stelarc 1998: 118). For as an individual's bodily capabilities are extended by technology, evolution no longer stands to benefit the species, but the self.

'EVOLUTION ENDS WHEN TECHNLOGY INVADES THE BODY' (Stelarc 1998: 118). When the TDK text implores us to 'Evolve to TDK', its hybrid, digital, simulation of technology and nature threatens the sanctity of a human species defined by the act of natural reproduction and genetic selection. The process of evolution, as it is popularly understood, depends on a random ordering of chromosomes to produce an individual displaying unique characteristics. When these genetically derived qualities result in the individual faring better than its peers, whether that be through its enhanced ability to collect food, disguise itself from predators or attract more mates, then it is more likely to survive and pass on its genes. In the case of the TDK baby, its uncanny semblance to technological systems promises an increased chance of survival in a technological age. This posthuman adaptation, however, defies a theory of evolution as proposed by Darwin because technological interventions augment or prop up the body to the point where 'weak' genes aren't eradicated through competition with stronger rivals.

It is no evolutionary accident or random mutation that caused the amplification of the TDK baby's viewing and hearing apparatus. The TDK newborn is the renegade product of a new model of evolution. The posthuman subject comes into being as an effect of the hyperreal, digital environment, not via a linear model of evolutionary 'progress' from human to posthuman. It offers a way of being that is without origins, a simulated construct emerging at the confluence of biology, technology and consumption. As subject and object collapse into each other, as biological and technological systems merge and fuse, what manifests is a mutant hybrid of technology and media networks. The baby as a privileged symbol of origins is refuted by the TDK image. Our mutant baby has no parents. As a simulated product of hyper-reality, it cannot reside in the real world. When bodily and technological components can no longer be distinguished from one another, traditional perceptions of the human are unsteadied. This situation creates a paradox: while technological culture threatens to end human evolution in the Darwinian sense, the evolutionary process is simultaneously accelerated beyond the species.

Re-reading the body/prosthesis relationship as an interface suggests an interactive exchange, whereby technological systems may extend the human body and mind, as well as implying that biological systems are extensions of electronic networks (Taylor 1997: 143). The body functions less like an organic system rendered obsolete by technology, and more like an interface with technological systems that allows for flows and exchanges of information *between* systems. In an interactive circuit where data streams flow across the screen interface, the subject becomes part of the technology as a sign-switcher that confuses the distinction between the medium and the message by existing as information.

Advertising the Posthuman

By configuring the body as interface, TDK's advertising constructs a radically altered relationship between advertising, media and consumers. By situating the posthuman entity in a circuit of communication precipitated by information technologies, TDK asks us to consider the role of the consumer in the sphere of advertising, communication and meaning formation. Positioning the posthuman as both subject and object of communication is achieved by collapsing the distinction between the subject and the technology it uses. Imploding the point of distinction between the consumer, the TDK products consumed, and the circuits through which information is relayed from one to another, enables new ways of thinking about our bodies and our relationship to media environments.

The paradoxically unsettling and appealing nature of the TDK image impelled me to ask for the poster in the music store. And, it is the confusion that is experienced when engaging with the TDK figuration that encourages a reconsideration of the traditional view of advertising as a site of identification or desire. The role of advertisements in establishing a relationship between the viewer and the image is conventionally understood as follows: 'advertising images are central to the construction of cultural ideas about lifestyle, self-image, self-improvement, and glamour. Advertising often presents an image of things to be desired, people to be envied, and life as it "should be"' (Sturken and Cartwright 2001: 189).

It could be said that the political efficacy of this posthuman image is compromised by its association with the advertising industry. 'Evolve to TDK' employs the commonplace strategy of disassociation between an advertisement and a material product. Nowhere in the image of the TDK baby are we presented with TDK's product range. As suggested by the TDK baby's oversized ears and square TV eyes, the image does not sell a particular product, but the promise of the heightened sensory awareness that consumers will experience when using TDK technology. No longer are we asked to associate with a product, but rather with the brand image TDK wishes to create (Klein 2000: 21).

The innocent smile of this gorgeous child is both appealing and captivating in a way that can be interpreted as perpetuating a romanticised myth of the global media and communications network that connects people across the world in a harmonious gesture of cross-cultural exchange. To an extent, TDK employs the seduction of technology, creating desire for a technologically mediated lifestyle and the possibility of becoming something else through technology. Yet the seductive aspects of technology sit alongside a long-standing fear that technology will come to control us. A degree of ambivalence complicates the ability to respond definitively or draw meaning from the TDK advertisement. In chapter four, we saw how an interpretation of the image as masking a reality is complicated an economy of simulation. So to suggest that the TDK baby depoliticises, or masks the power structures underlying global media, is to imply that there is a truth out there to be revealed, which resides behind the image. Instead, the posthuman figuration reveals nothing. There is no absolute reality regarding the media or the exchange of information.

This uncertainty surrounding what the advertisement might mean is in keeping with contemporary understandings of image culture. As one of the many forms of image production in a world overrun by visual signals, advertising can no longer be considered as creating a definitive meaning or message for the consumer. On the contrary, a study of TDK's advertising indicates that meaning is free-floating and diffuse, it cannot be traced to an 'original' reference point in reality. In much the same manner, technologies problematise a notion of origins by eroding the distinctions between human and machine, transforming the ways we enact our bodies and human existence. This is evidenced in areas as diverse as artificial intelligence, virtual reality and biotechnology. TDK does not pretend to envision an idealised life as it 'should be'. It offers us a fantasy, but part of the pleasure and appeal of the advertisement is that the fantasy is so immediate that there is no critical distance to be had, only the pleasure of immediacy and immersion. The incoherence produced by the posthuman is a theme that I will continue to pursue through an exploration of biotechnologies as they are represented in popular culture in the following chapter.

The TDK baby does not maintain a discrete differentiation between organic and mechanical systems, but its wide-eyed engagement with the world suggests that this posthuman functions as a system that is open to information and communication flows. Its senses extend outward to interface with the environment. This destabilisation or slippage between discrete categories functions strategically for a feminist engagement with posthuman figurations by enabling alternative ways of understanding subjectivity beyond the rhetoric of identity and difference. As the limits of the body are refigured, the modes by which women conceptualise the body and identity also undergo transformation. The body as interface disturbs established notions of what constitutes the material body, undermining the fixity of meaning attributed to an embodied identity.

6

Origins and Identity in a Biotech World

In the late nineties, Australian artist Patricia Piccinini created the photography and video series *Protein Lattice*, introducing a mutant rodent forged from an amalgam of a human ear and laboratory mouse. Her inspiration for the project derived from photographs of a then-recent biotechnological experiment, published in *Time* and *Arena* magazines. Speaking of this incident, Piccinini states:

> For a moment in late 1995 an image appeared in the world media that has stayed in my mind and in the minds of a huge number of other people who saw it. Perhaps it does not float on the surface, but if questioned most of the people I know would be able to recall the mouse with the human ear on its back. For a media second we saw the future and it was a sorry little rodent weighed down by an ear vastly out of scale with its emaciated body (Piccinini 1997).

In Piccinini's version, the rat is digitally rendered as a red-eyed, pink and hairless creature sprouting a human ear. One image from the series is particularly arresting (see figure 4). The rodent rests atop the manicured fingers of an exotic female model. Her sultry features are enhanced and emphasised—the skin of her face airbrushed into a seamless plastic mask. The model is made freakish in her absolute perfection. Her artifice is revealed in her facial features, which are too large, too sculpted, too glossy and glowing to pass as natural. The rat, too, is a construct. In this artwork, the once-separate biological systems of rodent and human are rendered as effortlessly fused. The rat's skin isn't marred by stitches, scars or any other markings that might suggest that the ear has been awkwardly spliced onto its back.

In the *Protein Lattice* series, we return to many of the issues that have been raised in this book so far: the blurring of boundaries between real and illusory, self and Other, organic and machinic. Rather than maintaining what were once distinct categories of rat and human, Piccinini's rodent appears to seamlessly articulate a fusion of self and Other. The interconnected biological systems of the human and animal species are made possible by both the tools of technoscience and the malleable qualities of digital image making.

Piccinini is one of a cluster of contemporary art practitioners exploring the posthuman moment where information and biological networks seamlessly merge. Eschewing the data–flesh interfaces typified by her Australian compatriot Stelarc, Piccinini's posthuman forms invert the human–machine prosthetic to render the potential effects of biotechnology on the body. In this respect, her work is more akin to Gilles Barbier's clones, Thomas Grunfeld's hybrid creatures or the Chapman Brothers' mutant twins. Her imagery raises the fundamental question of what constitutes identity, difference and being in a posthuman age. These questions invariably lead to the issue of gender difference, and its potential dissolution in a world of new biotechnologies and reproductive practices.

Building on the idea that posthuman figurations manifest from and exist in a culture of simulation, I want to explore how biotechnological narratives operate in this world of simulated images. It appears that popular media images of posthuman existence in a biotech age rest on a paradox. While science and technology are preoccupied with answering the question of our origins—whether it be through theories of the earth's formation such as the Big Bang, or the mapping of the human genome—the representation of biotechnological discourse in the popular cultural arena actively undermines the notion of origins by existing in a culture of simulation. Society is awash with multiple and competing narratives that simultaneously reproduce and undermine the authority of scientific dogma. It is from this slippage in the practice of signification that posthuman figurations might offer new ways of configuring narratives of gene discourse that move beyond origin stories.

In the article 'Patricia Piccinini: Plastic Realist', Peter Hennessey observes that 'Biotechnology forms the focus of much of Piccinini's work, because in many ways, biotechnology crystallises the particular moment where the artificial and the natural—the organic and the technological—begin to dissolve into each other' (Hennessey 1999: 250). Piccinini's work finds a theoretical complement in the writings of Donna Haraway, who (since her landmark cyborg manifesto of 1985) has challenged the myth of original unity and its associations with the categories of nature and woman. To this day, the cyborg retains currency as a key feminist figuration that allows for imaginings of alternative female subjectivities in a technologically mediated world.

Figure 4. Patricia Piccinini, *Protein Lattice–Red Portrait* (1997), digital C-type photograph, 80x80cm.

Transgressive Simulations: Nature Re-represented

Since writing about the cyborg, Haraway has identified the transgenic Oncomouse as another figuration that typifies the transgression of boundaries between the human and non-human. The cross-over of the species brought about by the fusion of human and rat components in this act of bioengineering puts Piccinini's rodent in good company with the Oncomouse. Like Piccinini's mutant imagery, the transgenic Oncomouse confuses the boundaries between nature and artifice. A transgenic organism, as explained by Haraway, 'contains genes transplanted from one strain or species…to another' (Haraway 1997: 60). In the case of the Oncomouse, it has been inserted with a human gene to promote the growth of cancerous breast tumours. So in this respect it differs somewhat from *Protein Lattice*, where the distinction between the species dissolves as the cells of the human ear and the rat conjoin in the process of tissue engineering. Nonetheless, both tissue engineering and transgenics question the status of the natural when human intervention, by way of technology, becomes the norm. Accordingly, Haraway interprets the insertion of genes from one species into another as a transgressive border crossing that transforms nature into culture by the process of human intervention (Haraway 1997: 60).

In her essay, 'Otherworldly Conversations, Terran Topics, Local Terms', Haraway asserts that the process of characterising nature as Other is conventionally configured as a project of policing borders and boundaries; of constructing a materialised and inert fiction of the natural that is locatable and originary (Haraway 1995: 70). Yet efforts to maintain nature as Other, as Haraway points out, are ultimately and increasingly untenable; ruptured in everyday instances of boundary displacement, such as the phenomenon of the Oncomouse. Haraway instead argues that the concept of nature in the popular psyche cannot and does not function as an essential reality in opposition to an equally inert and locatable notion of culture. Rather, she suggests that nature functions both as topos and trope; a rhetorical, artificial, constructed and all-pervasive 'common place'. She says:

> ...nature is not a physical place to which one can go, nor a treasure to fence in or bank, nor an essence to be saved or violated. Nature is not hidden and so does not need to be unveiled. Nature is not a text to be read in the codes of mathematics and biomedicine. It is not the 'other' who offers origin, replenishment and service. Neither mother, nurse, lover nor slave, nature is not a matrix, resource, mirror, nor tool for the reproduction of that odd ethnocentric, phallogocentric, putatively universal being called Man. Nor for his euphemistically named surrogate, 'the human' (Haraway 1995: 70).

By posing nature as topos and trope, instead of as the Other of binary thought, Haraway's critique exposes nature as a construct and displacement, which does not exist outside of the culture that names it. Rather, nature functions as a 'common-place', to use Haraway's terminology, which allows us to further understand the workings of culture. Moreover, Haraway claims that returning to the notion of an intrinsic nature fails as a strategy in the critique of transgenics. Upholding the natural in the face of the unnatural—in this instance the practices of genetic engineering—risks reasserting the themes of racial purity and natural type that underpin racist fears of the Other, the alien and the mixed (Haraway 1997: 60–3).

Despite her criticism of the categorisation of nature as inert and fixed, boundary transgression in the practice of biotechnology isn't something Haraway blindly endorses. In this regard, she aligns herself with the revisionist project undertaken by feminist critiques of science. These critiques provide one instance of the interventionist strategies used by feminism to reconsider the kinds of relations established between practices of representation, scientific knowledge and subject constitution. Understandably, feminism has expressed uneasiness at the relationship between knowledge and power in the realm of science. This concern stems from the recognition that men's experiences and perspectives traditionally inform the production of scientific knowledges, and these, in turn, produce reality. On top of this, the masculinist bias of scientific inquiry and observation is masked by the construction of science as a form of empirical or objective study that claims to present a world-view, unaffected by societal factors such as the gender and race of the knowledge-maker.

Feminist scholars of science reject the foundations of objective knowledge. They argue that biological science is not an empirical account of the world, but a form of constructed knowledge that is intimately tied to social control and power-effects (Fox Keller 1995b, Grosz and de Lepervanche 1988, Haraway 1991, Harding 1986, Hubbard 1990). These critiques recognise the gendering of science in binary terms, whereby science is a rational and empirical project, coded masculine, contra the natural and the feminine. In this schema, woman is positioned as the object, but rarely the subject or knowledge-maker of scientific inquiry. Clearly, the traditional power/knowledge relationship is a vital point of concern for a feminist critique of knowledge construction. This is partly because the construction of science as a neutral endeavour that transcends social and cultural contexts can't accommodate or take into account different perspectives and ways of knowing and experiencing the world, such as those of women and other groups who have been traditionally excluded from making scientific knowledge. In light of women's structural and cultural exclusion from the realms of science, medicine and technology, Ruth Hubbard has called for a feminist methodology in science to challenge the myth of objectivity that masks an implicit gender bias (Hubbard 1990: 29).

Haraway shares this approach, which has come to form the foundations of much of her scholarship.[1] The intimate association between transnational corporate capitalism and scientific funding and research is a consistent theme in her work (Haraway 1997). Although the role of power in knowledge production is central to an interrogation of the effects of biotechnologies, Haraway avoids interpreting power in basic terms of either resistance to or complicity with such technologies. Rather, an ethics of the transgenic organism is, for Haraway, 'about the manner in which we are responsible for these worlds' (Haraway 2000: 146). She states:

> The tendency by the political "left"...to collapse molecular genetics, biotechnology, profit and exploitation into one undifferentiated mass is at least as much of a mistake as the mirror-image reduction by the "right" of biological—or informational—complexity to the gene and its avatars, including the dollar (Haraway 1997: 62).

Haraway's response to biotechnological boundary transgressions circumvents an approach to scientific study and its products as irrevocably 'bad' for women. Rather, she considers who it is that might benefit from the creations of technoscience, and acknowledges the kinship women have with transgenic creatures such as the Oncomouse.

Similarly, *Protein Lattice* provides fertile ground on which to reconsider the role of images in feminist thinking about technoscience, namely emerging biotechnologies of genetic manipulation. Piccinini's images question the ethical implications of biotechnological engineering yet stop short of judging the creatures it produces. Instead, by circulating across the realms of contemporary media, biological and information technologies, they can complicate the origin myths promoted by science. At this site of instability posthuman figurations like the mutant rat open up possibilities and potentialities for alternative understanding of reality, subjectivity and gender in a technologically mediated society.

Like Haraway, Piccinini avoids a deterministic approach to technology that sees it as an unstoppable and inevitable threat to human existence. By emerging from the site at which natural and technological, real and illusion collapse, *Protein Lattice* disrupts the myth of a monolithic, dystopic technology that controls an equally immutable nature. Piccinini's depiction of the mutant rat shares Haraway's ambivalence toward the products of technoscience. This uncertainty arises from a culture where value systems of good or bad are too simplistic to understand the complex negotiations that constitute our engagements with the social world.

Ambivalent Images

Not only does the subject matter of *Protein Lattice* act ambivalently by securing and challenging our sense of reality, but the way that it is rendered and presented also complicates the status of representations as reflecting or constructing the real. In many ways Piccinini's works mimic the visual codes of advertising. The luxurious sheen that she gives to each form and her use of contrasting light and dark areas creates images that are, much like the ads in glossy magazines, seductive and aesthetically appealing. The viewer is drawn to look at something that is evocative and at the same time unsettling. Even though there is something not quite right about the marketing of the 'brave new world' of bioengineering as a lifestyle choice, it can nonetheless be pleasurable to consume.

Piccinini has spoken of working from a compromised space that acknowledges the appeal of popular media culture, 'a desire for the shiny stuff that consumer culture has to offer (Plastic, TV, sneakers, the FACE) although I know that they are not good for me' (Piccinini 1996). It is the artifice of Piccinini's images that opens up a mode of partaking in technological and popular cultural environments often deemed 'bad for us', an affront to human values and sensibilities. In the case of *Protein Lattice*, it is the construction of science as a commercial enterprise to be marketed and made appealing that is being questioned. One of the ways that it does this is by disrupting the division between scientific, artistic and commercial forms of image making. The other is by rejecting the idea that certain types of images are only accessed and interpreted in specific contexts.

In 1999, an image from the *Protein Lattice* series was displayed like a giant advertising billboard on the Republic Apartment Tower in Melbourne's central business district. This gesture indicates that art can, and does, move beyond the spaces of the gallery to inhabit the worlds of mass consumerism and popular media, just as the inverse also occurs (Gibbons 2005). As Jim Collins notes, 'radically eclectic forms of textuality' are a common feature 'across the entire spectrum of cultural production' (Collins 1995: 2). Given that the erosion between art and popular media and high and low culture has been a defining feature of the postmodern cultural condition (Jameson 1983: 112), Collins suggests that viewers have become adept at negotiating this 'array' of transhistorical and transnational signs and symbols in an information age. His ideas motivate us to ask: 'when images circulate outside of their once defined zones, is it really necessary for viewers to access and interpret the mutant mouse solely as a work of art, an advertisement or the depiction of a scientific breakthrough?'

If we take an anti-postmodern viewpoint, like the one expressed by Naomi Klein in her book *No Logo*, it would appear that it *is* important to define the purpose and the meaning of images. Klein comes to this conclusion by criticising the way that advertising encroaches on the spaces once occupied by images from the arts, culture and media, to the point where the elements that distinguish one type of image from another can no longer be discerned (Klein 2000: 29–44). She sees non-commercial spaces and forms of image culture as corrupted and infected by the dirty world of consumer advertising. While Klein argues that the breakdown of boundaries between high and low culture leads to the violation of public space by corporate interests,

Piccinini's 'placement strategy' shows that as this cultural collapse erodes the distinction *between* forms, we can no longer make definitive judgements about what is good or bad. Her tactic challenges the idea that the colonisation of non-commercial space by advertising is a one-way process that is largely negative. Mica Nava has suggested that the interconnection between art and commerce is shaped in part by young people's tendency to 'consume commercials independently of the product that is being marketed' (Nava 1992: 174). Her study contests the dominant view of advertising as directly tied to consumption, and like Collins, she interrogates the belief that art and advertising texts are necessarily consumed in radically different ways (Nava 1992: 181).

As noted earlier, Piccinini's inspiration for *Protein Lattice* was other media images. This tendency toward citing, revision and reworking of cultural artefacts is indicative of a postmodern experience that Jean Baudrillard observes is primarily of the order of the visual. In the context of cultural production increasingly shaped by the digital, Piccinini's rat emerges as a figuration that demands a particular understanding at the level of the representational economy where it is produced and circulated. And it is in the context of simulation culture, as discussed at length in chapter two, that we might begin to conceptualise the relation between representation and reality as no longer irrevocably opposed. Following the logic of simulation, the real no longer constitutes the referential point for representation because it has been substituted by the sign. In turn, it is the experience of hyperreality as a mode of signification that creates the possibility for understanding posthuman figurations beyond fixed interpretations.

The digitally constructed forms of *Protein Lattice* are indicative of a contemporary experience of the visual that severs the link between an original object and its reproduction. Piccinini collapses the real and its representational equivalent by digitally re-creating this mutant rodent. In doing so, she plays with the boundaries between human and animal, virtual and real, so that the purpose of the image is not to offer the viewer a copy of an original, nor to mirror the products of technoscience, but to complicate the idea of origins. Piccinini does not aim to depict reality. Indeed, it is the reality principle that her artwork destabilises. Rather than representing a fast approaching dystopic future, or advocating an unproblematic, utopian ideal of what the future will be, the *Protein Lattice* series circulates as potentialities, possibilities or processes beyond a dichotomy of what is real and what is illusion. What Piccinini constructs is a space to contemplate the complexity of contemporary culture, a site where the absolutisms of a dichotomous value system are replaced by a compromised vision. In a context where the distinctions between material and virtual worlds collapse, Piccinini favours imaginings that reside beyond the codes of signification and their enactment.

In Baudrillard's terms, our understanding of the subject isn't determined by its status as 'authentic' or 'true', but is, instead, characterised by the operational configuration of the '*precession of the model*' (Baudrillard 1994: 16, emphasis in text). As a digitally generated image, the rodent performs the function of the model, whereby '(o)nly affiliation to the model has any meaning, since nothing proceeds in accordance with its end anymore, but issues instead from the model, the "signifier of reference", functioning as a foregone, and the only credible, conclusion' (Baudrillard 1993: 56). The significance of this concept for reassessing the relationship between reality and representation is apparent throughout *Protein Lattice*, as the figure of the mouse is endlessly repeated, doubled and re-cited.

In one image from the *Protein Lattice* series, a female model sits on the floor surrounded by a teeming mass of digitally re-created rats. The naked woman wraps her left arm around her chest. Her right arm is outstretched, her hand touching the floor. With knees demurely drawn up toward her torso and downcast eyes, the model appears contemplative and a little bit vulnerable. Although the juxtaposition of the mutant rats and the woman could be interpreted through a critical framework as a statement about artifice versus nature, there is also an equivalence between the two forms, based on their shared status as unreal products of a consumer culture driven by desire and aesthetics that makes them fatal objects. Both the rats and model are naked, hairless and exposed; defenceless under the harsh gaze of the media spotlight that illuminates them. By comparing the rodents with the woman, Piccinini insinuates that gender is also a simulated construct. The smooth, plastic-looking skin of the model assures us that she is no more real than her hybrid friends. Just as the rat is a digitally generated image, so is the woman. In her artist's statement, Piccinini regards the association between rats and models as one of sympathy for these objectified constructions of a phallogocentric symbolic order. Both the rat and woman are, in her opinion, 'organic vessels destined to contain the desires of those who utilise them…both are used interchangeably, without any regard to their specific personality. There will always be another one' (Piccinini 1997).

By re-citing and repeating the image of the rodent, Piccinini ruptures conventional modes of signification that rely on a fixed point of origin. She instead enacts Baudrillard's assertion that '(a)t the end of this process of reproducibility, the real is not only that which can be reproduced, but *that which is always already reproduced*: the hyperreal' (Baudrillard 1993: 73). The proliferation of rats suggests that no origin or referent exists to precede the model, but that the model itself becomes what we understand to be reality, fracturing the dialectic of real/representation, origin/replica, from which difference is structured. Signification is broken up by the act of replication, preventing the possibility of a unified, originary, or fixed meaning to the text. That is not to say that reality is made meaningless in the free play of signification, but that reality becomes a contested zone.

The mutant rodents of *Protein Lattice* are '*conceived according to their very reproducibility*' (Baudrillard 1993: 56, emphasis in text). Their digital constructedness confounds the idea of origins. Yet to suggest that the anticipation of the model reduces or limits our engagements with the social world would be to misunderstand Baudrillard's political project. Rather, the infinite replication of the model causes a short-circuit in established modes of meaning based on dialectical thinking, allowing 'for all possible interpretations, even the most contradictory—all the time, in the sense that their truth is to be exchanged in the image of the models from which they derive, in a generalized cycle' (Baudrillard 1994: 17). Just as there is no original rat, only the digital information referred to as 'the mutant rodent', the myth of the originary or natural is exposed as an effect produced by simulation models.

By existing as digital constructs, the mutant rats disrupt the status of scientific discourse as offering a 'truer' or more legitimate account of this phenomenon. Baudrillard's theory of simulation reminds us that there is no longer any real, only coded information that simulates a real. To this end, the organic is itself an effect produced by the virtual, rather than existing as something that is outside the virtual. The digital image exists purely as information or data. As Baudrillard attests, a simulacrum doesn't even exist as a coherent image. Rather, simulation can only operate as pure information (Baudrillard 1994: 5). This is similar to the genetically engineered sheep called Dolly who, in 1996, became the first mammal to be cloned from adult cells. Prior to her (some say premature) death in 2003, Dolly existed as a model derived from the genetic information that makes up what we understand to be a sheep. What is significant about this is that this information cannot be differentiated from what we would consider to be 'real' or natural sheep. Dolly isn't a reality, but a virtuality. Likewise, the mutant rodent of *Protein Lattice* is a simulation model of a model, itself without origins, that ruptures the formal relation between representation and its reality. And it is this disruption of meaning that undermines the legitimacy of scientific rhetoric that perpetuates the idea of origins.

The Problem of Coding

The trend toward perceiving the world in terms of data isn't isolated to Dolly the sheep or the digital re-creation of genetically engineered rats. Many have suggested that the experience of reality as information has come to underpin all spheres of life, allowing for '*the translation of the world into a problem of coding'* (Haraway 1985: 83, emphasis in text). As information becomes the base unit through which the world can be quantified, the code 'serves as a translation between different discourse and spheres, DNA code, computer code, code as law, cultural code, aristocratic code, encrypted code' (Berry and Pawlik 2005: 2). Baudrillard has called the code the 'new *operational* configuration' of the society of simulacra (Baudrillard 1993: 57).

> Cybernetic control, generation through models, differential modulation, feedback, question/answer, etc.: this is the new *operational* configuration (industrial simulacra being *mere operations*). Digitality is its metaphysical principle...and DNA is its prophet' (Baudrillard 1993: 57).[2]

But Baudrillard is not alone in noting this phenomenon. Feminist commentators like Evelyn Fox Keller, Donna Haraway and Katherine Hayles have observed the tendency toward the coding of everyday life, especially with respect to the body. Each notes that metaphors of information and the code underpin a cultural shift in thinking about the organism as biological entity to one where it is regarded as technological system (Fox Keller 1995a: chapter three, Haraway 1991: chapter three, Hayles 1999: chapter nine). The body has become an information code. Nowhere is this more prevalent than at the level of the gene, where biological mechanisms are reduced to 'packets of information', in much the same way as digital data is read through a 0:1 code. Fox Keller makes the point that the basis of life has undergone a significant shift away from the bodily organism toward the cell, or more specifically its genetic component (Fox Keller 1995b: 52). As the life sciences become governed by capitalist imperatives, as Haraway suggests they have, the body comes to be understood in terms of information; as cybernetic systems and communications networks (Haraway 1991: 45).

While the representations of the posthuman discussed up to this point examine the body as it is extended into systems and networks (the posthuman figuration as plasticity, catastrophe, and interface), I want to now consider the inverse—what the implications might be for questions of identity and difference when the body is miniaturised to the level of the cell or gene. This process is intimately tied to simulation culture, as Baudrillard explains:

> The real is produced from miniaturized cells, matrices, and memory banks, models of control—and it can be reproduced an indefinite number of times from these. It no longer needs to be rational, because it no longer measures itself against either an ideal or negative instance. It is no longer anything but operational (Baudrillard 1994: 2).

Perhaps the most obvious example of this configuration of the body as data is the Human Genome Project (HGP).[3] Not only is this made clear by the project itself, which has identified the genes that make up the human body and analysed the sequences that form the 'building blocks' of life, but the way that the body as data is visually represented. If we look at the official US government website for information about the HGP (www.ornl.gov/sci/techresources/Human_Genome/home.shtml), it carries a logo which embodies this shift toward the coding and miniaturisation of the body. In a clear reference to a biological cell, the logo is circular, and is itself encircled by the names of scientific disciplines—'physics', 'ethics' 'informatics', 'engineering' 'chemistry' and 'biology'. Inside this sphere is a maroon silhouette of a body from the waist up against a pale blue background. A golden strand of DNA wraps around this figure.

The circle of science forms a unified barrier around the human form wrapped in a DNA strand, suggesting the construction of the body by scientific disciplines. Yet the sciences are also positioned as 'outside of' the body and the individual, perpetuating the myth of the objective, rational world-view of science, untainted by social or cultural bias. Given the iconography used to represent the HGP, the idea of the genetic code as representative of life is figuratively enacted as the body resides in the cell and the DNA coil. Rather than envisioning the organism as the primary subject constituted by an infinite multiplicity of cells, our conventional understanding of the body is radically reformulated. The body entwined in a DNA coil is smaller than both the cell and its genetic component, suggesting a shift in our understanding of the body toward a biologically essentialist position whereby DNA is the foundation of human existence. No longer the sum of its molecular parts, the body is subsumed by the cell, so that the cell becomes representative of personhood.

Evelyn Fox Keller tells us that part of making gene theory accessible to a lay audience is to re-create it as a story about humanity and its origins (Fox Keller 1995b: 63). This is precisely the paradox of simulation as Baudrillard understands it; that in order to secure reality, or conceal that the real is no longer real, we must convince ourselves of our origins. Of our simulated world, he observes that, 'there is a plethora of myths of origin and signs of reality—a plethora of truth, or secondary objectivity, and authenticity' (Baudrillard 1994: 6–7). The HGP icon is one such 'strategy of the real', whereby the genesis of human existence is made knowable and locatable inside the cell at the level of gene matter. This 'origin story' is also present in much of the literature used to describe the genome, which uses words like 'blueprint', 'centre', 'code' or 'essence' to reinforce the idea that the origins of life and the meaning of humanity lie in our DNA (Doyle 1997: 80).[4]

Another effect of this process of mapping the genome is the construction of the gene as a kind of fetish object; a 'thing unto itself' that is free of context, history or place. Temporal and spatial boundaries are erased as the body becomes cellular information. Haraway warns that when the gene is disassociated and fragmented from the body, it becomes a unitary object or site of origin that operates much like the fetish does in psychoanalytic discourse—as an interchangeable substitute, whereby the part (the gene) comes to stand for the whole (the organism) (Haraway 1997: 141–5).

Another example of the body as information code can be found in the Visible Human Project (VHP). Catherine Waldby explains this phenomenon as follows: 'VHP creates complete, anatomically detailed, three-dimensional representations of the male and female human body and makes these representations available on the Internet' (Waldby 2000: 25). To achieve these images, a cadaver undergoes a series of processes that involve the scanning, slicing and digital photographing of body sections. When uploaded into a computer program, this creates a digital archive of 'highly resolved transverse cross-sections through the body' (Waldby 2000: 25). These sections can be put together or disassembled in an infinite variety of ways through computer modelling to create a virtual corpse. In a reversal of the cyberpunk dream to 'leave the meat behind' by entering the virtual zone, the VHP reduces the fleshy body to information in order to reinsert it into cyberspace.

So what are the consequences of reducing the body to a code for our understandings of identity and difference? With respect to the coding of the body as DNA information, Richard Doyle observes that molecular biological discourse 'works by producing an invisibility of the body, whose object is no longer the living organism' (Doyle 1997: 59). Instead, the organism undergoes a shift toward an ahistorical, non-specific and dislocated myth of the molecule (Doyle 1997: 59). A number of feminists share this concern with the decontextualisation of the body in biomedicine. For Waldby, the political implications of flesh-made-data revolve around the management of bodies through digital technologies such as in-vitro fertilisation (IVF) and cloning (Waldby 2000: 29). The way that the body is represented in biomedicine can result in the standardisation, replication and commodification of the body, and lead to medical interpretations that reproduce gendered bodies in stereotypical and traditional ways (Cartwright 1998: 40, Waldby 2000: 32).

Not only is the complexity of human existence standardised by the codes of digital image making and genetic information, but as Dorothy Nelkin and Susan Lindee (1995) point out, 'differences between men and women and between racial groups are appearing in popular culture as genetically driven. Such genetic images encourage stereotypes of the nurturing female, the studious Asian, and the violent African American male' (Nelkin and Lindee 1995: 387). When the differences between the sexes or people of varying races are viewed as innate and genetically predetermined, we risk legitimating inequality against particular groups on the basis of a perceived genetic 'inferiority'. For a feminist political project that strives to recognise the contextual history, location and lived experience of the female subject, the perpetuation of difference as biologically determined fails to acknowledge the role of society in shaping subject constitution. For in order to define the specificities of female subjectivity beyond a universal and abstract concept of the human, feminism critically argues for an understanding of identity that is specific to the question of difference as it is configured within contextual, lived relations of the subject (Diprose 1995: 162). But what we see in the case of the HGP and the VHP is the negation of the specificities of bodily difference at the level of the social, and lived relations of the subject. When humanity is reduced to genetic code or flesh is made into data, it becomes reproducible and interchangeable, challenging both the integrity of the human subject, and the specificity of gender difference.

In her critique of the standardisation of the body for use as an object of exchange, Waldby writes about the analogy made by feminist scholar Rosi Braidotti between pornographic representation and the coding of the body. For Waldby, both pornography and the VHP are images that represent women in violent and hostile ways (Waldby 2000: 32). In a new economy of representation associated with digital technology, Wadlby finds the VHP disturbing because it can perfectly re-create the 'look' of the body-as-flesh without acknowledging the once-lived reality of that flesh (Waldby 2000: 28). But the problem with this argument is that it doesn't take into account the way that we experience signs and images in contemporary culture as simulations.

When she argues that the model shapes an understanding of reality, Waldby shares Baudrillard's assertion that the model precedes reality. But her argument differs from Baudrillard's in significant ways. For Waldby, the VHP is an inadequate representation of the body because it lacks grounding in a real life context. Yet she doesn't question what counts as real in a digital era. For Baudrillard, on the other hand, the VHP doesn't mask reality but is indicative of an ultra-reality, whereby the computer-simulated body becomes more real than real for us through the visual tools of science and technology. What is understood to be real in Waldby's case (that is, the fleshy body) is upheld as the true or original source behind the image, rather than the body being understood as an effect of the hyperreal. Furthermore by suggesting that the VHP functions as a technology of control and manipulation of the body, Waldby comes dangerously close to falling back into the binaries of technology, science and masculinity, contra nature, the body and femininity.

In what ways can we rethink posthuman bodies, like those of the VHP, to move beyond 'origins' and 'essentialisms' and dislocate a structural understanding of what the text means (that is, critical theory), in favour of a fatal theory, which proposes that 'representations are the world'? (Smith 2005: 3). Moreover, how might feminism engage with a simulation that abolishes definitive meaning and reduces all political and social events to pre-conceived models? One of the ways we might do this is to conceive of images as 'not the causes or effects of action' but as 'actions in their own right' (Smith 2005: 4). In an economy of symbolic exchange where signs only have value in relation to each other, the VHP is no more or less real than anything else. Instead of reading it against a 'real' body, the VHP can be approached in terms of the sign system that constitutes the current mode of figuring social reality.

Both the VHP and the mapping of the human genome embody the idea of the 'precession of the model' of the third-order simulacra. As a project whose aim is to produce the subject that it sets out to describe, the gene map, in Baudrillard's terms, is already configured: 'the map that precedes the territory…engenders the territory' (Baudrillard 1994: 1). As a model that is always already reproduced, the HGP is a hyperreality that at once signals the loss of reality as well as its possibility. The construction of the genome as the blueprint of human life and origins is complicated by its status as simulation. For the genome's currency no longer resides in the real, but circulates in a system of signs liberated from any referential locus or fixed point of meaning. The potential to undermine and refigure the humanist presuppositions informing the gene project may be located, according to Baudrillard, at the site of the 0:1 configuration of the code.

Generated from the code, the simulation model is thus a virtual entity. As such, the visual cannot be solely understood via the traditional modernist dimensions of space and time. As the new organising principle of contemporary society, the code is not governed by meaning but has no meaning. It carries no vestiges of structure or order through which to purposefully make sense of the world. So rather than saying that there is an 'original' person from which the image of the Visible Human was copied, there is only ever information. The idea that there once existed a real or natural person is an effect produced by simulation models inscribed within the code. The 0:1 of the digital cannot be figured in terms of an oppositional duality, where one term is inscribed with positive value and the other is its negation. Rather the 'bit' carries no meaning, as both presence (1) and absence

(0) exist as positive signals. And it is the endless proliferation of positivity in the operational configuration of the code that denies negativity or the possibility of Otherness.

Underpinning much of the fear about the code is the idea that the essence of humanity is threatened as the body is equated with the machine, or the digital with the gene. Yet by figuring the body as a code script locatable within the larger system of the 0:1 matrix, as Baudrillard does, the collapse in distinctions between genetic code and digital code can operate as an anti-humanist critique of the subject. Fixed formulations of the body and identity are redefined so that the sanctity of human essence and identity are replaced by the multiple configurations, interconnections and embodiments between organic and technological systems that define the posthuman.

By suggesting that the real is that which is replicable, Baudrillard offers an alternative construction of the self that does not rely on origin stories. According to Baudrillard, the assumptions underlying what was once constructed as the real—the notion of an originary or essential characteristic, as opposed to the dialectical Other of representation—has been replaced within a culture of simulation by 'miniaturized cells, matrices, and memory banks…reproduced an indefinite number of times' (Baudrillard 1994: 2). It is in a culture of endless replication that the relation between representation and reality escapes being positioned as irrevocably opposed. Instead, reality and representation collapse into each other, opening up a condition of possibility to refigure our understanding of the body as it is transformed by its encounters with technology, and vice-versa. In order to explore these ideas further, I want to look at what is perhaps the ultimate manifestation of the body as code: the clone.

The Posthuman Clone

One of the greatest anxieties appearing in popular press accounts of biotechnological advances is the cloning of human beings. But mixed with this fear is a morbid fascination regarding when and how this might happen, as well as the effects of cloning on who we think we are. Clones are the product of asexual reproduction. Yet, this does not wholly distinguish clones as unique from other organisms. As Nicholas Agar explains, there are a number of organisms that are produced asexually, which are not clones, such as male drone bees (Agar 2002: 21). So what is it, then, that characterises the clone? A clone is genetically, 'an exact duplicate of the organism from which it originated' (Agar 2002: 21). This is quite a different scenario from human reproduction, whereby the genetic material of a man and woman fuse to produce a unique individual. Since Dolly the sheep showed that animal cloning is possible, our attentions have turned to realising the fantasy of cloning ourselves. Indeed, there are regular claims in the press that this has been achieved, although none have yet been substantiated. Our preoccupation with the clone is not surprising, given our hyperreal existence where copies abound, and codes and models inform our perception of the world. The clone can be read as another manifestation of Baudrillard's claim that the subject has been displaced by the object at the point where the sign–origin relationship collapses. When subjects disappear through the circuits of the genetic code, digital information and communication forms, they risk becoming infinitely replaceable commodities in capitalism's wheel.

In films, literature and news reporting, cloning is often represented as a horror story or science fiction fantasy whereby the status of the human subject and identity is threatened (Huxford 2000: 187, Ferreira 2005). In writing about narratives of cloning in a number of well-known books, Maria Ferreira makes the following observation:

> From Aldous Huxley's *Brave New World* (1932) to Nancy Freedman's *Joshua Son of None* (1973) and Ira Levin's *The Boys from Brazil* (1976), Evelyn Lief's *The Clone Rebellion* (1980), and Michael Marshall Smith's *Spares* (1988), fictional representations of human cloning have been predominantly negative, arousing feelings of deep-seated horror in many readers. These and many other books and films have been largely responsible for spreading frightening visions of armies of clones taking over the earth. Indeed, misconceptions about cloning abound, producing heavily distorted pictures in the popular imagination of what might be an impending reality (Ferreira 2005: 4).

One of the reasons why the clone is horrifying is because it threatens the uniqueness of each individual. If you can make a clone of yourself, then who is the 'real' you? Will your clone look like you? Act like you? Or possibly come to replace you? In order to step outside of these entrenched perceptions of the clone as threatening and fascinating, I will to turn to another artwork by Patricia Piccinini, which I believe offers a welcome intervention into the often rigid utopian versus dystopian narratives of bioengineering practices, such as cloning, that appear in the popular media. What I want to show is how the clone stands as another posthuman form that calls into question our conventional understandings of subjectivity and reality.

In *Still Life with Stem Cells* (2002) Piccinini has created a contemplative and tender domestic scene in which a girl sits cross-legged on a large, carpeted area of the gallery floor among an array of indeterminate, biomorphic forms (see figure 5). These fleshy lumps display a humanness, an evocation of warm-blooded life. Their folds and wrinkles are reminiscent of human skin, textured with bumps, hairs and freckles. Veins and tiny capillaries criss-cross below the skin's surface. These creatures elude classification within the natural order of things, failing to resemble any known organism. And while they cannot be defined, they seem familiar. Going by the title, these forms envision the products of stem cell research. Cradling one of these inhuman 'lumps' in her arm while affectionately gazing at the others, the girl displays a maternalistic love for these mutant creatures. This rendering of domestic harmony could well be construed as perpetuating a myth of cloning technologies as part of everyday life.

The carpeted floor renders the sterility of the white-walled gallery homely and welcoming. Carpet evokes the domestic, the private, a feminised and nurturing space. This non-threatening space allows the viewer to conceptualise the stem cell creatures as something more than the failed monsters of technoscience. Removed from the scientific laboratory and its associations with masculinity and control, these products of biotechnological manipulation appear normal, a part of our everyday existence. There is an irresistible compulsion to touch, to sit down among these posthuman forms.

Such imagery runs counter to feminist theories that have been largely critical of the effects of new technologies on women's social power and subjectivity (Daly 1998). A radical feminist politic in particular has identified cloning technology as the realisation of 'the classic patriarchal myth of single parenthood by the male', which serves to devalue, if not eliminate, female reproductive power (Corea 1985: 260). Although cloning technologies have been assessed by radical feminism as incompatible with a feminist political project, other feminist critics have identified the potential of the clone to disable dominant formations of identity and subjecthood.

Applying her anthropological lens to cinematic representations of the clone, Debbora Battaglia suggests that the doubling process of cloning, as seen in a range of films including *The Terminator* (1984), *Jurassic Park* (1993) and *The Sixth Day* (2000), extends the cultural boundaries of selfhood and identity. It is through an examination of social exchange that Battaglia refocuses cloning debates; suggesting we consider 'which forms of social exchange and which patterns of *relation* set upon social connection, violate social futures, and which beget and elicit these in particular cultural and historical locations' (Battaglia 2001: 506). Here, Battaglia draws on Donna Haraway's examination of social relationships, or more accurately, 'socio-technical alliances' that reformulate the relationship between the human and non-human so to position the non-human actants as active players in the social process (Haraway 1997: 7). Both seek to examine the process of relation, rather than preordained structures of meaning, to make sense of the clone.

Motivated by the collapse of the natural and the technological, Piccinini,

Figure 5. Patricia Piccinini, *Still Life with Stem Cells* (2002), silicone, polyurethane, clothing, human hair, dimensions variable. Photo: Graham Baring.

too, presents us with a vision of collective life that revises traditional models of the relationship between the human and non-human. By looking at the interplay and connections between living and non-living forms, it is possible to configure cloning technologies beyond simple narratives of cloning as 'good' or 'bad'. Writing in the tradition of Heidegger, Latour and Haraway, social theorist Adrian McKenzie adopts this kind of approach to examine the processes by which technology is realised in collective life (2002). What he terms 'transduction' emphasises the linkages, interplay and points of engagement between the conventionally divergent realities of the human and non-human. Enlightenment concerns with identities, essences and origins are replaced by an examination of the network of relations between living and non-living things (McKenzie 2002: 52). Rather than view the organic and inorganic as separate domains, McKenzie suggests these distinctions dissolve in the process through which the products of biotechnology are realised. The cloning process co-implicates living (stem cells) and non-living (gene databases, agar plates, pipettes) elements so that technological and non-technological elements cannot be clearly differentiated.

The enmeshing of human and non-human elements creates alternative paradigms through which to understand the techno–human relationship. The connection between the girl and the lumps is ambivalent. Is she representative of a non-genetically engineered human, contrasted against the inhuman forms? Does she stand for the human self, opposed to the non-human Other? Rather than locate the girl as real and human, opposed to the inhuman lumps, Piccinini highlights that the girl, too, exists only as a simulation. This artificial, silicone construct simulates a humanness in her gently pulled-back ponytail, the tiny nails on her hands, the subtle colouration of her skin, her thoughtful smile. Like the lumps, the girl is a silicone simulation.

Piccinini hints at a possible biological relationship between the stem cell 'family' and in doing so she challenges the idea that techno–human engagements are adversarial. Perhaps the lumps are the girl's failed clones. That is, experiments that didn't quite work. Equally plausible is a scenario whereby these life forms are the by-products of scientific research to grow a heart or a liver or an arm from the girl's body cells. They would share the same DNA, being clones from the same genetic matter, only realised differently. By shifting our terms of reference away from an oppositional model of subjecthood, Piccinini's posthuman images disrupt a frame of meaning that positions cloning as the horror of the self realised as a double. Difference is no longer absolute. Rather, the relationship between the characters is one of degrees of difference.

The collapse between the natural and the artificial, the real and the virtual, is a recurrent theme in Piccinini's oeuvre. In another work called *Game Boys Advanced* (2002), Piccinini addresses the discourses of cloning and genetic manipulation more explicitly. In the tradition of the mannequin or the automaton, she has created a silicone sculpture of two young boy clones (see figure 6). Disconcertingly life-like, the boys are casually dressed in everyday street-wear—sneakers, track pants and t-shirts. They lean with their backs against the gallery wall, heads bowed together over a gameboy. One plays while the other looks on. Both are immersed in the world on the screen, oblivious to their gallery surrounds.

A closer inspection reveals that something is not quite right about these boys. Their hair is grey and their skin is sagging and covered in sun-spots. The boys are in a state of accelerated aging. The wrinkles around their eyes, neck and hands belong to someone 50 or 60 years their senior. Their translucent, papery skin evokes a grandparent's cheek, rather than the firmness and flawlessness of youth. While the children appear to be identical twins, the 'advanced' state they occupy indicates that they are not the offspring of natural reproductive practices but the products of cloning technologies gone awry. For Baudrillard, much of the anxiety created by cloning has

Figure 6. Patricia Piccinini, *Game Boys Advanced* (2002) (detail), silicone, polyurethane, clothing, human hair, dimensions variable. Photo: Graham Baring.

come about because of our changing perceptions of sex and reproduction in a biotechnological age. In his essay 'The Hell of the Same'[5] Baudrillard reflects on the consequences of a form of reproduction that relies on the propagation of genes from one cell:

> Father and mother are gone, but their disappearance, far from widening an aleatory freedom for the subject, instead leaves the way clear for a *matrix known as a code.* No more mother, no more father: just a matrix. And it is this matrix, this genetic code, which is destined to 'give birth', from now till eternity, in an operational mode from which all chance sexual elements have been expunged (Baudrillard 1999: 115).

Biotechnological modes of reproduction see the 'disassociation of reproduction from sex', replacing the mother with the matrix in a commonly voiced concern for the negation of the body within the technoscientific landscape (Sofia 1992: 14–6). As the product of the replication of genetic material from an individual cell, the clone is not forged through the mixing of parental DNA. As the exact replication of the genetic information contained in a single cell, the clone is the model of simulation par excellence—an accumulation of positivities that is described by Baudrillard as the 'reiteration of the same: 1+1+1+1, etc.' (Baudrillard 1999: 116). And it is this possibility for serial propagation that differentiates the clone from the twin. For it is true that identical twins share the same DNA, yet unlike the clone, twins are the product of two—a mother and a father. Compare this to cloning, where sex between two people isn't necessary.

Yet is a fear of the clone based on the eradication of procreation between the two sexes unfounded? After all, sex isn't necessary for the birth of many children these days. In the Western world, artificially assisted reproductive techniques like IVF and intracytoplasmic sperm injection (ICSI) have become commonplace procedures that are viewed by many as just as legitimate forms of reproduction as the old-fashioned sex act. It is no longer seen as strange for reproduction to be separated from sex and vice-versa. Nor has it been for some time, says Baudrillard, who highlights that the sexual revolution and contraception have already challenged the assumption that sexual activity is determined solely by reproduction (Baudrillard 2000: 10).

What is more unnerving than the disassociation of sex from reproduction in cloning technologies is, for Baudrillard, the disassociation of life from death. He writes that 'the question concerning cloning is the question of immortality' (Baudrillard 2000: 3). One of the ways that humans and other organic life forms are distinguished from inorganic matter is through the cycle of life and death. If humans can be cloned, then an individual need never die. The 'self' can be endlessly remade or their life endlessly prolonged by spare body parts supplied by clones of oneself.

Cloning is, as Valerie Hartouni effectively articulates, 'a question about identity that assumes and invokes while also signaling a shift in prevailing cultural beliefs about who and what "we" are' (Hartouni 1997: 112). The parameters of what counts as natural, and what technological interventions are acceptable, depend upon changing configurations of culture. Certainly, as Hartouni points out, cloning is not the first example of shifting boundaries to challenge the constitution of the human. By alerting us to the most common objections to cloning—the history of eugenics, the commodification of the body and human life, the disruption of generational kinship structures, and the dissolution of identity and individuality—Hartouni reminds us that the controversies surrounding cloning are not new, but a continuation of a history of engagements between humans and technology that disturb and reset the boundaries of what it means to be human (Hartouni 1997: chapter seven).

What the feminist interventions of Hartouni, Battaglia and Haraway illuminate is that the clone does not necessarily violate subjectivity, inasmuch as it is a product of a particular cultural and historical moment where our understandings of what it means to be human—the body and history, as well as identity and difference—are being radically redefined. The potency of the clone for feminism resides with its disruption of a dominant narrative of the human, which in turn, enables formulations of the subject beyond an identity politics structured in terms of self and Other. A poststructural and postmodern feminist project to revise an Enlightenment model of the subject that privileges masculinity, reason, autonomy and selfhood, is not dissimilar to what Jean Baudrillard proposes in his reading of the clone. Baudrillard conceives the elimination of differences by the sameness of the clone as a replacement of dichotomies of value with pure differences, which cannot find recourse in binary oppositions. A difference construed as the Other of dominant discourse is replaced within the sign system by a difference that functions beyond the limits of signifying practice. Baudrillard's vision of the clone might just serve as a useful tactic for feminism to rethink identity as it is realised through traditional narratives of human identity and essences.

It appears as though the clone displaces the body as the locus of a unified individual in favour of the code, in much the same way as the HGP remakes the body as genetic information. Yet while the HGP miniaturises the body, the clone extends and propagates a singular cell to create a human form. It is the cell that exists as the prosthesis of the body. Unlike the external prosthesis of the mechanical era, the digital age sees the prosthesis internalised (Baudrillard 1999: 119). By doing away with the subject/object divide in the form of the clone, Baudrillard positions the subject within a hell of sameness 'doomed to self-metastasis, to pure repetition' (Baudrillard 1999: 122). Although the clone signals the disappearance of the autonomous and unique self, I don't think that this means that we can't speak about what it means to be a subject in a biotechnological age. Humanity isn't necessarily over and we aren't all destined to an existence where zombie-like clones inhabit the earth.

Neither am I convinced that Baudrillard's insights can only offer us a pessimistic account of cloning, as it has been suggested (Ferreira 2005: 24). An ambiguity pervades Baudrillard's vision of the clone. When he tells us that subjects come to occupy an indeterminate space as neither self nor Other through biotechnological processes such as cloning, we might begin to think about subjectivity outside of dialectical frames (Baudrillard 1999: 122). Despite the bleakness that accompanies the doom and hell of sameness, I suggest that it is through the disappearance of the 'authentic' self that new modalities of the subject may emerge to accommodate a proliferation of differences beyond a dichotomous system of values. For it is only through radical Otherness that one may escape the Hell of the Same; an Otherness constituted without reference to a self—not as a negativity but a point of excess that fractures the coherence and primacy of being.

Piccinini's artwork, like Baudrillard's theories, doesn't seek to represent cloning as the demise of the individual through technology. Nor does it judge cloning technologies to be a threat to the sanctity of the human. These clones are more akin to what Donna Haraway has theorised as 'natural technical entities—human, technological, and organic—with problematic selfhood boundaries' (Haraway 1997: 71). Certainly, the potential consequences of cloning are alluded to in the premature ageing of the boys. In her catalogue essay for the Piccinini retrospective *Respectology: The World According to Patricia Piccinini*, curator Juliana Engberg recognises the ambiguous response that the cloned boys elicit. She reminds us that 'cloning has the potential for great medical advances, but this medical frontier looks uncanny and unsettling and still unresolved from the point of view of these new replicants' (Engberg 2002: 44).

Amid the uncertainty that surrounds cloning technologies, Piccinini refrains from presenting us with the horror of the Frankenstein myth. As we watch the children engrossed in their game, we accept them, acknowledging the shifting status of the body and identity with the advent of new communications and biotechnologies. The boys are neither like us nor unlike us, but are indicative of the confusion between nature and technology, self and Other that typifies simulation society. It is at the site of Piccinini's art practice that we might begin to think of technoscientific representations as enabling new formulations of the subject beyond an identity politics structured in terms of self and Other. This is not to deny the issues raised by cloning such as the patenting of life by multinational corporations and the risk to biodiversity (Haraway 1997: 60–1, Tokar 2001). Rather, Piccinini's clones are emblematic of our current cultural condition where the status of the human, identity and the body are no longer fixed.

Haraway and Baudrillard

By way of conclusion, I want to return to the theories of two central figures in the debates about techno–human relationships and the status of the human—Donna Haraway and Jean Baudrillard. Given that both have featured significantly throughout this book, summarising the affinities and differences in their thinking at this point serves as a way of promoting greater dialogue between their ideas. In light of the posthuman texts I have explored here, there are various points of connection between Haraway's writing on nature and Baudrillard's notion of simulation. For both authors, there is little question that the subject is reformulated through the interfaces and interconnections of technological interaction. Despite their different approaches to the subject's relationship with technological worlds, both agree that the rearticulation of the organism blurs the boundaries between virtual and real, exposing the paradox of scientific fact grounded in non-origins.

Haraway and Baudrillard also share a commitment to reassessing the status of the natural, origins and the real, which tend to be legitimated through processes of signification based in dialectical logic. Each theorist interrogates the kind of oppositional thinking that has informed and limited an understanding of representation. They reorient the question of difference so that it becomes one of degrees instead of absolutes. For Haraway, difference is disturbed by challenging the definitions and boundaries structured by binary thought. She maintains a definitive semiotic relation between the production and circulation of signs, and their location in material reality. In Baudrillard's writings, the challenge to ontological presuppositions depends upon a free play of meaning beyond signification that interrogates notions of the real.

Perhaps the most significant distinction to be made between Haraway and Baudrillard's understandings of science and culture is located at the site of 'material–semiotic practice'. A term invented and used by Haraway, 'material–semiotic practice' is a way of configuring the world that is associated with the collapse of the material and the metaphorical, and the reassertion of boundaries through which science is understood. To put this term into context, for example, Haraway's transgenic mice 'inhabit an unfixed but not infinite material–semiotic field where possible lives are at stake' (Haraway 1997: 119). In making this claim, Haraway reiterates the need to recognise the relation between the material and the cultural, reality and its representation. The free play of signification that Baudrillard endorses is only partly acknowledged by Haraway, for whom materiality operates as a limit point to making sense of the world.

Both theorists acknowledge the shift in contemporary social operations from an industrial age typified by consumption and production to an emerging order of digitality, media and information. As those familiar with Haraway's writing would know, this shift is what she terms an 'informatics of domination' (Haraway 1985: 80), in later works theorised as the 'New World Order, Inc.' (Haraway 1997: 6–7). In the process of defining this new order of information culture, Haraway lists the various changes in thinking that have occurred in the transition from industrial to information society. And while she names simulation as the mode of figuring reality that replaces representation, Haraway does not ask what it might mean for our conceptualisation of reality when simulation becomes the organising principle of society. In another context, Haraway claims that a 'higher order structure' such as the genome 'is a figure of the "already written" future' (Haraway 1997: 100). This echoes clearly Baudrillard's third order of the simulacra, where the precession of the model already determines the mapping of the genome. Although Haraway refers to key Baudrillardian concepts like obsolescence, inertia, surface and simulation in her definition of a new cultural moment (Haraway 1985: 80), she resists engaging with such terms as they are used by Baudrillard to contest the ontological grounding of traditional value systems. Instead, Haraway maintains a notion of the political located within the material and ideological.

Instead of interpreting the genome as a simulation devoid of signifying power, Haraway asserts that figurations such as the transgenic Oncomouse and genome map can tell us something about the biotechnological world, as it is constructed through the intersections of materiality, cultural fiction, biology and politics. Indeed, the strength of her argument resides in her recognition of the complex tensions between these domains, and the collapse of the distinctions between nature and culture, science and society, materiality and representation that define and determine the workings of culture. But at the same time, by upholding the primacy of signifying practice when reading and interpreting the products of science, reality is secured as something that exists 'outside of' representation.

As the discourses of biotechnology and information technology reshape our understandings of what it means to be human, feminists have critically considered the implications of digital and virtual representational practices that redefine the status of the body. For Haraway, there is always an embodied reality situated within a material context, despite her recognition of the numerous connections, affiliates and hybrid associations between the technological and the natural that usurp the fixity of such categories. Hers is a socialist feminism underpinned by an assumed relation between the image and the real, where representations shape meaning and make realities. These realities are located in, and impact on, the social, political and cultural frameworks in which they circulate. In this regard, Haraway differs significantly from Baudrillard on questions of representation and the body because for Baudrillard there is no truth or definitive meaning behind either in a culture of simulation.

Baudrillard's writings and Piccinini's images call into question the structural equation between reality and representation that informs the practices of reading and analysing the products of scientific discourses. Representations of technoscience are traditionally interpreted as constructing reality, as well as functioning as a mirror or reflection of the real. While this approach maintains a relationship between representation and the real, both Baudrillard and Piccinini contest the possibility of constructing an equivalence between the image and reality, as it is these very terms which can no longer be upheld in a system of signs that ensures the image has no definitive meaning. By tapping into the confused cultural space of simulation, Piccinini offers us a site of ambiguity, a transitional place where established dichotomies are no longer sustainable. The potency of her posthuman figurations for feminist thinking lies in an engagement with contemporary simulation culture, which functions to create new possibilities for what a subject might be in technoculture.

Conclusion

Throughout *Cyborgs and Barbie Dolls*, the themes of techno–human relations and simulation culture have been pursued to advocate a new approach to images, reality and subjectivity in the context of twenty-first century technologies. Using a selection of visual texts, this book has explored the ways that the posthuman encourages new imaginings for women; imaginings that celebrate the ambiguities and contradictions of a posthuman existence as it is represented in popular culture. I have resisted interpreting female identity in terms of origins, essentialisms or the natural body, preferring to favour a transformative approach that circumvents dialectical value systems. Baudrillard's theory of simulation based on non-origins has provided the framework to consider the gendered self at the collapse of the sign/origin relationship. Simulation culture, Baudrillard argues, is fleeting, indeterminate, and never grounded in a real.

One of the central concerns arising from any study of the popular is the ephemeral nature of cultural texts and trends. Since writing this book, it's likely that Marilyn Manson's monstrous posthuman appeal has been superseded by other fads in the affections of many young consumers. Barbie's number one status is under attack from the rival Bratz dolls, which have captured the imagination of girls with their streetwise attire and savvy attitude. Even the concerns of Piccinini's *Protein Lattice* and *Still Life with Stem Cells* have 'evolved' along with new directions in biotechnological research. One of her more recent projects is a series of sculptures titled *Natures Little Helpers* (2005) that reflects on the symbiotic relations between humans and non-humans.

Despite the high turnover of signs and images in a world of hyperconsumerism, an understanding of our engagements with popular culture doesn't need to take the form of rampant consumption followed by the sheepish rejection of a dying trend. Neither does an analysis of popular forms need grounding in something more substantial to ensure their longevity and legitimate their value. Dick Hebdige has described the process of textual engagement as an attempt to 'walk the flickering line between images and things but not, I'd like to think, just any old images, any old things—choosing rather those images which burn for me, those things that I think really matter' (Hebdige 1988: 12). These cultural moments become part of an inter-textual circuit, the circulation of signifiers that exist and derive value in relation to each other. This is the sign system of simulation that Baudrillard speaks about when he denounces the reference to forms, causes and origins in favour of the recurrent circulation of signs against each other.

At the start of this book, I raised the issue of reality in feminist narratives of the posthuman in order to ask 'how might rethinking the relationship between reality and images function as a strategically useful tactic for feminist engagements with posthuman representations?' By questioning the status of the real in feminist scholarship on the posthuman, I sought to offer new ways of engaging with representations of the posthuman that move beyond identity toward alternative formulations of the subject. En route to answering that question, I critically reviewed the feminist debates regarding the relationship between women and technology.

Feminist critiques of technology revealed the associations between masculinity and technology as perpetuating men's domination over women. In response to the notion that women and technology are incompatible, many contemporary theorists have critically considered the affirmations and pleasures to be experienced from an alliance of the technological and the feminine. In reviewing these debates, I chose not to view technology as either 'good' or 'bad' for women. Instead, I suggested that alternative interpretations of women's relationship with technology were needed to account for the ambiguity and contradictory nature of posthuman representations. An overview of feminist writings on technology allowed me to explore the question of bodily boundaries in an information age, and this in turn, led to an examination of the posthuman's potential to generate new bodily imaginings.

As indicated by Sherry Turkle's study of computer culture, our engagements with technology promote alternative means of thinking about the self. Yet I argued that throughout Turkle's scholarship, a distinction remains between what is technological and what is human. In such accounts, the status of the real contra the virtual, the self versus the Other, remains intact. How, then, can representation operate to disavow, rather than legitimate, the meanings ascribed to the techno–human relationship? The substantive body of feminist critique on the subject and technology motivated me to develop an account of the posthuman that focused beyond signification and the limits of the real.

Chapter two asked what a posthuman, post-gender existence might mean for women in a current media age where the idea of the self and reality is under attack. Jean Baudrillard's theory of simulation was introduced as the conceptual framework through which to consider this question. It was within the representational economy of simulation culture that I located posthuman figurations as exceeding signification. That chapter argued for the generation of alternative understandings of the relationship between bodies, technology and representation through the collapse of the association between an image and its referent. The collapse of origin-derived meaning has been a key theme throughout *Cyborgs and Barbie Dolls*. If, as I have argued, new forms of the visual demand an alternative understanding of the real, then the possibility arises to think about the subject beyond a system of dialectics. By putting an end to stable oppositions, simulation promotes the generation of diverse subject formations not confined to the rule of opposites. Accordingly, the idea that an original underpins our understanding of images, the body, or subjectivity, is disturbed.

We saw earlier how simulation offers a platform to re-engage with the question of popular images from a feminist perspective. The process of charting the debates on representation, from 1970s feminist film aesthetics through poststructural critiques of ideology, has indicated a diversity of responses from feminist thought. While contemporary feminist visual and media studies theorists share with Baudrillard a commitment to approaching images in different ways, they still interpret them in critical terms—as having meaning, albeit multiple ones. In my contribution to the debate Baudrillard's concept of the simulacra is used to argue that images can operate outside of this representational paradigm, offering a way of approaching the posthuman and the gendered self as transformative.

It was through an analysis of Barbie that I applied my thinking about images as transformational to feminist debates on women, technology and the body. Chapter three developed the themes of plasticity and play to explore the possibilities that Barbie might hold for new formulations of selfhood. In looking at such an established icon of ideal femininity, I questioned the feminist interpretation of Barbie as a bad role model for girls. Through a historical reading of the mannequin and contemporary understandings of Barbie, the deep-rooted associations between femininity, consumption and the body were exposed. Locating Barbie in this trajectory provided a point from which to rethink this long-standing approach to the commodification of femininity.

Rather than reading Barbie as a fixed ideal of femininity, I positioned her as a posthuman precursor, or a type of plastic transformer that embodies the potential for identity to be mutable and unfixed. In Barbie's plastic body, transformation becomes a contamination of forms; a rejection of a stable female identity through the disruption of oppositions such as self and Other, subject and object. When Debbora Battaglia writes of the difficulty of representing 'the nonsteady state of selfhood in different cultural situations, and varying degrees and relations of determinacy', she highlights the importance of new modes of theorising the self where the distinction between things collapse and take on new forms (Battaglia 1995: 1).

This collapse is most apparent, I argued, at the site of the body as 'cultural plastic'. Our engagements with technology in everyday life challenge the perception of the body as the limit point of subjectivity. Certain feminist critiques of plastic surgery, fitness clubs and anti-aging products stress the role of such cultural practices in subordinating women. Others focus on the agency women express relative to such practices. I suggest that positioning women as 'victims' or 'agents' limits the ways that subjectivities can be envisioned through a range of possible modalities of the body. Posing the plastic body as a transformative potentiality allows us to move beyond the determinism of a materialist 'return to the body'.

Chapter four turned to Marilyn Manson and his depiction on the cover of the CD *Mechanical Animals* to consider the idea that social and biological differences are erased in posthuman representations. This question of difference has been central to feminist studies of the monstrous, and, like the monster, the posthuman is a boundary figure. An exploration of feminist engagements with the monstrous provided a model through which to establish the continuities and discontinuities between posthuman images and those of the monster. By way of such comparison, the limits of feminist theorisations of the monstrous to interpreting the posthuman were exposed. Posthuman figurations were found to differ from their predecessors by residing within a digital economy of representation that disrupts the organic potency of the monster as described by feminism. Theorising Manson in terms of Baudrillard's concept of catastrophe, I approached the posthuman in a way that demonstrated how digital images promote a proliferation of differences to replace dialectical value systems.

From the space of tension between the real and the image, *Cyborgs and Barbie Dolls* sees subjecthood in terms of a difference that goes beyond oppositional thinking. It is at this site of ambiguity that posthuman figurations such as Manson exceed their role as signifiers. The collapse between image and reality was also shown to offer new possibilities for understanding contemporary biotechnological myths. Contrasting Barthes' structural analysis of myth to Baudrillard's order of the sign provided a means to engage with difference as it was represented by the posthuman. Moreover, it illuminated the difficulty of sustaining a theory of myth as the naturalisation of culture in terms of ideology and semiotics. While Barthes' analysis of myth exists within a pre-determined regime of signs to position the viewing subject, posthuman images exist in an order of simulation where the image has no relation to the real. By existing in the context of digital media, Manson creates new ways of thinking about gender and representation.

So, too, do posthuman images offer a way of understanding ourselves in the accelerated flows of media and communications. In chapter five, I argued for a model of the body as a posthuman interface that takes pleasure in negotiating diverse media forms. Reading one of the images from the TDK advertising campaign 'Evolve to TDK', I challenged the ways of thinking about the subject in the media as either an active or passive respondent in the act of information exchange. By arguing for the body as an interface, I pursued a strategy by which women might engage with images of the posthuman beyond the spectres of identity politics. Conceiving of the body as an interface system offers an alternative to conceptualising the virtual and the real as oppositional terms, which in turn changes our understanding of the relationship between women and communication technologies.

In the final chapter, I returned to the theme of the dissolution of the natural in order to consider images of the posthuman in the context of a biotechnological age. Until this point, posthuman reworkings of the subject extended the boundaries of the body. Posthuman qualities of plasticity, catastrophic acceleration and interfacing challenged particular understandings of corporeal identity by going beyond perceived borders of the body. An exploration of genome narratives in this chapter examined the inverse—the cultural trend toward the miniaturisation of the body and reduction of subjecthood to the level of the cell and the gene. A critique of the Human Genome Project website showed how such inversions of the body operate and what the implications of such reformulations are on notions of identity and difference.

Feminist critiques of science have established a framework through which to approach the nexus of scientific knowledge, representational practice and subject formation. While recognising the importance of such critiques, I argued for something more than a structuralist approach to gene narratives. What we see in images such as *Protein Lattice* is a slippage between a scientific, empiricist project grounded in an objective world-view and a simulation culture that disowns origins. By occupying the site between the original and its representation, between nature and technology, the artworks of Patricia Piccinini complicate the myth of origins that science strives to uphold.

One of the central aims of this book has been to explore the benefits that arise from the dialogue between feminist thought and the theories of Jean Baudrillard. In concluding, it highlighted the parallels and differences between Baudrillard's ideas and those of Donna Haraway. Baudrillard offers feminist engagements with the techno–human relationship a way of conceptualising social relations beyond dialectical logic. His understandings of the order of the image serve as an incisive tool for feminist analyses of contemporary culture like mass media, communications and information technologies. By contesting the categorical distinctions between the real and illusion, self and Other, origin and sign, Baudrillard effectively denies the possibility of origins, realities or essentialisms in the reading of contemporary images. In problematising concepts such as identity, reality and the body in the context of simulation, *Cyborgs and Barbie Dolls* has evaluated how such displacements may be understood. It has also envisioned new possibilities for theorising posthuman images in a society of simulation.

Notes

Chapter 1

1 I offer a more comprehensive assessment of Donna Haraway's cyborg figuration in my discussions of the women and technology debates later in this chapter.

2 A substantive theory defines technology as a force that shapes the ways that society and self experience the world. For a discussion of 'substantive' and 'instrumental' approaches to technology, see Feenberg, Andrew. (1991). *Critical Theory of Technology*, New York and Oxford: Oxford University Press.

3 The term 'substrate' is used by Katherine Hayles to connote the medium through which information is made meaningful. She states: 'for information to exist, it must *always* be instantiated in a medium, whether that medium is the page from the *Bell Laboratories Journal* on which Shannon's equations are printed, or computer-generated topological maps used by the Human Genome Project, or the cathode ray tube on which virtual worlds are imagined' (Hayles 1999: 13). In Hayles, N. Katherine. (1999). *How We Became Posthuman: Virtual Bodies in Cybernetics, Literature and Informatics*, Chicago and London: University of Chicago Press.

4 According to Hayles, the posthuman is predicated on the formation of subject constitution via the human relationship with technology that does not necessarily require the invasion of the corporeal by non-biological components (Hayles 1999: 4). This is in keeping with the function of the figuration as a site for re-imagining subjectivities that does not demand a physical transformation at the actual site of the body.

5 Sadie Plant's reading of the convergence of woman and machine is informed by Luce Irigaray's politics of a productive feminine difference, and more specifically, her writings on the mimetic qualities of woman.

6 MOOs, chat rooms, Second Life, and other online role play games perform similar functions to MUDs, with respect to the reconfiguration of individual and collective identity in virtual space.

Chapter 2

1 This book's emphasis is not on Baudrillard's early Marxist-inspired semiological examinations of the circulation and operation of sign systems in society. It is Baudrillard's later approach to the production of the social order in terms of the simulation effect that is of interest to this study of the posthuman.

2 To make his point about the strategy of deterrence as the mode by which simulation functions against reality to signal the death of the real, Baudrillard uses the well-documented example of Disneyland. In Baudrillard, Jean. (1994). *Simulacra and Simulation*, (Sheila Faria Glaser, trans.), Michigan: University of Michigan Press, 12ff.

3 For a lucid introduction to the history of simulation and its contemporary theoretical incarnations (including the theories of Baudrillard alongside those of Debord, Eco and Virilio), see Cubitt, Sean. (2001). *Simulation and Social Theory*, London, Thousand Oaks, New Delhi: Sage Publications.

4 While Baudrillard presents the orders of the image sequentially, the introduction of a new order does not necessitate the abolition of the old. Instead, they may function simultaneously, with particular orders constituting the dominant schema during their corresponding cultural eras. Baudrillard explains these formal distinctions in terms of particles, whereby the discovery of a new particle 'does not replace those discovered earlier: it simply joins their ranks, takes its place in a hypothetical series' (Baudrillard 1999: 5). In Baudrillard, Jean. (1999). *The Transparency of Evil: Essays on Extreme Phenomena*, (James Benedict, trans.), London and New York: Verso.

5 While the camera obscura was developed in the Renaissance, the first documentation of the optical principles underpinning the camera obscura is to be found in the writings of Aristotle. This knowledge was passed on through eleventh-century Arab scholars to form the basis of the viewing technologies of the Quattracento, as explained in Gersheim, Helmut. (1965). *A Concise History of Photography*, London: Thames and Hudson, 10–11.

6 David Macey observes that 'the idea of modernity always implies that of a break with or departure from something earlier, and "modern" is often used as the opposite of "traditional"' (Macey 2000: 259). Macey reminds us of the different traditions of the new by distinguishing between historical understandings of modernity in the Renaissance, seventeenth-century enlightenment period, and modernity of the nineteenth century. See Macey, David. (2000). *The Penguin Dictionary of Critical Theory*, London and New York: Penguin, 259–60.

7 Benjamin has portrayed the modern city, with its crowds, speed and urban flows in terms of the shock of new stimuli upon the *flâneur* as viewing subject in Benjamin, Walter. (1968a). 'On Some Motifs in Baudelaire', in Walter Benjamin, *Illuminations*, (Harry Zohn, trans.), New York: Harcourt, Brace and World, 176–7.

8 The gendered distinctions between public and private space are explored by

Griselda Pollock in the context of art produced by male and female artists of modernity. See the chapter 'Modernity and the Spaces of Femininity' in Pollock, Griselda. (1988). *Vision and Difference: Femininity, Feminism and, Histories of Art*, London and New York: Routledge, 50–90.

9 See the argument of cyberfeminists as outlined in chapter one for the ways in which Internet technologies have reconceptualised bodies and corporeality.

10 In a feminist methodological tactic to refigure gendered stereotypes of women and consumption, Meaghan Morris' analysis of the space of the contemporary shopping mall bypasses an interpretation of the act of consumption in terms of the objects consumed by women, to instead consider the 'unique sense of place' created within the modernist space (Morris 1993: 318). This contemporary redressing of a female relationship to modernity signals a shift in conceptions of the female observer as consumer, favouring instead to identify the ambivalence and indeterminate relationship of women with the spaces of consumption. See Morris, Meaghan. (1993). 'Things to do with Shopping Centres', in Simon During (ed.), *The Cultural Studies Reader*, London and New York: Routledge, 295–319.

11 At the same time that photography was being heralded as an indexical tool for capturing an accurate and objective depiction of the world, it was employed to create pictorial effects through manipulation of the image by using expressive qualities such as light, posing, soft focus and composition. Influenced by art practice, this use of photography created an image, rather than reflecting a given reality. See Bartram, Michael. (1985). *The Pre-Raphaelite Camera: Aspects of Victorian Photography*, London: Weidenfeld and Nicolson. Yet despite its non-realist tendencies, this type of photography still maintained an experience of vision predicated on a relationship between reality and representation, as noted in Sontag, Susan. (1977). *On Photography*, New York: Farrar, Straus and Giroux, pp. 5–6.

12 Feminists such as Braidotti denounce Baudrillard's nihilistic trend toward the implosion of differences in favour of Deleuze's dynamic and affirmative politics of the molecular and multiple as a way of figuring the female subject without origins. See Braidotti, Rosi. (1994b) 'Toward a New Nomadism: Feminist Deleuzian Tracks; or, Metaphysics and Metabolism', in Constantin V. Boundas and Dorothea Olkowski (eds.), *Gilles Deleuze and the Theater of Philosophy*, New York and London: Routledge, 159–186. See also Buchanan, Ian and Colebrook, Claire (eds.). (2000). *Deleuze and Feminist Theory*, Edinburgh: Edinburgh University Press, for an introduction to the key writers on Deleuze and feminism.

13 Central to this paradigm shift in practices of reading and reception is Barthes' pivotal essay 'The Death of the Author' in Barthes, Roland. (1977). *Image, Music, Text*, London: Fontana, 142–8.

Chapter 3

1 For more about the fashion doll, which existed prior to the nineteenth-century mannequin and was aimed at adults and used primarily to model clothing designs, see Peers, Juliette. (2004). *The Fashion Doll. From Bébé Jumeau to Barbie*, Oxford and New York: Berg, 15ff

2 This is consistent with Gillian Swanson's argument from chapter two, which highlighted how the female subject of nineteenth-century modernity, who occupied public spaces, was constructed as pathological and deviant. In Swanson, Gillian. (1995). '"Drunk with Glitter": Consuming Spaces and Sexual Geographies', in Sophie Watson and Katherine Gibson (eds.), *Postmodern Cities and Spaces*, Oxford: Blackwell, 80–98.

3 For a more comprehensive examination of the representation of women in surrealist practices, see Belton, Robert J. (1995). *The Beribboned Bomb: The Image of Woman in Male Surrealist Art*, Calgary: University of Calgary Press. Caws, Mary Ann; Kuenzli, Rudolf E.; Raaberg, Gwen (eds.). (1991). *Surrealism and Women*, Cambridge, Massachusetts: MIT Press. Finkelstein, Haim. (1979). *Surrealism and the Crisis of the Object*, Michigan: University Microfilms International. Foster, Hal. (1993). *Compulsive Beauty*, Cambridge, Massachusetts, London, England: MIT Press. Krauss, Rosalind and Livingston, Jane. (1985). *L'Amour Fou: Photography and Surrealism*, New York: Abbeville.

Chapter 4

1 My use and understanding of the terms 'gender' and 'sex' are consistent with these theories.

2 Zakiya Hanafi observes the early associations between God and monsters 'as an indication of divine will' (Hanafi 2000: 3). See Hanafi, Zakiya. (2000). *The Monster in the Machine. Magic, Medicine, and the Marvelous in the Time of the Scientific Revolution*, Durham and London: Duke University Press.

3 The final chapter of this book offers a comprehensive engagement with feminist studies of science that exposes the masculinist assumptions underpinning scientific discourse.

4 The term 'faciality', as it appears in Deleuze, Gilles and Guattari, Felix. (1988). *A Thousand Plateaus: Capitalism and Schizophrenia*, London: Athlone Press, signals a mechanism by which the concept of the unitary, or majoritarian subject (White Man) is constructed in terms of the opposing aspects of the face (Deleuze and Guattari 1988: 176). This face is described as an overcoding system constituted by the white wall of the signifier and black hole of subjectivity (Deleuze and Guattari 1988: 167). The dual aspects of the 'white wall/black hole system' operate according to organisations of power that fix the identity of the subject in a regime of binary relations, so that 'it is a man *or* a woman, a rich person or a poor one, an adult or a child, a leader or a subject, "an x *or* a y."' (Deleuze and Guattari 1988: 177).

Chapter 5

1 According to Virilio, the concepts of 'real time' and 'delayed time' have replaced the three traditional tenses of past, present and future once used to connote decisive action. See Virilio, Paul. (1994). *The Vision Machine.* (Julie Rose, trans.), Bloomington and Indianapolis: Indiana University Press, 66–7.

2 Stelarc's performances, including those discussed here, can be viewed on his website at <http://www.stelarc.va.com.au>.

Chapter 6

1 Haraway's commitment to exploring the role of gender and power in the constitution of scientific knowledges has formed the basis of three monographs, as well as numerous articles. See Haraway, Donna J. (1989). *Primate Visions: Gender, Race and Nature in the World of Modern Science*, New York and London: Routledge. Haraway, Donna J. (1991). *Simians, Cyborgs and Women: The Reinvention of Nature*, New York: Routledge. Haraway, Donna J. (1997). *Modest_Witness@Second_Millenium.FemaleMan©_Meets_Oncomouse™: Feminism and Technoscience*, New York and London: Routledge.

2 It is worth noting the claim of various commentators that Baudrillard is insufficiently clear in his definition and use of the code. They include Connor, Steve. (1997). *Postmodernist Culture: An Introduction to Theories of the Contemporary* (3rd edn.). London: Blackwell. Levin, Charles. (1996). *Jean Baudrillard: A Study in Cultural Metaphysics*, London and New York: Prentice Hall, Harvester Wheatsheaf. Kellner, Douglas. (1989). *Jean Baudrillard: From Marxism to Postmodernism and Beyond*, Cambridge: Polity.

3 See the *Human Genome Project Information* website for a full history of the HGP and its aims. Retrieved 19 June 2006, <http://www.ornl.gov/sci/techresources/Human_Genome/home.shtml>. See also Marks, Joan H. (1994). 'The Human Genome Project: A Challenge in Biological Technology', in Gretchen Bender and Timothy Druckrey (eds.), *Culture on the Brink: Ideologies of Technology*, Seattle: Bay Press, 99–106.

4 Examples of this tendency include the following: Bodmer, Walter and McKie, Robin. (1994). *The Book of Man: The Quest to Discover our Genetic Heritage*, London: Little, Brown and Company. Cooper, Necia Grant (ed.). (1994). *The Human Genome Project: Deciphering the Blueprint of Heredity*, California: University Science Books. Hood, Leroy and Kelves, Daniel J. (1992). *The Code of Codes: Scientific and Social Issues in the Human Genome Project*, Cambridge and Massachusetts: Harvard University Press. Lee, Thomas F. (1991). *Human Genome Project: Cracking the Genetic Code of Life*, New York: Plenum.

5 This essay forms one of the chapters of Baudrillard, Jean. (1999). *The Transparency of Evil: Essays on Extreme Phenomena*, (James Benedict, trans.), London and New York: Verso.

Bibliography

Adorno, Theodor and Horkheimer, Max. (1973). 'The Culture Industry: Enlightenment as Mass Deception', in Theodor Adorno and Max Horkheimer, *Dialectic of Enlightenment*, (John Cumming, trans.), London: Allen Lane, 120–167.

Agar, Nicholas. (2002). *Perfect Copy: Unravelling the Cloning Debate*, Cambridge: Icon.

Albury, Kath. (2003). 'The Ethics of Porn on the Net', in Catharine Lumby and Elspeth Probyn (eds.), *Remote Control: New Media, New Ethics*, Cambridge: Cambridge University Press, 196–211.

Althusser, Louis. (1984). 'Ideology and Ideological State Apparatuses (Notes Towards an Investigation)', in Louis Althusser, *Essays on Ideology*, London: Verso, 1–60.

Ang, Ien. (1985). *Watching Dallas: Soap Opera and the Melodramatic Imagination*, (Della Couling, trans.), London and New York: Methuen.

Appadurai, Arjun. (1990). 'Disjuncture and Difference in the Global Cultural Economy', in Mike Featherstone (ed.), *Global Culture: Nationalism, Globalisation and Modernity*, London: Sage, 295–310.

Arditti, Rita; Duelli Klein, Reante; and Minden, Shelly (eds.). (1984). *Test Tube Women: What Future for Motherhood?*, London: Pandora Press.

Attfield, Judy. (1996). 'Barbie and Action Man: Adult Toys for Girls and Boys, 1959–93', in Pat Kirkham (ed.), *The Gendered Object*, Manchester and New York: Manchester University Press, 79–89.

Badmington, Neil (ed.). (2000). *Posthumanism*, New York: Palgrave.

Balsamo, Anne. (1995). 'Forms of Technological Embodiment: Reading the Body in Contemporary Culture', in Mike Featherstone and Roger Burrows (eds.), *Cyberspace, Cyberbodies, Cyberpunk: Cultures of Technological Embodiment*, London: Sage, 215–237.

Balsamo, Anne. (1996). *Technologies of the Gendered Body: Reading Cyborg Women*, Durham and London: Duke University Press.

Barthes, Roland. (1973). *Mythologies*, (Annette Lavers, trans.), London: Paladin.

Barthes, Roland. (1977). 'The Death of the Author', in Roland Barthes, *Image, Music, Text*, (Stephen Heath, trans.), London: Fontana, 142–148.

Barthes, Roland. (2000). *Camera Lucida*, (Richard Howard, trans.), London: Vintage.

Bartram, Michael. (1985). *The Pre-Raphaelite Camera: Aspects of Victorian Photography*, London: Weidenfeld and Nicolson.

Batchen, Geoffrey. (1996). 'Spectres of Cyberspace', *Artlink* 16(2&3), 25–28.

Battaglia, Debbora (ed.). (1995). *Rhetorics of Self-Making*, Berkeley, Los Angeles, London: University of California Press.

Battaglia, Debbora. (2001). 'Multiplicities: An Anthropologist's Thoughts on Replicants and Clones in Popular Film', *Critical Inquiry* 27, Spring, 493–514.

Baudelaire, Charles. (1964). *The Painter of Modern Life and Other Essays*, (Johnathan Mayne, trans. and ed.), London: Phaidon.

Baudrillard, Jean. (1981). *For a Critique of the Political Economy of the Sign*, (Charles Levin, trans.), St Louis: Telos Press.

Baudrillard, Jean. (1983). 'The Ecstasy of Communication', in Hal Foster (ed.), *The Anti-Aesthetic: Essays in Postmodern Culture*, Seattle: Bay Press, 126–134.

Baudrillard, Jean. (1986). 'The Year 2000 Will Not Take Place', in E.A. Grosz, Terry Threadgold, David Kelly, Alan Cholodenko and Edward Colless (eds.), *FUTUR*FALL: Excursions into Post-Modernity*, Sydney: Power Institute, 18–28.

Baudrillard, Jean. (1988a). *America*, (Chris Turner, trans.), London and New York: Verso.

Baudrillard, Jean. (1988b). 'Interview with Jean Baudrillard', *Block 14, Special Issue: The Work of Art in the Electronic Age*, 8–10.

Baudrillard, Jean. (1990a). *Seduction*, (Brian Singer, trans.), Basingstoke: Macmillan.

Baudrillard, Jean. (1990b). *Fatal Strategies*, (Phillip Beitchman and W.G.J. Niesluchowski, trans.), New York and London: Semiotext(e)/Pluto.

Baudrillard, Jean. (1993). *Symbolic Exchange and Death*, (Iain Hamilton Grant, trans.), London: Sage.

Baudrillard, Jean. (1994). *Simulacra and Simulation*, (Sheila Faria Glaser, trans.), Michigan: University of Michigan Press.

Baudrillard, Jean. (1998a). *The Consumer Society: Myths and Structures*, London, Thousand Oaks, New Delhi: Sage.

Baudrillard, Jean. (1998b). *Paroxysm: Interviews with Philippe Petit*, (Chris Turner, trans.), London and New York: Verso.

Baudrillard, Jean. (1999). *The Transparency of Evil: Essays on Extreme Phenomena*, (James Benedict, trans.), London and New York: Verso.

Baudrillard, Jean. (2000). *The Vital Illusion*, Julia Witwer (ed.), New York: Colombia University Press.

Baudrillard, Jean. (2005). 'Violence of the Virtual and Integral Reality', *International Journal of Baudrillard Studies* 2(2), 1–16. Retrieved 20 June 2006, <http://www.ubishops.ca/baudrillardstudie/vol2_2/baudrillardpf.htm>.

Belton, Robert J. (1995). *The Beribboned Bomb: The Image of Woman in Male Surrealist Art*, Calgary: University of Calgary Press.

Benjamin, Walter. (1968a). 'On Some Motifs in Baudelaire', in Walter Benjamin, *Illuminations*, (Harry Zohn, trans.), New York: Harcourt, Brace and World.

Benjamin, Walter. (1968b). 'The Work of Art in the Age of Mechanical Reproduction', in Walter Benjamin, *Illuminations*, (Harry Zohn, trans.), New York: Harcourt, Brace and World, 219–253.

Benthien, Claudia. (2002). *Skin: On the Cultural Border Between the Self and the World*, (Thomas Dunlap, trans.), New York: Colombia University Press.

Berman, Marshall. (1982). *All That is Solid Melts into Air: The Experience of Modernity*, New York: Simon and Schuster.

Berry, David M. and Pawlik, Jo. (2005). 'What is a Code? A Conversation with Deleuze, Guattari and Code', *Kritikos* 2, December, 1–16. Retrieved 14 February 2006, <http://garnet.acns.fsu.edu/%7Enr03/berry%20and%20Pawlik.htm>.

Billyboy. (1987). *Barbie and Her Life and Times and the New Theatre of Fashion*, Morebank: Transworld.

Bodmer, Walter and McKie, Robin. (1994). *The Book of Man: The Quest to Discover Our Genetic Heritage*, London: Little, Brown and Company.

Bolt, Barbara. (2004). *Art Beyond Representation. The Performative Power of the Image*, London and New York: I.B.Tauris.

Bolter, Jay David and Grusin, Richard. (2000). *Remediation. Understanding New Media*, Cambridge, Massachusetts: MIT Press.

Bordo, Susan. (1991). '"Material Girl": The Effacements of Postmodern Culture', in Laurence Goldstein (ed.), *The Female Body: Figures, Styles, Speculations*, USA: University of Michigan Press, 106–130.

Bornstein, Kate. (1994). *Gender Outlaw*, New York: Routledge.

Braidotti, Rosi. (1991). *Patterns of Dissonance: A Study of Women in Contemporary Philosophy*, (Elizabeth Guild, trans.), New York and London: Routledge.

Braidotti, Rosi. (1994a). *Nomadic Subjects: Embodiment and Sexual Difference in Contemporary Feminist Theory*, New York: Columbia University Press.

Braidotti, Rosi. (1994b). 'Toward a New Nomadism: Feminist Deleuzian Tracks; or, Metaphysics and Metabolism', in Constantin V. Boundas and Dorothea Olkowski (eds.), *Gilles Deleuze and the Theater of Philosophy*, New York and London: Routledge, 159–186.

Braidotti, Rosi. (1996). 'Signs of Wonder and Traces of Doubt: On Teratology and Embodied Differences', in Nina Lykke and Rosi Braidotti (eds.), *Between Monsters, Goddesses and Cyborgs: Feminist Confrontations with Science, Medicine and Cyberspace*, London and New Jersey: Zed Books, 135–152.

Braidotti, Rosi. (2000). 'Teratologies', in Ian Buchanan and Claire Colebrook (eds.), *Deleuze and Feminist Theory*, Edinburgh: Edinburgh University Press, 156–172.

Brillo magazine. (1996). 'Hacking Barbie with the Barbie Liberation Organization', Issue #1: Armed and Dangerous. Retrieved 7 June 2006, <http://www.brillomag.net/No1/blo.htm>.

Buchanan, Ian and Colebrook, Claire (eds.). (2000). *Deleuze and Feminist Theory*, Edinburgh: Edinburgh University Press.

Buck Morss, Susan. (1986). 'The Flâneur, The Sandwichman, and the Whore: The Politics of Loitering', *New German Critique* 39 Fall, 99–140.

Bukatman, Scott. (1993). *Terminal Identity: The Virtual Subject in Postmodern Science Fiction*, Durham: Duke University Press.

Butler, Judith. (1990). *Gender Trouble: Feminism and the Subversion of Identity*, New York and London: Routledge.

Butler, Judith. (1993). *Bodies that Matter: On the Discursive Limits of "Sex"*, New York and London: Routledge.

Butler, Judith. (2004). *Undoing Gender*, New York and London: Routledge.

Butler, Rex. (1999). *Jean Baudrillard: The Defence of the Real*, London, Thousand Oaks, New Delhi: Sage.

Caidin, Martin. (1972). *Cyborg: A Novel*, New York: Arbor House.

Cartwright, Lisa. (1998). 'A Cultural Anatomy of the Visible Human Project', in Paula A. Treichler, Lisa Cartwright and Constance Penley (eds.), *The Visible Woman. Imaging Technologies, Gender, and Science*, New York and London: New York University Press.

Caws, Mary Ann; Kuenzli, Rudolf E.; Raaberg, Gwen (eds.). (1991). *Surrealism and Women*, Cambridge, Massachusetts: MIT Press.

Chen, Kuan-Hsing. (1987). 'The Masses and the Media: Baudrillard's Implosive Postmodernism', *Theory, Culture and Society* 4, 71–88.

Cixous, Hélène. (1980). 'Sorties', in Elaine Marks and Isabelle De Courtivron (eds.), *New French Feminisms: An Anthology*, Amherst: University of Massachusetts Press, 90–98.

Cockburn, Cynthia. (1985). *Machinery of Dominance: Women, Men, and Technical Know-How*, London: Pluto Press.

Cockburn, Cynthia. (1991). *Brothers: Male Dominance and Technological Change*, London: Pluto Press.

Cohen, Jeffrey Jerome. (1996a). 'Preface: In a Time of Monsters', in Jeffrey Jerome Cohen (ed.), *Monster Theory: Reading Culture*, Minneapolis and London: University of Minnesota Press, vii–xiii.

Cohen, Jeffrey Jerome. (1996b). 'Monster Culture (Seven Theses)', in Jeffrey Jerome Cohen (ed.), *Monster Theory: Reading Culture*, Minneapolis and London: University of Minnesota Press, 3–25.

Collins, Jim. (1995). *Architectures of Excess. Cultural Life in the Information Age*, New York and London: Routledge.

Connor, Steve. (1997). *Postmodernist Culture: An Introduction to Theories of the Contemporary* (3rd edn.). London: Blackwell.

Conor, Liz. (2004). *The Spectacular Modern Woman: Feminine Visibility in the 1920s*, Bloomington and Indianapolis: Indiana University Press.

Cooper, Joel and Weaver, Kimberlee D. (2003). *Gender and Computers: Understanding the Digital Divide*, New Jersey and London: Lawrence Erlbaum Associates.

Cooper, Necia Grant (ed.). (1994). *The Human Genome Project: Deciphering the Blueprint of Heredity*, California: University Science Books.

Corea, Gena. (1985). *The Mother Machine: Reproductive Technologies from Artificial Insemination to Artificial Wombs*, London: The Women's Press.

Covino, Deborah Caslav. (2004). *Amending the Abject Body. Aesthetic Makeovers in Medicine and Culture*, New York: State University of New York Press.

Crary, Johnathan. (1992). *Techniques of the Observer: On Vision and Modernity in the Nineteenth Century*, Cambridge, Massachusetts: MIT Press.

Creed, Barbara. (1987). 'Feminist Film Theory: Reading the Text', in Annette Blonski, Barbara Creed and Freda Freiberg (eds.), *Don't Shoot Darling! Women's Independent Filmmaking in Australia*, Richmond: Greenhouse, 280–313.

Creed, Barbara. (1993). *The Monstrous Feminine: Film, Feminism, Psychoanalysis*, London and New York: Routledge.

Creed, Barbara. (2003). *Media Matrix: Sexing the New Reality*, Sydney: Allen & Unwin.

Csicsery-Ronay Jr., István. (1991). 'The SF of Theory: Baudrillard and Haraway', *Science–Fiction Studies*, 18(3), 387–403.

Cubitt, Sean. (2001). *Simulation and Social Theory*, London, Thousand Oaks, New Delhi: Sage.

Daly, Mary. (1998). *Quintessence: Realising the Archaic Future: A Radical Elemental Feminist Manifesto*, Boston: Beacon Press.

Daston, Lorraine and Park, Katharine. (1998). *Wonders of the Order of Nature 1150–1750*, New York: Zone Books.

Davis, Kathy. (2003). *Dubious Equalities and Embodied Differences: Cultural Studies on Cosmetic Surgery*, Lanham: Rowman and Littlefield.

Dawkins, Richard. (1976). *The Selfish Gene*, Oxford: Oxford University Press.

De Lauretis, Teresa. (1987). *Technologies of Gender: Essays on Theory, Film and Fiction*, Bloomington and Indianapolis: Indiana University Press.

De Lauretis, Teresa. (1994). *Practices of Love: Lesbian Sexuality and Perverse Desire*, Bloomington and Indianapolis: Indiana University Press.

Deleuze, Gilles and Guattari, Felix. (1988). *A Thousand Plateaus: Capitalism and Schizophrenia*, London: Athlone Press.

Dent, Grace. (2005). 'Moaning Minnies', *The Guardian*, Friday 4 February. Retrieved 14 July 2006, <http://www.guardian.co.uk/women/story/0,3604,1405577,00.html>.

Diamond, Elin. (1997). *Unmaking Mimesis: Essays on Feminism and Theatre*, New York and London: Routledge.

Diprose, Rosalyn. (1995). 'A "Genethics" that Makes Sense', in Vandana Shiva and Ingunn Moser (eds.), *Biopolitics: A Feminist and Ecological Reader on Biotechnology*, London and New Jersey: Zed Books, 162–174.

Doane, Mary Ann. (1990). 'Technophilia: Technology, Representation, and the Feminine', in Mary Jacobus, Evelyn Fox Keller and Sally Shuttleworth (eds.), *Body/Politics: Women and the Discourses of Science*, New York and London: Routledge, 163–176.

Dolan, Jill. (1998). 'The Discourse of Feminisms: The Spectator and Representation', in Lizbeth Goodman and Jane de Gay (eds.), *The Routledge Reader in Gender and Performance*, New York and London: Routledge, 288–294.

Doyle, Richard. (1997). *On Beyond Living: Rhetorical Transformations of the Life Sciences*, Stanford: Stanford University Press.

Dreyfus, Hubert L. (1993). 'Heidegger on the Connection Between Nihilism, Art, Technology, and Politics', in Charles Guignon (ed.), *The Cambridge Companion to Heidegger*, Cambridge: Cambridge University Press, 289–316.

du Cille, Ann. (1995). 'Dyes and Dolls: Multicultural Barbie and the Merchandizing of Difference', in Jessica Munns and Gita Rajan (eds.), *A*

Cultural Studies Reader: History, Theory, Practice, London and New York: Longman, 550–567.

Dworkin, Andrea. (1981). *Pornography: Men Possessing Women*, London: The Women's Press.

Dyer, Richard. (1997). *White*, London and New York: Routledge.

Engberg, Juliana. (2002). *Respectology: The World According to Patricia Piccinini*, Melbourne: Australian Centre for Contemporary Art.

Farnell, Ross. (1999). 'In Dialogue with "Posthuman Bodies": Interview with Stelarc', *Body and Society* 5(2–3), 129–147.

Feenberg, Andrew. (1991). *Critical Theory of Technology*, New York and Oxford: Oxford University Press.

Fenichell, Stephen. (1996). *Plastic: The Making of a Synthetic Century*, New York: HarperCollins.

Ferreira, Maria Aline Salgueiro Seabra. (2005). *I am the Other: Literary Negotiations of Human Cloning*, Westport: Praeger.

Finkelstein, Haim. (1979). *Surrealism and the Crisis of the Object*, Michigan: University Microfilms International.

Firestone, Shulamith. (1970). *The Dialectic of Sex: The Case for Feminist Revolution*, New York: Morrow.

Fiske, John. (1987). *Television Culture*, New York and London: Routledge.

Foster, Hal. (1991). 'Amour Fou', *October* 56 Spring, 64–97.

Foster, Hal. (1993). *Compulsive Beauty*, Cambridge, Massachusetts: MIT Press.

Foster, Thomas. (2005). *The Souls of Cyberfolk: Posthumanism as Vernacular Theory*, Minneapolis: University of Minnesota Press.

Foucault, Michel. (1977). *Discipline and Punish: The Birth of the Prison*, London: Penguin.

Foucault, Michel. (1980). *Power/Knowledge: Selected Interviews and Other Writings, 1972–1977*, New York: Pantheon.

Foucault, Michel. (1984a). 'Nietzsche, Genealogy, History', in Paul Rabinow (ed.), *The Foucault Reader*, London: Penguin, 76–100.

Foucault, Michel. (1984b). 'What is Enlightenment?', in Paul Rabinow (ed.), *The Foucault Reader*, London: Penguin, 32–50.

Foucault, Michel. (1984c). 'The Subject and Power', in Brian Wallis (ed.), *Art After Modernism: Rethinking Representation*, New York: New Museum of Contemporary Art, 417–433.

Fox Keller, Evelyn. (1995a). *Refiguring Life: Metaphors of Twentieth Century Biology*, Columbia: Columbia University Press.

Fox Keller, Evelyn. (1995b). 'Fractured Images of Science, Language and Power: A Post-Modern Optic, or Just Bad Eyesight?', in Vandana Shiva and Ingunn Moser (eds.), *Biopolitics: A Feminist and Ecological Reader on Biotechnology*, London and New Jersey: Zed Books, 52–67.

Freud, Sigmund. (1955a) *The Standard Edition of the Complete Psychological Works of Sigmund Freud*, (James Strachey, trans.), London: Hogarth.

Freud, Sigmund. (1955b). 'The "Uncanny"', in Sigmund Freud, *The Standard Edition of the Complete Psychological Works of Sigmund Freud (vol XVII: An Infantile Neurosis and Other Works)*, (James Strachey, trans.), London: Hogarth, 219–256.

Freud, Sigmund. (1969). *Civilization and its Discontents*, (Joan Riviere, trans.), London: Hogarth.

Friedberg, Anne. (1993). *Window Shopping: Cinema and the Postmodern*, Berkeley, Los Angeles, Oxford: University of California Press.

Friedberg, Anne. (2004). 'The Virtual Window', in David Thorburn and Henry Jenkins (eds.), *Rethinking Media Change. The Aesthetics of Transition*, Cambridge, Massachusetts: MIT Press, 334–353.

Fukuyama, Francis. (2002). *Our Posthuman Future: Consequences of the Biotechnology Revolution*, New York: Farrar, Straus and Giroux.

Gallop, Jane. (1987). 'French Theory and the Seduction of Feminism', in Alice Jardine and Paul Smith (eds.), *Men in Feminism*, New York and London: Methuen, 111–115.

Gane, Mike. (1991a). *Baudrillard's Bestiary: Baudrillard and Culture*, New York and London: Routledge.

Gane, Mike. (1991b). *Baudrillard: Critical and Fatal Theory*, London and New York: Routledge.

Gane, Mike (ed.). (1993). *Baudrillard Live: Selected Interviews*, New York and London: Routledge.

Gates, Bill. (1995). *The Road Ahead*, New York and London: Viking Penguin.

Genosko, Gary. (1994). *Baudrillard and Signs: Signification Ablaze*, New York and London: Routledge.

Gersheim, Helmut. (1965). *A Concise History of Photography*, London: Thames and Hudson.

Gibbons, Joan. (2005). *Art and Advertising*, London and New York: I.B.Tauris.

Gilman, Sander. (1985). *Difference and Pathology; Stereotypes of Sexuality, Race and Madness*, Ithaca: Cornell University Press.

Giroux, Henry A. (1994). 'Consuming Social Change: The "United Colors of Benetton"', *Cultural Critique* 26 Winter, 5–32.

Gledhill, Christine. (1984). 'Developments in Feminist Film Criticism', in Mary Ann Doane, Patricia Mellencamp and Linda Williams (eds.), *Re-Vision: Essays in Feminist Film Criticism*, Maryland: University Publications of America, 18–47.

Goshorn, Keith A. (1994). 'Valorizing "the Feminine" while Rejecting Feminism?—Baudrillard's Feminist Provocations', in Douglas Kellner (ed.), *Baudrillard: A Critical Reader*, Oxford and Cambridge: Blackwell, 256–291.

Grace, Victoria. (2000). *Baudrillard's Challenge: A Feminist Reading*, London and New York: Routledge.

Grace, Victoria. (2005). 'Editorial: What is Baudrillard "Doing"?', *International Journal of Baudrillard Studies* 2(2), 1–6. Retrieved 20 June 2006, <http://www.ubishops.ca/baudrillardstudies/vol2_2/grace_edpf.htm>.

Graham, Elaine L. (2002). *Representations of the post/human: Monsters, Aliens and Others in Popular Culture*, Manchester: Manchester University Press.

Griggers, Camilla. (1997). *Becoming–Woman*, Minneapolis: University of Minnesota Press.

Gronberg, Tag. (1997). 'Beware Beautiful Women: The 1920s Shopwindow Mannequin and a Physiognomy of Effacement', *Art History* 20(3), 375–396.

Grosz, Elizabeth. (1987). 'Notes Toward a Corporeal Feminism', *Australian Feminist Studies* 5, 1–15.

Grosz, Elizabeth and de Lepervanche, Marie. (1988). 'Feminism and Science', in Barbara Caine, E.A. Grosz and Marie de Lepervanche (eds.), *Crossing Boundaries: Feminism and the Critique of Knowledges*, Sydney: Allen & Unwin, 5–27.

Halberstam, Judith. (1995). *Skin Shows: Gothic Horror and the Technology of Monsters*, Durham and London: Duke University Press.

Halberstam, Judith. (1998). *Female Masculinity*, Durham and London: Duke University Press.

Halberstam, Judith. (2005). *In a Queer Time and Place: Transgender Bodies, Subcultural Lives*, New York and London: New York University Press.

Halberstam, Judith and Livingstone, Ira, (eds.). (1995). *Posthuman Bodies*, Bloomington and Indianapolis: Indiana University Press.

Hall, Stuart. (1995). 'The Whites of Their Eyes: Racist Ideologies and the Media', in Gail Dines and Jean M. Humez (eds.), *Gender, Race and Class in Media*, California: Sage, 18–22.

Hall, Stuart. (1996). 'Signification, Representation, Ideology: Althusser and the Post-Structuralist Debates', in James Curran, David Morley and Valerie Walkerdine (eds.), *Cultural Studies and Communications*, London: Arnold, 11–34.

Hanafi, Zakiya. (2000). *The Monster in the Machine. Magic, Medicine, and the Marvelous in the Time of the Scientific Revolution*, Durham and London: Duke University Press.

Haraway, Donna J. (1985). 'A Manifesto for Cyborgs: Science, Technology, and Socialist Feminism in the 1980s', *Socialist Review* 15(2), 65–107.

Haraway, Donna J. (1989). *Primate Visions: Gender, Race and Nature in the World of Modern Science*, New York and London: Routledge.

Haraway, Donna J. (1991). *Simians, Cyborgs and Women: The Reinvention of Nature*, New York and London: Routledge.

Haraway, Donna J. (1992). 'The Promise of Monsters: A Regenerative Politics for Inappropriate/d Others', in Lawrence Grossberg, Cary Nelson and Paula A. Treichler (eds.), *Cultural Studies*, New York and London: Routledge, 295–329.

Haraway, Donna J. (1995). 'Otherworldly Conversations, Terran Topics, Local Terms', in Vandana Shiva and Ingunn Moser (eds.), *Biopolitics: A Feminist Ecological Reader on Biotechnology*, London and New Jersey: Zed Books, 69–93.

Haraway, Donna J. (1997). *Modest_Witness@Second_Millenium.FemaleMan©_Meets_Oncomouse™: Feminism and Technoscience*, New York and London: Routledge.

Harding, Sandra. (1986). *The Science Question in Feminism*, Ithaca and London: Cornell University Press.

Hartouni, Valerie. (1997). *Cultural Conceptions: On Reproductive Technologies and the Remaking of Life*, Minneapolis and London: University of Minnesota Press.

Hartsock, Nancy. (1990). 'Foucault on Power: A Theory for Women?', in Linda J. Nicholson (ed.), *Feminism/Postmodernism*, New York and London: Routledge, 157–175.

Hassan, Ihab. (1977). 'Prometheus as Performer: Toward a Posthumanist Culture?', in Michael Benamon and Charles Caramella (eds.), *Performance in Postmodern Culture*, Milwaukee: Centre for Twentieth Century Studies, University of Wisconsin-Milwaukee, 201–217.

Hassan, Ihab. (1993). 'Toward A Concept of Postmodernism', in Terry Docherty (ed.), *Postmodernism: A Reader*, New York: Columbia University Press, 146–156.

Hawthorne, Susan. (1999). 'Cyborgs, Virtual Bodies and Organic Bodies: Theoretical Feminist Responses', in Susan Hawthorne and Renate Klein (eds.), *Cyberfeminism: Connectivity, Critique and Creativity*, Melbourne: Spinifex, 213–249.

Hayles, N. Katherine. (1999). *How we Became Posthuman: Virtual Bodies in Cybernetics, Literature and Informatics*, Chicago and London: University of Chicago Press.

Heath, Stephen. (1981). *Questions of Cinema*, London and Basingstoke: Macmillan Press.

Hebdige, Dick. (1988). *Hiding in the Light: On Images and Things*, London and New York: Routledge.

Hegarty, Paul. (2004). *Jean Baudrillard: Live Theory*, London and New York: Continuum.

Heidegger, Martin. (1977). 'The Question Concerning Technology', in David Farnell Krell (ed.), *Martin Heidegger: Basic Writings*, New York: Harper and Row, 287–317.

Hennessey, Peter. (1999). 'Patricia Piccinini: Plastic Realist', in Blair French (ed.), *Photo Files: An Australian Photography Reader*, Sydney: Power Publishing and Australian Centre for Photography, 247–254.

Hood, Leroy and Kelves, Daniel J. (1992). *The Code of Codes: Scientific and Social Issues in the Human Genome Project*, Cambridge and Massachusetts: Harvard University Press.

Hubbard, Ruth. (1990). *The Politics of Women's Biology*, New Brunswick: Rutgers University Press.

Human Genome Project Information Website. (2006). Retrieved 19 June 2006, <http://www.ornl.gov/sci/techresources/Human_Genome/home.shtml>.

Huxford, John. (2000). 'Framing the Future: Science Fiction Frames and the Press Coverage of Cloning', *Continuum* 14(2), 187–199.

Huyssen, Andreas. (1986). 'The Vamp and the Machine: Fritz Lang's "Metropolis"', in Andreas Huyssen, *After the Great Divide*, Bloomington and Indiana: Indiana University Press, 65–81.

Jackson, Cindy. (2006). *Welcome to My Official Website.* Retrieved 7 June 2006, <http://www.cindyjackson.com/>.

Jameson, Fredric. (1983). 'Postmodernism and Consumer Society', in Hal Foster (ed.), *The Anti-Aesthetic: Essays in Postmodern Culture*, Seattle: Bay Press, 111–125.

Jameson, Fredric. (1991). *Postmodernism, or, the Cultural Logic of Late Capitalism*, Durham: Duke University Press.

Jardine, Alice and Feher, Michael. (1987). 'Of Bodies and Technologies: Discussion', in Hal Foster (ed.), *Discussions in Contemporary Culture* 1, DIA Art Foundation, Seattle: Bay Press, 156–172.

Jay, Nancy. (1991). 'Gender and Dichotomy', in Sjena Gunew (ed.), *A Reader in Feminist Knowledge*, London and New York: Routledge, 89–106.

Jones, Steven G. (ed.). (1995). *Cybersociety: Computer-Mediated Communication and Community*, London: Sage.

Kellner, Douglas. (1989). *Jean Baudrillard: From Marxism to Postmodernism and Beyond*, Cambridge: Polity.

Kelly, Mary. (1983). *Post-Partum Document*, London and Boston: Routledge and Kegan Paul.

Kindler, Marsha. (2000). 'From Mutation to Morphing: Cultural Transformations in Greek Myth to Children's Media Culture,' in Vivian Sobchack (ed.), *Meta-Morphing: Visual Transformation and the Culture of Quick Change*, Minneapolis: University of Minnesota Press, 59–80.

Kirby, Vicki. (1994). 'Viral Identities: Feminism and Postmodernisms', in Norma Grieve and Ailsa Burns (eds.), *Australian Women: Contemporary Feminist Thought*, Melbourne: Oxford University Press, 120–132.

Klein, Naomi. (2000). *No Logo*, London: Flamingo.

Klein, Renate. (1996). '(Dead) Bodies Floating in Cyberspace: Post-modernism and the Dismemberment of Women', in Diane Bell and Renate Klein (eds.), *Radically Speaking: Feminism Reclaimed*, North Melbourne: Spinifex Press, 346–358.

Kohanski, Alexander S. (1977). *Philosophy and Technology: Towards a New Orientation in Modern Thinking*, New York: Philosophical Library.

Kramer, Jana and Kramarae, Cheris. (2000). 'Women's Political Webs: Global Electronic Networks', in Annabelle Sreberny and Liesbet van Zoonen (eds.), *Gender Politics and Communication*, New Jersey: Hampton Press, 205–222.

Krauss, Rosalind and Livingston, Jane. (1985). *L'Amour Fou: Photography and Surrealism*, New York: Abbeville.

Kristeva, Julia. (1982). *Powers of Horror: An Essay on Abjection*, (Leon S. Roudies, trans.), New York: Columbia University Press.

Kroker, Arthur and Kroker, Marilouise. (1996). 'Code Warriors: Bunkering In and Dumbing Down', in Arthur Kroker and Marilouise Kroker (eds.), *Hacking the Future: Stories for the Flesh-Eating 90s*, New York: St Martins, 75–88.

Kuhn, Annette. (1985). *The Power of the Image: Essays on Representation and Sexuality*, London: Routledge and Kegan Paul.

Lacan, Jacques. (1977). 'The Mirror Stage as Formative of the Function of the I as Revealed in Psychoanalytic Experience', in Jacques Lacan, *Ecrits: A Selection*, (Alan Sheridan, trans.), London: Routledge, 1–7.

Lash, Scott. (2001). 'Technological Forms of Life', *Theory, Culture and Society* 18(1), 105–120.

Lee, Thomas F. (1991). *Human Genome Project: Cracking the Genetic Code of Life*, New York: Plenum.

Levin, Charles. (1996). *Jean Baudrillard: A Study in Cultural Metaphysics*, London and New York: Prentice Hall, Harvester Wheatsheaf.

Levinson, Paul. (2004). *Cellphone: The Story of the World's Most Mobile Medium and How It Has Transformed Everything!*, New York: Palgrave Macmillan.

Linker, Kate. (1984). 'Representation and Sexuality', in Brian Wallis (ed.), *Art After Modernism: Rethinking Representation*, New York: New Museum of Contemporary Art, 391–415.

Lister, Martin. (ed.). (1995). *The Photographic Image in Digital Culture*, London and New York: Routledge.

Lloyd, Genevieve. (1984). *The Man of Reason: 'Male' and 'Female' in Western Philosophy*, Minneapolis: University of Minnesota Press.

Lord, M.G. (1994). *Forever Barbie: The Unauthorized Biography of a Real Doll*, New York: William Morrow.

Lumby, Catharine. (1997). *Bad Girls: The Media, Sex and Feminism in the 90s*, Sydney: Allen & Unwin.

Macey, David. (2000). *The Penguin Dictionary of Critical Theory*, London and New York: Penguin.

MacKinnon, Catherine A. (1979). *The Sexual Harassment of Working Women: A Case of Sex Discrimination*, New Haven: Yale University Press.

Manovich, Lev. (1996). 'The Automation of Sight: From Photography to Computer Vision', in Timothy Druckrey (ed.), *Electronic Culture: Technology and Visual Representation*, New Jersey: Aperture, 229–239.

Manson, Marilyn. (1998). *Mechanical Animals* [CD], Los Angeles: Nothing/ Interscope Records.

Marks, Joan H. (1994). 'The Human Genome Project: A Challenge in Biological Technology', in Gretchen Bender and Timothy Druckrey (eds.), *Culture on the Brink: Ideologies of Technology*, Seattle: Bay Press, 99–106.

McKenzie, Adrian. (2002). *Transductions: Bodies and Machines at Speed*, London and New York: Continuum.

McLuhan, Marshall. (1964). *Understanding Media: Extensions of Man*, London: Sphere.

McRobbie, Angela. (1978). *Jackie: An Ideology of Adolescent Femininity*, Birmingham: Centre for Contemporary Studies.

McRobbie, Angela. (1997). 'Second-Hand Dresses and the Role of the Ragmarket', in Ken Gelder and Sarah Thornton (eds.), *The Subcultures Reader*, Routledge: London and New York, 191–199.

McRobbie, Angela. (1999). *In the Culture Society: Art, Fashion and Popular Music*, London and New York: Routledge.

Meikle, Jeffrey L. (1995). *American Plastic: A Culture of History*, New Brunswick and New Jersey: Rutgers University Press.

Modleski, Tania. (1982). *Loving with a Vengeance: Mass Produced Fantasies for Women*, New York: Methuen.

Moravec, Hans. (1988). *Mind Children. The Future of Robot and Human Intelligence*, Cambridge, Massachusetts: Harvard University Press.

Morris, Meaghan. (1988). 'Room 101 Or A Few Worst Things In The World', in Meaghan Morris, *The Pirate's Fiancée: Feminism, Reading, Postmodernism*, London and New York: Verso, 187–211.

Morris, Meaghan. (1993). 'Things to do with Shopping Centres', in Simon During (ed.), *The Cultural Studies Reader*, London and New York: Routledge, 295–319.

Motz, Marilyn Ferris. (1983). '"I Want to Be a Barbie Doll When I Grow Up": The Cultural Significance of the Barbie Doll', in Christopher D. Geist and Jack Nachbar (eds.), *The Popular Culture Reader* (3rd edn.). Ohio: Bowling Green University Popular Press, 122–136.

Mulvey, Laura. (1989a). 'Visual Pleasure and Narrative Cinema', in *Visual and Other Pleasures*, London: Macmillan, 14–26.

Mulvey, Laura. (1989b). 'Afterthoughts on "Visual Pleasure and Narrative Cinema" Inspired by King Vidor's "Duel in the Sun"', in *Visual and Other Pleasures*, London: Macmillan, 29–38.

Mulvey, Laura. (1996). *Fetishism and Curiosity*, Bloomington and Indianapolis: Indiana University Press.

Nava, Mica. (1992). 'Discriminating or Duped? Young People as Consumers of Advertising/Art', in Mica Nava, *Changing Cultures: Feminism, Youth and Consumerism*, London: Sage, 171–182.

Nelkin, Dorothy and Lindee, M. Susan. (1995). 'The Media-ted Gene: Stories of Gender and Race', in Jennifer Terry and Jacqueline Urla (eds.), *Deviant Bodies: Critical Perspectives on Difference in Science and Popular Culture*, Bloomington and Indianapolis: Indiana University Press, 387–402.

Nunes, Mark. (1995). 'Jean Baudrillard in Cyberspace: Internet, Virtuality, and Postmodernity', *Style* 29(2), Summer, 314–327.

Ockman, Carol. (1999). 'Barbie Meets Bouguereau: Constructing an Ideal Body for the Late Twentieth Century', in Yona Zeldis McDonough (ed.), *The Barbie Chronicles: A Living Doll Turns Forty*, Sydney and Auckland: Bantam, 75–88.

O'Connell, Karen. (2005). 'The Devouring: Genetics, Abjection, and the Limits of the Law', in Margit Shildrick and Roxanne Mykitiuk (eds.), *Ethics of the Body: Postconventional Challenges*, Cambridge, Massachusetts: MIT Press.

O'Sickey, Ingeborg Majer. (1994). 'Barbie Magazine and the Aesthetic Commodification of Girls' Bodies', in Shari Benstock and Suzanne Ferris (eds.), *On Fashion*, New Brunswick and New Jersey: Rutgers University Press, 21–40.

Panofsky, Erwin. (1991). *Perspective as Symbolic Form*, New York: Zone.

Peers, Juliette. (2004). *The Fashion Doll. From Bébé Jumeau to Barbie*, Oxford and New York: Berg.

Pepperell, Robert. (2005). 'The Posthuman Manifesto', *Kritikos* 2, February, 1–15. Retrieved 14 February 2006, <http://garnet.acns.fsu.edu/%7Enr03/The%20Posthuman%20Manifesto.htm>.

Piccinini, Patricia. (1996). 'Artist's Statement for *The Mutant Genome Project* 1994–1995'. Retrieved <http://patriciapiccinini.net/pp/tmgp.htn>.

Piccinini, Patricia. (1997). 'Artist's Statement for *Protein Lattice* 1997'. Retrieved 3 August 2001 <http://patriciapiccinini.net/pp/plt.htn>.

Pile, Steve and Thrift, Nigel (eds.). (1995). *Mapping the Subject: Geographies of Cultural Transformation*, London and New York: Routledge.

Plant, Sadie. (1993). 'Baudrillard's Woman: The Eve of Seduction', in Chris Rojek and Bryan S. Turner (eds.), *Forget Baudrillard?*, London and New York: Routledge, 88–106.

Plant, Sadie. (1995). 'The Future Looms: Weaving Women and Cybernetics', in Mike Featherstone and Roger Burrows (eds.), *Cyberspace, Cyberbodies, Cyberpunk: Cultures of Technological Embodiment*, London: Sage, 45–64.

Plant, Sadie. (1996). 'On the Matrix: Cyberfeminist Simulations', in Rob Shields (ed.), *Cultures of Internet: Virtual Spaces, Real Histories, Living Bodies*, London: Sage, 170–183.

Pollock, Griselda. (1988). *Vision and Difference: Femininity, Feminism, and Histories of Art*, London and New York: Routledge.

Poster, Mark. (1990). *The Mode of Information: Poststructuralism and Social Context*, Cambridge: Polity.

Prado, C.G. (1995). *Starting with Foucault: An Introduction to Genealogy*, Boulder, San Francisco, Oxford: Westview.

Rakow, Lana F. and Rakow, Caitlin S. (1999). 'Educating Barbie', in Sharon R. Mazzarella and Norma Odom Pecora (eds.), *Growing Up Girls: Popular Culture and the Construction of Identity*, New York: Peter Lang, 11–20.

Rand, Erica. (1995). *Barbie's Queer Accessories*, Durham and London: Duke University Press.

Rheingold, Howard. (1991). *Virtual Reality*, New York and London: Summit.

Rodaway, Paul. (1995). 'Exploring the Subject in Hyper-Reality', in Steve Pile and Nigel Thrift (eds.), *Mapping the Subject: Geographies of Cultural Transformation*, London and New York: Routledge, 241–266.

Rogers, Mary F. (1999). *Barbie Culture*, London, Thousand Oaks, New Delhi: Sage.

Rothenbuhler, Eric W. and Peters, John Durham. (1997). 'Defining Phonography: An Experiment in Theory', *Musical Quarterly* 81(2), 242–262.

Rothfield, Philipa. (1990). 'Feminism, Subjectivity, and Sexual Experience', in Sneja Gunew (ed.), *Feminist Knowledges: Critique and Construct*, London and New York: Routledge, 121–141.

Rozak, Theodore. (1970). *The Making of a Counter Culture*, London: Faber and Faber.

Schoonmaker, Sara. (1994). 'Capitalism and the Code: A Critique of Baudrillard's Third Order Simulacrum', in Douglas Kellner (ed.), *Baudrillard: A Critical Reader*, Oxford and Cambridge: Blackwell Publishers, 168–188.

Sekula, Allan. (1986). 'The Body and the Archive', *October* 39 Winter, 3–64.

Shelley, Mary. (1969). *Frankenstein*, Oxford and New York: Oxford University Press.

Shildrick, Margrit. (1999). 'This Body Which is Not One: Dealing with Differences', *Body and Society* 5(2–3), 77–92.

Shildrick, Margrit. (2000). 'Monsters, Marvels and Metaphysics: Beyond the Powers of Horror', in Sarah Ahmed, Jane Kilby, Celia Lury, Maureen McNeil and Beverley Skeggs (eds.), *Transformations: Thinking Through Feminism*, London and New York: Routledge, 303–315.

Smith, Richard G. (2005). 'Lights, Camera, *Action*: Baudrillard and the Performance of Representations', *International Journal of Baudrillard Studies* 2(1), 1–8. Retrieved 6 June 2006, <http://www.ubishops.ca/baudrillardstudies/vol2_1/smithpf.htm>.

Sobchack, Vivian. (1987). *Screening Space: The American Science Fiction Film* (2nd edn.). New Brunswick, New Jersey and London: Rutgers University Press.

Sobchack, Vivian. (1991). 'In Response to Baudrillard. Baudrillard's Obscenity', *Science–Fiction Studies* 18(3), 327–329.

Sobchack, Vivian. (1994). 'Meta-Morphing', *Art/Text* 58 August/October, 43–45.

Sobchack, Vivian. (ed.). (2000a). *Meta-Morphing: Visual Transformation and the Culture of Quick-Change*, Minneapolis and London: University of Minnesota Press.

Sobchack, Vivian. (2000b). '"At the Still Point of the Turning World": Meta-Morphing and Meta-Stasis', in Vivian Sobchack (ed.), *Meta Morphing: Visual Transformation and the Culture of Quick-Change*, Minneapolis and London: University of Minnesota Press, 130–158.

Sofia, Zoe. (1992). 'Virtual Corporeality: A Feminist View', *Australian Feminist Studies* 15, 11–24.

Sontag, Susan. (1977). *On Photography*, New York: Farrar, Straus and Giroux.

Spallone, Patricia and Steinberg, Deborah Lynn (eds.). (1987). *Made to Order: The Myth of Reproductive and Genetic Progress*, Oxford and New York: Pergamon.

Spender, Dale. (1995). *Nattering on the Net: Women, Power and Cyberspace*, North Melbourne: Spinifex Press.

Spigel, Lynne (2001). 'Barbies without Ken: Femininity, Feminism, and the Art–Culture System', in Lynne Spigel, *Welcome to the Dreamhouse: Popular Media and Postwar Suburbs*, Durham and London: Duke University Press, 310–353.

Squires, Judith. (2000). 'Fabulous Feminist Futures and the Lure of Cyberculture', in David Bell and Barbara M. Kennedy (eds.), *The Cybercultures Reader*, London and New York: Routledge, 360–373.

Stacey, Jackie. (1994). *Star Gazing: Hollywood Cinema and Female Spectatorship*, London and New York: Routledge.

Stafford, Barbara Maria. (1996). *Good Looking. Essays on the Virtue of Images*, Cambridge, Massachusetts: MIT Press.

Stelarc. (1998). 'From Psycho-Body to Cyber-Systems: Images as Post-Human Entities', in Joan Broadhurst-Dixon and Eric J. Cassidy (eds.), *Virtual Futures: Cyberotics, Technology and Post-Human Pragmatism*, New York and London: Routledge, 116–123.

Stelarc. (2002). *Stelarc Official Website.* Retrieved 8 July 2002 <http://www.stelarc.va.com.au/>.

Stone, Allucquere Roseanne. (1992). 'Virtual Systems', in Jonathan Crary and Sanford Kwinter (eds.), *Incorporations* 6, New York: Zone, 609–621.

Stone, Allucquere Roseanne. (1995). *The War of Desire and Technology at the Close of the Mechanical Age*, Cambridge, Massachusetts: MIT Press.

Sturken, Marita and Cartwright, Lisa. (2001). *Practices of Looking: An Introduction to Visual Culture*, New York: Oxford.

Swanson, Gillian. (1995). '"Drunk with Glitter": Consuming Spaces and Sexual Geographies', in Sophie Watson and Katherine Gibson (eds.), *Postmodern Cities and Spaces*, Oxford: Blackwell, 80–98.

Taylor, Mark C. (1997). *Hiding*, Chicago: University of Chicago Press.

Terranova, Tiziana. (1996). 'Posthuman Unbounded: Artificial Evolution and High-Tech Subcultures', in George Robinson, Melinda Mash, Lisa Tickner, Jon Bird, Barry Curtis, Tim Putnam (eds.), *FutureNatural: Nature, Science, Culture*, London: Routledge, 165–180.

Tokar, Brian (ed.). (2001). *Redesigning Life? The Worldwide Challenge to Genetic Engineering*, London and New York: Zed Books.

Turkle, Sherry. (1984). *The Second Self: Computers and the Human Spirit*, New York: Simon and Schuster.

Turkle, Sherry. (1988). 'Computational Reticence: Why Women Fear the Intimate Machine', in Cheris Kramarae (ed.), *Technology and Women's Voices*, London: Routledge.

Turkle, Sherry. (1996). 'Constructions and Reconstructions of Self in Virtual Reality', in Timothy Druckrey (ed.), *Electronic Culture: Technology and Visual Representation*, New York: Aperture Foundation, 354–365.

Turkle, Sherry. (1997). *Life on the Screen: Identity in the Age of the Internet*, London: Phoenix.

Urla, Jacqueline and Swedlund, Alan C. (1995). 'The Anthropometry of Barbie: Unsettling Ideals of the Feminine Body in Popular Culture', in Jennifer Terry and Jacqueline Urla (eds.), *Deviant Bodies: Critical Perspectives on Difference in Science and Popular Culture*, Bloomington and Indianapolis: Indiana University Press, 277–313.

Veltman, Kim H. (1996). 'Electronic Media: The Rebirth of Perspective and the Fragmentation of Illusion', in Timothy Druckrey (ed.), *Electronic Culture: Technology and Visual Representation*, New Jersey: Aperture, 209–227.

Virilio, Paul. (1988). Interview with Paul Virilio, *Block 14, Special Issue: The Work of Art in the Electronic Age*, 4–7.

Virilio, Paul. (1991). *The Aesthetics of Disappearance*, (Philip Beitchman, trans.), New York: Semiotext(e).

Virilio, Paul. (1994). *The Vision Machine*, (Julie Rose, trans.), Bloomington and Indianapolis: Indiana University Press.

Wajcman, Judy. (1991). *Feminism Confronts Technology*, Cambridge and Oxford: Polity Press.

Wajcman, Judy. (2004). *Technofeminism*, Cambridge: Polity Press.

Wakeford, Nina. (1997). 'Networking Women and Grrrls with Information/Communication Technology: Surfing Tales of the World Wide Web', in Jennifer Terry and Melodie Calvert (eds.), *Processed Lives: Gender and Technology in Everyday Life*, London and New York: Routledge, 51–66.

Waldby, Catherine. (2000). 'The Visible Human Project: Data into Flesh, Flesh into Data', in Janine Marchessault and Kim Sawchuk (eds.), *Wild Science: Reading Feminism, Medicine and The Media*, London and New York: Routledge, 24–38.

Waldby, Catherine. (2002). 'The Instruments of Life: Frankenstein and Cyberculture', in Darren Tofts, Annemarie Jonson, Alessio Cavallaro (eds.), *Prefiguring Cyberculture: An Intellectural History*, Sydney: Power Publications and Cambridge: MIT Press, 28–37.

Weiss, Gail. (1999). 'The Durée of the Techno-Body', in Elizabeth Grosz (ed.), *Becomings: Explorations in Time, Memory, and Futures*, Ithaca and London: Cornell University Press, 161–175.

Willis, Susan. (1991). *A Primer for Daily Life*, London and New York: Routledge.

Wong, Kristina Sheryl. (2003). 'Pranks and Fake Porn: Doing Feminism My Way', in Rory Dicker and Alison Piepmeier (eds.), *Catching a Wave: Reclaiming Feminism for the 21st Century*, Boston: Northeastern University Press, 294–307.

Index